MW00851806

EMOTIONS AND AFFECT
IN WRITING CENTERS

Writing Program Administration
Series Editors: Christopher Carter and Laura R. Micciche

The series provides a venue for scholarly monographs and projects that are research or theory-based and that provide insights into important issues in the field. We encourage submissions that examine WPA work broadly defined and thus not limited to studies of first-year composition programs.

Books in the Series

EMOTIONS AND AFFECT IN WRITING CENTERS

Edited by Janine Morris and
Kelly Concannon

Parlor Press
Anderson, South Carolina
www.parlorpress.com

Parlor Press LLC, Anderson, South Carolina, USA

Printed in the United States of America
S A N: 2 5 4 - 8 8 7 9

Library of Congress Cataloging-in-Publication Data on File

978-1-64317-312-2 (paperback)
978-1-64317-313-9 (hardcover)
978-1-64317-314-6 (pdf)
978-1-64317-315-3 (epub)

1 2 3 4 5

Writing Program Administration
Series Editors: Christopher Carter and Laura R. Micciche

Cover art: "Curiosity" by Darlean Morris. Used by permission.
Cover design by David Blakesley.

Printed on acid-free paper.

Parlor Press, LLC is an independent publisher of scholarly and trade titles
in print and multimedia formats. This book is available in paper, hardcover,
and ebook formats from Parlor Press on the World Wide Web at https://
parlorpress.com or through online and brick-and-mortar bookstores. For
submission information or to find out about Parlor Press publications, write
to Parlor Press, 3015 Brackenberry Drive, Anderson, South Carolina, 29621,
or email editor@parlorpress.com.

CONTENTS

ACKNOWLEDGMENTS

This project began in our writing center, through many conversations with our undergraduate and graduate students about the emotions involved in tutoring and how to best care for themselves. We are thankful for the incredible students we work with and learn from every day. We are extremely indebted to Nicole Chavannes, Veronica Diaz, and Noemi Nunez, who first wrote with us about affect and emotions and whose conversations changed how we think about mentorship, mindfulness, and emotional labor. We are also thankful for Monique Scoggin's research assistantship as we started researching the origins of emotions and affect in writing center scholarship.

While working on this collection, we have benefitted from the wisdom of our colleagues at Nova Southeastern University. Kevin Dvorak and Shanti Bruce have consistently encouraged us and provided us with support to pursue this project. Likewise, Star Vanguri, Whitney Lehmann, Juliette Kitchens, and Claire Lutkewitte were instrumental in offering guidance in working on an edited collection and navigating the publishing process.

We are grateful for the many people involved in making this collection. We are so appreciative of the authors featured, and we are thankful for the dedication they have shown to this project. We are also thankful for the patience and guidance from Laura Micciche, Chris Carter, David Blakesley, and an anonymous reviewer who helped shape the project and whose feedback greatly strengthened the collection.

The cover art, *Curiosity*, for *Emotions and Affect in Writing Centers* is by Janine's late aunt, Darlean Morris. Darlean was an artist, educator, and the first member of Janine's family to earn a PhD. We are thankful that Gary Austin, her husband, allowed us to use her artwork for this collection and for took the time to choose and explain the sentiments behind several of Darlean's pieces. In her artist's statement, Darlean wrote, "My art informs my vision and my vision informs my art. Many strong, dormant, images remained alive in my mind but unexpressed until after I retired from my first career as an art teacher and administrator. After years of being concerned with linear communication in education, I began to explore the multi-leveled, emotionally charged message that my art offers." We find her vision especially fitting for a collection on emotion in the context of writing centers and higher education.

Janine. Along with those mentioned above, I am grateful for my writing group—Christina LaVecchia, Hannah Rule, and Allison Carr—who were there to review early drafts of our proposal and talk through the process of working on an edited collection. Although they might not see themselves reflected in this work, I am also thankful for my family, who were willing to listen to me talk about the collection, and friends, who provided useful distractions from work. Aileen Farrar, Star Vanguri, Hollie Adams, Vanessa Shields, Alex Gayowsky, Sabrina Habrun, and Carla Sarr have been part of my longtime support network, and I'm grateful for their friendship. I'm ever thankful for Mario D'Agostino, whose meals, jokes, reassurance, and love made finishing this collection possible. Finally, I am so grateful for my late mom, Sharon Morris. She taught me many lessons about perseverance, dedication, and collaboration. As the collection progressed, I spent many afternoons working at the table in her backyard and evenings sharing updates with her over meals. I'm sorry she isn't here to see the completed book but feel very strongly that she has been a major part of its creation.

Kelly. I am primarily grateful for all of our amazing colleagues at Nova Southeastern University, who provided love, support, and guidance. We are truly blessed to be guided by leadership in both the Writing and Communication Center (WCC) as well as within our department. For me, this book truly illustrates principles of collaboration and mentorship. I am grateful for my mentors who continue to inspire my work—Dr. Ken Lindblom and Dr. Margaret Himley—as I continue to be moved by the students I have been afforded the privilege to mentor throughout this research project. Finally, I would like to acknowledge my daughter, Grace, my why, who inspires me to navigate uncertain from a position of hope, as we create space for alternate ways of connecting with others.

Introduction: Circulating Emotions and Affect in Writing Centers

Janine Morris and Kelly Concannon

> *So rather than asking 'What are emotions?' I will ask, 'What do emotions do?' In asking this question, I will not offer a singular theory of emotion, or one account of the work that emotions do. Rather, I will track how emotions circulate between bodies, examining how they 'stick' as well as move.*
>
> —Sara Ahmed, *The Cultural Politics of Emotion*

At the beginning of each semester, the two of us lead a workshop where tutors in our writing center explore the role emotions and affect play in our work. We begin the workshop by asking tutors to identify instances where emotions and affect impact their experiences in the center, with the intention of creating strategies for navigating emotions and affect throughout the semester. In the workshop, we draw from scholarship on emotions and affect to create rich and complex definitions of these terms that tutors can return to (Ahmed; Micciche, *Doing*). Tutors share stories about stressful consultations, tips for cultivating mindfulness between sessions, and the joys that come out of the work they do. Our purpose is to create a space where tutors recognize how they are impacted by affective and emotional encounters and understand how emotions move between and among them. We aim to recognize emotions and affect as central to writing center work, rather than something left at the periphery.

During the workshop, tutors share stories and strategies with one another, and we often leave the session with an enhanced sense of community and connection. We try to set in motion multiple ways to name, discuss, and validate how emotions and affect permeate the work we do. Yet, in spite of the positive feelings in the moment, those initial discussions about emotions and affect fade away as the semester progresses. Our talk about emotions and affect gets absorbed into the being and doing that take place during the semester. However, emotions linger, and we experience them even if they are unnamed. Consequently, throughout the course of the semester, we often return to our earlier conversations around emotions and affect—and attempt to push the boundaries of the comfortable and neutral narratives that often characterize writing center work and experiences.

Stories shape the work that we do, producing both reassurance and dissonance as we reconcile lore to the lived reality of writing center scholarship and practice. Multiple writing center scholars have examined how stories shape current and future practices (Briggs and Woolbright; Denny; Geller et al.; *Writing Center Journal*). In *Peripheral Visions for Writing Centers*, Jackie Grutsch McKinney argues that "writing center work is complex, but the storytelling of writing center work is not" (3). She reveals that the "grand narrative" of writing center work, that "writing centers are comfortable, iconoclastic spaces where all students go to get one-on-one tutoring on their writing," creates a divide between what we do and what we say (3). The consequence of this divide and these narratives is that only "certain activities are legible in writing center work and others are not" (5). Along with Grutsch McKinney, we believe that things that fall outside the legible scope often remain invisible and unintelligible to others. While we might not always acknowledge emotions and affect, they are always there, always at the surface of our work. This project is motivated by our awareness of how writing center work is emotional and affective. We are committed to making that work visible. To that end, we recognize how the stories that circulate around writing center work create particular types of structures for how we *should* experience emotions and affect in our respective spaces.

We recognize and value the role that emotions and affect have in the learning, training, and the daily practices of our academic lives. However, we find the discussion of emotions and affect in writing center scholarship leaves us wanting more, and we argue for a space that brings together varied examinations of emotions and affect showing up in our everyday writing center practices. We see this collection achieving that goal and complementing the existing scholarship on writing center and writing program administrator emotional labor (Adams Wooten et al., *The Things*; Caswell et al.; Jackson et al.; Saleem), graduate student administrative experiences (Elder et al.), and the affective and emotional challenges of daily administrative work (Adams Wooten et al., *WPAs*; Cole and Hassel; Jacobs and Micciche; Micciche, "More Than"; Davies; Holt et al.; Ritter; Sura et al.). Adding to these existing discussions about administrative labor, contributors examine becoming and leaving administrative positions (Grutsch McKinney et al.; Navickas et al.), navigating burnout and imposter syndrome in graduate student administrative identities (Chavannes et al.), and maintaining positive workplace relationships with various institutional stakeholders (Giaimo; Hull and Brooks-Gillies; Cirillo-McCarthy and Leahy). Contributors highlight the often collaborative structures involved in writing center administration and the complex layers of interaction among administrators, tutors, and the students we serve.

This collection goes beyond administrative experiences to bring together multiple perspectives from writing center scholars, administrators, and tutors who experience and grapple with emotions and affect in everyday writing center work and research. *Emotions and Affect in Writing Centers* explores how emotions and affect circulate and are studied, understood, and represented within writing centers. In developing this collection, we argue that emotions and affect continue to play an ever-present but under-emphasized role in writing center scholarship. Although emotions have certainly been acknowledged in writing center research (Evertz and Fitzpatrick; Follett; Giaimo and Hashlamon; Hudson; Jackson et. al; Lawson; Meuse; Mills; Nicklay; Perry; *Praxis* Admin; Rowell; Saleem; Taylor; Yoon and Stutelberg), this collection centralizes emotions and affect at the forefront of writing center work. To date, there are no single collections exploring emotions and affect from the perspectives of writing center administrators *and* tutors. Thus, this collection builds on existing scholarship by bringing together these diverse perspectives and introducing multiple methods of studying and understanding emotions and affect. Collectively, contributors raise questions concerning how to study, experience, and reflect on emotions and affect within a variety of institutional contexts and specific rhetorical situations. *Emotions and Affect in Writing Centers* demonstrates how a more complex understanding of emotions and affect problematize, support, and expand writing center theories and practices.

We align ourselves with Sara Ahmed, who explains that we need to ask better questions when it comes to engaging with emotions— namely how emotions and affect directly impact theory and practice, as well as the methods we use to share our stories and experiences (4). Ahmed suggests focusing more critically on the roles that emotions play in allowing and disallowing engagement, connection, and practitioner work. Thus, Ahmed argues for a clear shift from solely focusing on what emotions and affect *are* to focusing more on their functionality, or what they *do*. Across this collection, contributors explore the active role of emotions and affect in researching, training, tutoring, and administrating writing centers.

The collection deliberately seeks to create spaces for an exploration of emotions and affect from multiple positions. It does so by anchoring emotions and affect in stakeholder positions: writing center directors, administrators, and individuals in leadership positions, including graduate and undergraduate students. *Emotions and Affect in Writing Centers* adds to these existing conversations on administrative work and emotional labor in writing centers and would find an appropriate audience in individuals in leadership positions—namely those who work in academic affairs, tutoring and testing centers, teaching and academic learning centers, and the like. Along with appealing to administrators, we hope this collection will be adopted by writing centers for tutor training or in graduate and undergraduate classrooms focusing on writing center pedagogy. Concerns about graduate student emotional labor and well-being are particularly important to writing center scholarship and practice (Nicolas), and a collection emphasizing emotions in training adds to that body of scholarship. Because the collection focuses on emotion from theoretical and practical angles, our work affords students and administrators a complex analytic to assist in making sense of the complex role that emotions and affect play in writing centers.

Defining Key Terms

Underlying this collection is an attempt to clarify and make visible the role emotions and affect play in writing centers. Authors in this collection have chosen when and how to use and distinguish among emotions, affect, and feelings in their chapters. Here, we situate those terms and offer a brief overview of how they relate to and differ from one another. We build on the histories of emotions and affect in writing studies and writing centers (Lape; Lawson; Micciche, *Doing*; Micciche, "Staying;" Nelson) by charting emotional and affective workings in everyday writing center practices and research settings. We stress the importance of recognizing and studying how affect and emotion are *both* at play in writing centers. By exploring things like sighs or affective nonlexical vocalizations (Haen), emotional performance (Iantorno), crying (Brentnell et al.), individual tutoring sessions (Bell), and listening (Lerner and Oddis; Corbett and Villarreal), contributors make visible how emotions and affect circulate, are embodied, and have unintentional consequences on relationships and interactions. Contributors also argue that emotions and affect are valuable sites of analysis and exploration and look into how emotions and affect manifest in administrative identities and relationships (Chavannes et al.; Grutsch McKinney et al.), decisions to stay or leave (Hull and Brooks-Gillies; Navickas et al.), tutor training (Del Russo), and larger institutional power structures (Giaimo; Napoleone).

Like Ahmed, we avoid distinguishing between *good* and *bad* emotions and instead acknowledge the importance of how emotions are shaped, circulated, read, and interpreted (6). Across the collection, contributors explore how "emotions shape the very surfaces of bodies, which take shape through the repetition of actions over time, as well as through orientations towards and away from others. Indeed, attending to emotions might show us how all actions are reactions, in the sense that what we do is shaped by the contact we have with others" (Ahmed 4). The idea of contact, repetition of actions over time, and orientations underlie chapters as contributors view the ways emotions linger, affect, and shape bodily responses, spaces, interactions, and relationships. For example, in her chapter on how attitudes towards writing develop over time, Lisha Daniels Storey argues that dispositions accumulate and are both individually experienced and socially constructed, impacted by past experiences, environments, and relations. These past experiences come to reside in the body and lead to embodied reactions and responses to present spaces and occurrences. Like Micciche explains, "emotions *do* something besides express individuals' feelings . . . emotions function as the adhesive that aligns certain bodies together and binds a person/position/role to an affective state" (*Doing* 75). Through their chapters, contributors demonstrate the ways that emotions, over time, impact interactions and workplace experiences, and have material consequences on administrator and tutor health, well-being, decision-making, training, and interpersonal relationships.

Central to our view of emotions and affect is that they have embodied and material consequences. Conceptualized in an active sense, we see emotions involving movement between people (Jacobs and Micciche 3), encompassing an expression of feelings (Micciche, *Doing* 15), and involving others (Seibel Trainor 647). Emotions are personal, socially constructed, biological, cognitive, and embodied. We gravitate towards Lynn Worsham's definition of emotion as "the tight braid of affect and judgement, socially and historically constructed and bodily lived, through which the symbolic takes hold of and binds the individual, in complex and contradictory ways, to the social order and its structure of meaning" (216). As our contributors demonstrate, our emotional responses are wrapped up in how we feel, how we learn to feel, and how we interpret and express those feelings. Throughout the collection, contributors emphasize the emotional consequences of attitudes and dispositions (Del Russo; Iantorno; Storey), class (Napoleone), race and gender (Chavannes et al.; Brentnell et al.), and cultural backgrounds (Bell). The feelings we have and emotional expressions we display function to: circulate between others, "stick:, and consequently impact our varying relationships. The feelings we have and emotional expressions circulate between others, "stick," and impact our relationships (Micciche, *Doing* 36).

Affect, as part of our emotional expressions, is experienced pre-discursively and is conceptualized as a change of states or changes between people (Edbauer Rice; Nelson). As Micciche writes, affect "refers more to a sense and an atmosphere than it does to a specific, intentioned act of making or unmaking" (*Doing* 15). Affect involves an ephemeral quality or sense that changes between states, distinguishing it from the outward expression of emotion. Affect exists corporeally and is transmitted between bodies and people socially, biologically, and physiologically (Brennan). For example, in Lisa Bell's chapter, she considers the affective and relational qualities underlying tutor interactions with L2 students. By focusing her study on the subtle attitudes and interactions taking place within tutorials, she shows how affect exists below the surface of tutor awareness. Throughout the collection, contributors bring together emotion and affect, using it in different ways.

The affective turn in composition studies and rhetoric has already influenced how administrators and teachers situate and recognize the role of affect and emotion in education, technology, and workplace settings (Benesch; Boler; Caswell; Davies; Doe et al.; Jacobs and Micciche; Jensen and Wallace; Lindquist; Micciche, *Doing*; Stenberg; Ticineto Clough and Halley; Weisser et al.; Williams; Worsham). Aligning with this scholarship, we argue that writing center administrators, practitioners, and tutors alike could benefit from recognizing the practical and theoretical elements of emotions and affect and incorporating those theories and lessons into tutor training and writing center interactions. We offer this collection to more fully complicate how emotions and affect influence writing center work. This collection both theorizes the centrality of emotion and affect and provides suggestions for making intelligible the material realities of emotion and affect in writing center scholarship.

METHODOLOGICAL APPROACHES TO EMOTIONS AND AFFECT

This collection explores what emotions and affect *do* by adopting various methods and methodological lenses to study emotions and affect. The way to disrupt and complicate writing center grand narratives, and make more aspects of writing center work visible, is to find ways of studying emotions and affect that go beyond a surface acknowledgement that emotions and affect exist. Contributors embody Grutsch McKinney's ideal for writing center scholars to conduct "serious, interesting, [and] groundbreaking research" (*Strategies* xxii). Contributors study emotions and affect through longitudinal studies (Grutsch McKinney et al.), mixed methods (Bell; Lerner and Oddis), action research (Navickas et al.), conversation analysis (Haen), reflective journals (Del Russo), case studies (Corbett and Villarreal), surveys (Iantorno), and personal narratives (Chavannes et al.; Brentnell et al.; Cirillo-McCarthy and Leahy).

In writing centers, many have challenged researchers to move away from the "stories and [. . .] gut feelings" that make up reports about writing center work (Wells 88). As Jaclyn Wells explains, "Many recent scholars have advocated for replacing the lore and anecdote that often drive writing center studies with research, and more specifically, research that fits Richard H. Haswell's (2005) replicable, agreeable, and data-supported (RAD) criteria" (88). Part of the push for more data-driven research is to help legitimize the work being done in writing centers and justify that work to outside stakeholders (Liggett et al.). Moving beyond either/or debates about particular methods, *Emotions and Affect in Writing Centers* features a plurality of methods, with contributors often employing multiple methods in their chapters. We agree with Sarah Liggett et al. in "view[ing] the nature of writing processes and writing center practices as complex enough to warrant making and using knowledge simultaneously in different ways" (55). In this collection, chapters by Grutsch McKinney et al.; Bell; Neal Lerner and Kyle Oddis; and Steven Corbett and Katherine Villareal show how relying on multiple methods (like surveys, interviews, case studies, and longitudinal research) and shifting methodological approaches over time can provide different kinds of insight into emotional and affective work.

In writing studies, methodological conversations have acknowledged and validated researcher positionality in the process of conducting research. For example, in Maureen Daly Goggin and Peter Goggin's introduction to *Serendipity in Rhetoric, Writing, and Literacy Research*, they focus on the benefits of happenstance in conducting research (6). Contributors in their collection use narratives about serendipity in research to challenge "notions of objectivity, impartiality, and pure data in research" (7). Likewise, in Will Banks et al.'s *Re/Orienting Writing Studies*, editors begin the collection by focusing on researcher "orientation, about how (and why and even to what extent) the researcher turns toward the objects, participants, or contexts of study" (4). For both Goggin and Goggin and Banks et al., an acknowledgement of researcher orientation goes beyond describing firsthand experience to critically examining how researchers approach meaning making in understanding their emotional and affective experiences in data collection and analysis. In this collection, contributors make visible and examine their own positionalities in relation to the research they conduct. For instance, Kate Navickas et al.'s chapter includes action research and interviews of the authors based on their experiences. Comparatively, in Corbett and Villarreal's chapter, they look extensively at Corbett's role as a researcher in previous case studies he conducted. In these instances, researcher identity and affect surrounding research become central components of data collection and knowledge making practices.

The collaborative nature of the contributions and inclusion of contributor narratives illustrate the ways that writing center work and research is strengthened by multiple perspectives and personal involvement. Throughout the collection, many of the chapters are co-authored and focus on interpersonal relationships in writing centers. These contributions, particularly by Kelin Hull and Marilee Brooks-Gillies; Nicole Chavannes et al.; Lauren Brentnell et al.; and Erica Cirillo-McCarthy and Elizabeth Leahy demonstrate how even within similar institutional contexts or familiar relationships, emotions and affect manifest in varied and complex ways. The decision to explore emotions and affect together further emphasizes the social nature of emotions and affect and mirrors the ethos of writing centers as spaces where relationships form, where togetherness is physically structured into place.

COLLECTION ORGANIZATION

Emotions and Affect in Writing Centers is organized into fifteen chapters in three sections. We grouped chapters into sections focusing on administration, tutoring and training, and relational encounters. Contributors explore how lived, embodied, and material experiences of emotions and affect in writing centers are studied, theorized and researched. Many of our contributors identify how marginalized identities, experiences, and histories can be mobilized through a more careful attention to emotions and affect. To this end, contributors offer readers particular recommendations throughout the collection, including suggestions for training and future conversations between writing center stakeholders. The sections are organized based on the identified positionality of the contributor. In recognizing that emotions and affect are experienced in different ways, this collection emphasizes administrators' and tutors' perspectives, while additionally creating space for researchers to reflect on their methods and methodological orientations. In turn, we hope to mobilize how to study, reflect on, and continue to complicate the roles that emotions and affect can potentially play in our futures.

Themes. Contributors explore how affect and emotions gather and impact identities, relationships, and dispositions over time (rather than limiting them to experiences happening in fleeting moments). Thus, themes of leaving, becoming, and belonging cross the chapters and sections. Significantly, contributors identify the emotions and affect involved in performing particular assumed or agreed upon roles; they explore and expose how emotions and affect impact their membership within an academic community; and finally, they document how emotions and affect impact their choices to remain in writing center positions. It is important to note how contributors are complicating the idea of circulation. Contributors reveal the tension between the types of emotions and affect that are traditionally rendered intelligible and consequently repeated. Thus, the power of this collection is that contributors bring to light conversations surrounding emotions and affect that are usually ignored, marginalized, and/or suppressed. Therefore, contributors create spaces for how emotions and affect impact the work that they do and how they are able to connect with others—within and beyond their respective writing centers. This shift creates new possibilities for future writing center scholarship.

The first portion of the collection outlines how emotions and affect impact administrative roles and relationships. In *Part I: Writing Center Administration*, contributors argue that more careful and nuanced approaches to studying administrative emotions are needed—a process that will disrupt concepts like community, collaboration, egalitarianism, and burnout. This focus mobilizes conversations of administrative affect and emotions on an institutional and structural level. Contributors explore why administrators leave, what it means to become an administrator, the embodied work of administration, and the emotions involved in graduate student administration.

In the first chapter, Jackie Grutsch McKinney, Nicole Caswell, and Rebecca Jackson demonstrate that because emotions accumulate over time, recognizing them in the moment provides only a partial picture of what administrators experience. Using case study results and subsequent surveys of over one-hundred writing center administrators, Grutsch McKinney et al. examine administrator satisfaction and intention to leave and make a case for studying emotional labor. Similarly, Kelin Hull and Marilee Brooks-Gillies use storytelling to explore how administrators establish community while navigating their relationships and shifting roles in their centers. Hull and Brooks-Gillies articulate the importance of creating space for the messiness and emotional involvement of writing center work—themes that echo across the chapters. Building further on administrative identities, Kate Navickas, Kristi Murray Costello, and Tabatha Simpson-Farrow ground their exploration of internal struggle and conflicts tied to administrator identities by drawing on rhetorical genre studies to explore sites where those roles are enacted. They use this chapter to examine the emotional labor involved in becoming and unbecoming writing center administrators and identify how emotional labor decreases over time once administrators become comfortable in their positions. Accordingly, as administrators become more comfortable, they experience increased confidence and positive feelings in their roles. To conclude the first section, Nicole Chavannes, Monique Cole, Jordan Guido, and Sabrina Louissaint use narratives to share their perspectives as graduate students in administrative positions and the emotional labor, imposter syndrome, and burnout they experienced when transitioning into their roles. Focusing on the complexities of navigating multiple roles as graduate students, Chavannes et al. offer strategies for increasing communication and making space for emotional dialogue in writing center work. While contributors in this section focus on their experiences as researching administrators, the larger questions around belonging, becoming, leaving, and accepting positions within writing centers also apply to tutors and people working in writing centers or coming into higher education positions.

Part II: Tutoring and Training focuses on emotions that come up in tutors' day-to-day experiences in writing centers, including face-to-face and online sessions. Often conceiving of writing centers as boundary or liminal spaces, contributors in this section explore how tutors and students identify with and are positioned within writing centers and tutoring relationships. Chapters examine how emotions and affect impact tutor identities, consultations, training initiatives, and encounters with one another and students visiting writing centers. Class performance, linguistic backgrounds, social justice, and power structures are emphasized and considered in light of policy making and training initiatives.

Contributors in this section go beyond the surface features of tutoring interactions and critically examine how emotions and affect create particular ways of being and knowing that oftentimes dictate how individuals express identities. To begin this section, Anna Rita Napoleone argues that the performance of emotions and affect is embodied and socially situated; thus, she explores the types of "affective orientations" that influence writing center practices. Napoleone concludes by indicating that writing center tutors can make visible often unexplored aspects of class performance as products of academic spaces. Similarly, Neal Lerner and Kyle Oddis examine how rhetorical listening and emotions are represented in online, text-based, synchronous consultations. Lerner and Oddis examine how questions, exclamations, and emoticons are used to build and maintain rapport. Their chapter points administrators and scholars to examine how relationship-building happens online and the ways that emotions and affect are involved in those sessions. Lisa Bell's chapter continues the trajectory of studying emotion within rapport-building in tutoring sessions by examining how tutors approach working with L2 students. Bell examines the dispositions and associations tied to tutors being positioned as *experts* and students as *deficient*. Using mixed methods data analysis, Bell suggests the importance of training tutors for the relational and affective aspects of tutoring to enhance learning and growth.

The need to shift tutor training to account for the affective dimensions of writing center work extends across chapters and oftentimes accounts for issues related to social justice. For example, Celeste Del Russo's chapter relies on reflective empathy narratives to examine tutors' commitments to social justice work in writing centers. Del Russo argues for cultivating critical empathy in tutor training and using training interventions as a tool for both reflection and application. She argues that this process creates more engaged and reflective conversations and understandings of social justice work in writing centers. Similarly, Lauren Brentnell, Elise Dixon, and Rachel Robinson illustrate how crying serves as a powerful move to disrupt institutional structures. Drawing from multiple narratives, the authors demonstrate embodied vulnerability in writing center work. They suggest that creating spaces for vulnerability can lead to critical conversations and enhanced understandings of emotions and affect.

The final two chapters in this section examine affective and emotional displays, questioning their function in tutoring sessions. Mike Haen's chapter examines sighs and groans as emotional displays that build affiliation in tutoring sessions rather than signal conflict or negative affect. Haen argues the non-verbal aspects of conversations can help tutors become more reflective in their work. Bringing together different performances and emotional displays, Luke Iantorno's chapter explores how positive emotional displays relate to tutor burnout. Iantorno's chapter reveals the ways that tutors respond and react to their own and others' emotions and how they view emotional control as part of working in writing centers. Along with other chapters in this section, Iantorno reveals the importance of integrating emotional and affective awareness into tutor training and education.

Part III: Relational Encounters concludes the collection by suggesting new areas of research and directions of study. Contributors think through the embodied implications of emotive and affective work as it connects writing centers to outside stakeholders, including research participants, faculty, and upper administration. They highlight how the embodied qualities of emotions and affect resonate outwards—impacting not only our everyday work in writing centers but also our research relationships and interactions with others, spaces, dispositions, and wellness initiatives as we move beyond the center.

Together, these final chapters illustrate the reach of emotional and affective encounters and outline the ways that emotions and affect are never just contained within individuals or specific interactions. In Steven Corbett and Katherine Villarreal's chapter, they posit feminist listening *with* research participants as a strategy for conducting RAD—replicable, aggregate, and data-driven—research. Their re-orientation to research has transformative potential for establishing stronger connections and deeper understandings of research and participant identities and experiences. Their call to linger and listen resonates with the embodied approach other contributors in this section take by understanding the impact of emotions and affect in various contexts. Moving beyond tutoring interactions, Erica Cirillo-McCarthy and Elizabeth Leahy argue for cultivating *metis*—an embodied knowledge—when emotions surface in conflict with faculty outside writing centers. Cirillo-McCarthy and Leahy's metic approach acknowledges and recognizes frustrations and felt emotions rather than running or turning away from them. When practiced regularly, cultivating metis intelligence allows administrators to more strategically and thoughtfully respond in key moments.

Embodied knowledges not only inform our interactions with others, but they also interact with larger movements and impact orientations toward writing and educational spaces. In Lisha Daniels Storey's chapter, she draws on critical affect and emotion studies to explore how dispositions towards writing form, often devalue, and result in embodied tendencies. By learning how lived experiences contribute to dispositions towards writing, Storey argues for a more nuanced understanding of how and why writers might have the orientations and feelings they do. The collection concludes with a return to administrative concerns and questions about leadership responsibility within larger wellness movements. Genie Giaimo's chapter asks administrators to question the necessity and responsibility they have in encouraging wellness at the micro level when austerity measures are imposed by those who have greater power. Turning to game theory as a way to strategically engage with university administration, Giaimo argues that writing center administrators need to collectively develop sustainable solutions to issues of administrative labor, find ways to articulate the importance of our work, and advocate for additional resources at the macro level to avoid exploitation.

To conclude the collection, authors share their perspectives on emotion and affect research and practices in light of the COVID-19 pandemic. Through short reflections, authors consider how rapport-building, emotional displays, and resource inequity have impacted relationships and writing center work. Taken together, contributors in this collection are just beginning to understand the many ways that emotions and affect intersect with writing center work and experiences. This collection represents an invitation for additional research, building on the methods, applying them in different contexts, and diversifying approaches to understand and work with emotions at all levels of writing center encounters.

Works Cited

Ahmed, Sara. *The Cultural Politics of Emotion*. Routledge, 2004.

Adams Wooten, et al., editors. *WPAs in Transition: Navigating Education Leadership Positions*. Utah State UP, 2018.

—, et al., editors. *The Things We Carry: Strategies for Recognizing and Negotiating Emotional Labor in Writing Program Administration*. Utah State UP, 2020.

Banks, William P., et al., editors. "Re/Orienting Writing Studies: Thoughts on In(queer)y." *Re/Orienting Writing Studies: Queer Methods, Queer Projects*. Utah State UP, 2019, pp. 3–23.

Benesch, Sarah. *Considering Emotions in Critical English Language Teaching: Theories and Praxis.* Routledge, 2012.

Boler, Megan. *Feeling Power: Emotions and Education.* Routledge, 1999.

Brennan, Teresa. *The Transmission of Affect.* Cornell UP, 2004.

Briggs, Lynn Craigue, and Meg Woolbright. *Stories from the Center: Connecting Narrative and Theory in the Writing Center.* National Council of Teachers of English, 2000.

Caswell, Nicole, et al. *The Working Lives of New Writing Center Directors.* Utah State UP, 2016.

—. "Writing Assessment, Emotions, Feelings and Teachers." *The CEA Forum*, vol. 40, no. 1, 2011, pp. 57–70.

Cole, Kristi, and Holly Hassel, editors. *Surviving Sexism in Academia: Strategies for Feminist Leadership.* Routledge, 2017.

Davies, Laura J. "Grief and the New WPA." *WPA: Writing Program Administration*, vol. 40, no. 2, 2017, pp. 40–51.

Denny, Harry C. *Facing the Center: Toward an Identity Politics of One-to-One Mentoring.* Utah State UP, 2010.

Doe, Sue, et al. "What Works and What Counts: Valuing the Affective in Non-Tenure Track Advocacy." *Contingency, Exploitation, and Solidarity: Labor and Action in English Composition*, edited Seth Kahn, et al. WAC Clearinghouse, 2017, pp. 213–34.

Edbauer Rice, Jenny. "The New 'New': Making a Case for Critical Affect Studies." *Quarterly Journal of Speech*, vol. 94, no. 2, 2008, pp. 200–12.

Elder, Cristyn, et al. "Strengthening Graduate Student Preparation for WPA Work." *WPA: Writing Program Administration*, vol. 37, no. 2, 2014, pp. 13–35.

Evertz, Kathy, and Renata Fitzpatrick. "Guest Editor's Note." Special issue on the affective dimensions of writing center work, *WLN: A Journal of Writing Center Scholarship*, vol. 42, no. 9–10, 2018, p. 1.

Follett, Jennifer R. "How Do You Feel about This Paper?" A Mixed-Methods Study of How Writing Center Tutors Address Emotion. 2016. Indiana U of Pennsylvania, PhD dissertation.

Geller, Anne Ellen, et al. *The Everyday Writing Center: A Community of Practice.* Utah State UP, 2006.

Giaimo, Genie, and Yanar Hashlamon. "Guest Editors' Note." Special issue on wellness and self-care in writing centers, *WLN: A Journal of Writing Center Scholarship*, vol. 44, no. 5–6, 2020, p. 1.

Goggin, Maureen Daly, and Peter N. Goggin, editors. "Stumbling into Wisdom in Rhetoric, Writing, and Literacy Research: An Introduction." *Serendipity in Rhetoric, Writing, and Literacy Research.* UP of Colorado, 2018, pp. 13–24.

Grutsch McKinney, Jackie. *Peripheral Visions for Writing Centers.* Utah State UP, 2013.

Holt, Mara, et al. "Making Emotion Work Visible in Writing Program Administration." *A Way to Move: Rhetorics of Emotion and Composition Studies,* edited Dale Jacobs and Laura Micciche, Heinemann, 2003, pp. 147–60.

Hudson, Tracy. "Head 'Em Off at the Pass: Strategies for Handling Emotionalism in the Writing Center." *The Writing Lab Newsletter,* vol. 25, no. 5, 2001, pp. 10–12.

Jacobs, Dale, and Laura R. Micciche, editors. *A Way to Move: Rhetorics of Emotion and Composition Studies.* Heinemann, 2003.

Jackson, Rebecca, et al. "Writing Center Administration and/as Emotional Labor." *Composition Forum,* vol. 34, 2016.

Jensen, Katharine Ann, and Miriam Wallace. Introduction. "Facing Emotions." Special issue on emotions, *PMLA,* by Jensen and Wallace, vol. 130, no. 5, 2015, pp. 1249–68.

Lape, Noreen. "Training Tutors in Emotional Intelligence: Toward a Pedagogy of Empathy." *The Writing Lab Newsletter,* vol. 33, no. 2, 2008, pp. 1–6.

Lawson, Daniel. "Metaphors and Ambivalence: Affective Dimensions in Writing Center Studies." *WLN: A Journal of Writing Center Scholarship,* vol. 40, no. 3–4, 2015, pp. 20–26.

Liggett, Sarah, et al. "Mapping Knowledge-Making in Writing Center Research." *The Writing Center Journal,* vol. 31, no. 2, 2011, pp. 50–88.

Lindquist, Julie. "Class Affects, Classroom Affectations: Working through the Paradoxes of Strategic Empathy." *College English,* vol. 67, no. 2, 2004, pp. 187–209.

Meuse, Julia. "Tutoring Sessions as Safe Spaces: Affective Writing and the Personal Personal Statement." *Another Word,* 9 Feb. 2016, writing.wisc.edu/blog/tutoring-sessions-as-safe-spaces-affective-writing-and-the-personal-personal-statement/.

—. *Strategies for Writing Center Research.* Parlor Press, 2015.

Micciche, Laura R. *Doing Emotion: Rhetoric, Writing, and Teaching.* Heinemann, 2007.

—. "More than a Feeling: Disappointment and WPA Work." *College English*, vol. 64, no. 4, 2002, pp. 432–58.

—. "Staying with Emotion." *Composition Forum*, vol. 34, 2016.

Mills, Gayla. "Preparing for Emotional Sessions." *The Writing Lab Newsletter*, vol. 35, no. 6, 2011, pp. 1–5.

Nelson, Julie D. "An Unnecessary Divorce: Integrating the Study of Affect and Emotion in New Media." *Composition Forum*, vol. 34, 2016.

Nicklay, Jennifer. "Got Guilt? Consultant Guilt in the Writing Center Community." *The Writing Center Journal*, vol. 32, no. 1, 2012, pp. 14–27.

Nicolas, Melissa, editor. *(E)merging Identities: Graduate Students in the Writing Center*. Fountainhead Press, 2008.

Perry, Alison. "Training for Triggers: Helping Writing Center Consultants Navigate Emotional Sessions." *Composition Forum*, vol. 34, 2016.

Praxis Admin. "Emotions in the Writing Center." *Axis: The Blog*, 2016, www.praxisuwc.com/praxis-blog/2016/7/17/emotions-in-the-writing-center.

Ritter, Kelly. "'What Would Happen if Everybody Behaved as I Do?': May Bush, Randall Jarrell, and the Historical 'Disappointment' of Women WPAs." *Composition Studies*, vol. 39, no. 1, 2011, pp. 13–39.

Rowell, Christina. *Let's Talk Emotions: Re-envisioning the Writing Center through Consultant Emotional Labor*. 2015. East Carolina U, Master's Thesis.

Saleem, Muhammad Khurram. "The Languages in Which We Converse: Emotional Labor in the Writing Center and Our Everyday Lives." *The Peer Review*, vol. 2, no. 1, 2018.

Seibel Trainor, Jennifer. "From Identity to Emotion: Frameworks for Understanding, and Teaching Against, Anticritical Sentiments in the Classroom." *JAC: A Journal of Composition Theory*, vol. 26, no. 3–4, 2006, pp. 643–55.

Stenberg, Shari. "Teaching and (Re)learning the Rhetoric of Emotion." *Pedagogy*, vol. 11, no. 2, 2011, pp. 349–69.

Sura, Tom, et al. "Praxis and Allies: The WPA Boardgame." *WPA: Writing Program Administration*, vol. 32, no. 3, 2009, pp. 75–88.

Taylor, David. "Peer Tutoring's Hidden World: The Emotional and Social Issues." *The Writing Lab Newsletter*, vol. 13, no. 5, 1989, pp. 1–4.

Ticineto Clough, Patricia, and Jean Halley, editors. *The Affective Turn: Theorizing the Social*. Duke UP, 2007.

Weisser, Christian, et al. "From the Editors." Special issue on emotions, *Composition Forum*, vol. 34, 2016.

Wells, Jacyln. "Why We Resist 'Leading the Horse': Required Tutoring, RAD Research, and Our Writing Center Ideals." *The Writing Center Journal*, vol. 35, no. 2, 2016, pp. 87–114.

Williams, Bronwyn. "Having a Feel for What Works: Polymedia, Emotion, and Literacy Practices with Mobile Technologies." *Social Writing/Social Media: Publics, Presentations, Pedagogies*, edited by Douglas M. Walls and Stephanie Vie, WAC Clearinghouse, 2017, pp. 127–43.

Worsham, Lynn. "Going Postal: Pedagogic Violence and the Schooling of Emotion." *JAC: A Journal of Composition Theory*, vol. 18, no. 2, 1998, pp. 213–45.

Writing Center Journal. "From the Editors." Special issue on writing center narratives, *The Writing Center Journal*, vol. 28, no. 1, 2008, pp. 1–2.

Yoon, Stephanie Rollag, and Erin B. Stutelberg. "Rose's Writing: The Generative Power of Affect in a High School Writing Center." *WLN: A Journal of Writing Center Scholarship*, vol. 42, no. 9–10, 2018, pp. 18–25.

Part I: Writing Center Administration

1 Studying Emotion and Emotional Labor over Time and in Context

Jackie Grutsch McKinney, Nicole Caswell, and Rebecca Jackson

One could make the case that writing studies has taken an emotional turn. While rhetorical studies can trace a focus on emotions experienced by an audience since at least Aristotle's time, it was not until the 1980s that composition scholars began to take up questions about the role emotions play in our understanding of how students learn to write (Brand, "The Why;" Brand, *Psychology*). More recently, scholars such as Kia Richmond, Sally Chandler, and Amy Robillard have written about the influence of emotions within composition classrooms in instances such as teacher-student relationships, self-reflection papers, and plagiarism. Others, like Laura Micciche, argue that a community's values are expressed through emotion—that is, emotions are cultural artifacts and they are "a central component in social relation[s]" ("More Than" 452). Micciche writes specifically of the social relations and cultural values implicit in writing program administration; she untangles how emotions and the related work of "emotional labor" impact writing program and writing center administrative work ("More Than"). While in the past, publications on emotion in writing studies or writing center studies were hard to come by, this emotional turn means we now have special issues on emotion (*Composition Forum*; *WLN*), an edited collection on emotion and emotional labor (Adams Wooten et al.), and a generally more sustained interest in emotion within the discipline (McLeod; Worsham; Lindquist; Ritter; Winans; Mihut; Babb and Corbett).

As we have witnessed this emotional turn, the questions, *what is emotion? what is emotional labor?* and *how do we study emotion?* become pressing and, we argue, not yet answered adequately within writing studies. This chapter endeavors to define what emotion and emotional labor are and how we might study them in writing center work by discussing two longitudinal studies we have designed on writing center administrators' labor and leaving. We begin this chapter by reviewing how emotions and emotional labor have been approached within writing center scholarship. Then, we discuss how we methodologically approach emotion and emotional labor within our research to make the case for longitudinal methods to examine emotion and emotional labor within writing center work. Our discussion centers on the emotional dimension and the cumulative effect of emotions and emotional labor on those working in writing centers.

WHAT ARE EMOTIONS? WHAT IS EMOTIONAL LABOR?

Outside of writing studies, emotions can be understood as biological, neurological, sociological, and cultural phenomena. We argue that emotions are biologically, physiologically, and culturally constructed states of mind and body, emerging from the social-contextual interactions that shape individuals' behaviors or responses. While emotions are biological—all individuals have neuropathways that automatically fire when an emotional trigger happens—emotions are also social and cultural—environments shape individuals' knowledge of how and when to display emotions and even what counts as an emotion. Emotions are the names for states of mind and body we feel; self-recognition and individual expression of these states of mind and body vary due to an individual's psychology, neurology, exposure, and even the situation or trigger.

Many in writing studies have defined emotions similarly. Laura Micciche uses Sara Ahmed's definition of emotion as the "stickiness" between contexts and bodies (*Doing* 1). Similarly, Julie Lindquist argues "emotions are situated and constructed" (201), and Nicole Caswell has advocated for a cross-disciplinary approach in researching emotions ("Affective Tensions"). Moreover, Ligia Mihut ties together emotion and literacy—what she calls "literacy as affinity"—describing it as "a discursive repertoire comprised of language of empathy, personal experiences, and even social relations embedded in the literate experience" (58).

The other related term in this emotional turn is emotional labor. As with emotion, definitions vary by discipline and scholar. However, we define emotional labor as one of two performances of emotion that a person engages in while at work. One of these is often called emotion management. For this one, workers are urged to display certain emotions on the job and to repress or hide other emotions (Hochschild, "Emotion;" Tsang). Typically, workers are expected to be content, engaged, and happy to help. Instructions to "smile" and "look friendly" while working are instances of emotion management.

The other type of emotional labor refers to work that is relational and requires empathy, connection, mediation, and compassion to complete. Called "emotional work" by Holt et al., this form of emotional labor consists of "responsive attention to the emotional aspects of social life, including attention to the personal feelings, the emotional tenor of the relationships, empathy and encouragement, mediation of disputes, building emotional solidarity in groups, and using one's own or others' *outlaw emotions* to interrogate structures" (147). Sometimes this form of emotional labor is evident in job descriptions as "mentoring" or "handling issues as they arise," but more often than not, this labor is institutionally invisible but necessary to do the tasks that are in a job description. For instance, a new writing center director tasked with starting a writing fellows' program has to build relationships and trust with administrators and faculty; has to feel out the new culture and learn how and when to ask for support or budget lines; and has to earn the trust of those hired to be fellows so they enact the vision the new director has. All of this requires forging deep connections, maintaining an empathetic stance, performing negotiations, and working as a go-between—in brief, relational work. It is emotional labor because the new director is compelled to connect and relate to those at the workplace in order to accomplish the given task. The director must make and maintain "good" relationships to be a "good fit" or simply a "good director."

One small but crucial distinction we would like to make is that we do not call the emotions one has while at work emotional labor. For us, emotional labor is work that emerges as a consequence of specific emotions—relational labor—and mandates to display particular emotions—managed emotion. A writing center director might beupset or disappointed with a tutor who is late for a shift but having those feelings on the job does not fall within the definition we describe. Rather, emotional labor would be the relational work the writing center director engages in to address the tutor's late arrival, despite or because of the emotions the writing center director experiences.

How Have Writing Center Scholars Studied Emotions and Emotional Labor?

Publications on emotions exist in writing center studies, but it is assumed readers know what is meant by the constructs *emotion* and *emotional labor* without the scholar defining them. Generally, the research tends to forefront the individual component of emotion and disregard the cultural. Nonetheless, writing center scholars have focused on the emotions at play in consultant, writer, and administrator lives. Emotions have been framed both as intruders to tutoring that must be handled swiftly (Hudson; Nicklay) and as welcome facets of the community of writers that work within writing center spaces (Perry). Writing center scholarship has focused on specific emotions—like guilt (Nicklay)—or on emotions more broadly within the center (Haen; Perry).

There are various styles of inquiry and methods used by writing center scholars to study emotion. Tracy Hudson and Alison Perry each write about emotion from their own vantage points using practitioner reflection on real or imagined tutoring sessions and offer advice on how tutors might engage or not engage in emotions in writing center work. Using sample tutoring sessions, Hudson offers advice on how tutors can remain professional and detached from writers; for Hudson, emotions within sessions are distractions that take away from the goal of writing improvement (12). Perry, alternatively, advocates for tutors to remain emotionally engaged in their work.

Other scholars have used empirical research strategies like surveys and conversation analysis to understand emotion in writing centers. Jennifer Nicklay, for example, uses a survey to study tutors' emotions. Nicklay focuses on the principles that drive consulting methods and asks tutors if they feel guilty for using strategies that do not align with their tutoring principles. For the eleven consultants who responded, using directive tutoring methods prompted guilt (21-22). Then, there is Mike Haen, who uses conversational analysis to identify emotional moments within writing center session transcripts. Focusing specifically on the negative stances writers bring to sessions, Haen's analysis provides avenues for how tutors can productively respond (8).

There has been less written on emotional labor in writing center work. Exceptions include our case study project, *The Working Lives of Writing Center Directors*, outlined in the next section and Muhammad Khurram Saleem's article, "The Languages in Which We Converse: Emotional Labor in the Writing Center and Our Everyday Lives." Drawing on theoretical and practitioner inquiry, Saleem advocates for tutors to engage in relationship building within sessions and lean into emotional labor to do so. Situating himself theoretically with Arlie Hochschild (*Managed*), Saleem defines emotional labor as "acts that let [people] know [they] are loved, cared for, welcome[d], and valued" (para 22).

All types of inquiry have benefits and limitations. While we can and do learn from writers' personal experiences and from short-term empirical studies, we make the case for longitudinal, contextual studies—practitioner, qualitative, or quantitative—in understanding emotion and emotional labor within writing center work. Perhaps ironically, because emotions can bubble up and then pass within a few minutes, we have found that the cumulative effect of emotions and emotional labor is consequential to writing center work and is best studied over time. Longitudinal research allows for greater trust and deeper connection with participants, better clarity on dominant or residual emotions, rather than fleeting ones, and an understanding of participants' perspectives on the effects of emotions and emotional labor on their job over time. Further, looking at emotions and emotional labor in context helps provide us perspective. There is no question that humans have emotions at work and that writing center administration involves emotional labor; however, if we look at those elements in isolation, we may overemphasize their impact or importance.

PROJECT ONE: THE CASE STUDY

Our advocacy for longitudinal, contextual studies comes from our experience collaborating on two studies involving emotions and emotional labor among writing center administrators at work. The first was a case study project that resulted in *The Working Lives of New Writing Center Directors*. Over the course of one academic year, we studied nine new writing center directors in different institutions in the US and Europe to answer our two main research questions: *Who directs writing centers?* and *what is the work of directing a writing center?* We interviewed each director about once a month—via phone or video chat—and asked them about their roles and their labor. We were particularly interested in the tasks they did, the tasks they wanted to do, and what prevented them from completing those tasks.

This longitudinal, qualitative research project allowed us to form a level of intimacy with participants that is not possible—sometimes is not even appropriate—in other types of research. Relationship building was vital since we knew we would be asking directors questions that they might not answer if they did not trust us and that they would not answer without confidentiality. In this respect, our research approach and process are themselves grounded in emotional labor as relational work. From the start of the project, we wanted to know about the emotions that participants were having on the job. Nikki had previously studied the emotions that instructors had while grading and responding to writing (Caswell, "Affective;" "Dynamic;" and "Writing"), which sparked our curiosity about the emotions experienced during writing center work. Thus, one question we asked during most monthly interviews was "what emotions did you experience during the past month?" As expected, participants had a variety of emotions while working—both positive and negative—that they shared with us in response to this question and other questions. For example, on the positive side, we heard Allison tell us she is "over the moon about the quality of [her] tutors." Every participant also had negative feelings. Darya tells us at one point she was "really frustrated and sounded maybe a little abrupt and snappy with my colleagues" because they will not support her. Again, we believe shaping the study as longitudinal and qualitative, and thus relational, allowed participants to trust us with their emotions at work. Moreover, interviewing participants frequently throughout the academic year meant participants were not asked to think back to the emotions they had over the whole year at, say, the end of the year, but rather were asked in the moment, month to month, what emotions they were experiencing.

Conversely, we did *not* set out to study emotional labor; however, it became clear in our data analysis that emotional labor, too, was part of the story of working as a new writing center director. In our first round of coding, we identified the many tasks that participants did. As we tried to group the tasks, we looked at the data and at the literature for theoretical frameworks for how to talk about the labor. We found many of the tasks fell into the categories used by Anne Ellen Geller and Harry Denny—everyday administrative and intellectual labor)—but some tasks—like mentoring, relationship building, conflict negotiations—fell into another category that we saw as and named emotional labor.

We eventually coded two types of emotional labor for our participants, as described in our definition earlier in this chapter, emotion management and relational work. When directors told us about emotional management, we got a glimpse of the disconnect they had between the emotions they were feeling inwardly and those they felt permitted to perform outwardly. For instance, Joe, a tenure-track director at a midwestern public university, told us he makes sure to keep a smile on his face when he walks across campus just in case anyone sees him—he wants to make sure they know he is a friendly writing center director.

We saw relational work frequently among participants as the work of administering a writing center is highly interpersonal. Participants give "responsive attention" to tutors, writers, colleagues, and supervisors (Holt et al. 147). Katerina, for instance, a director of a brand-new writing center at an Eastern European boarding high school, has to continually make nice with her fellow teachers who are suspicious of her course release to direct the writing center. She makes time to stop by their classrooms and talk about the writing center and other topics to warm the chilly relationships.

We believe building flexibility and recursiveness into our interview protocol allowed us to ask follow-up questions on any interview topic we wanted to hear more about and allowed us to circle back to issues that came up in previous interviews. If a participant was having difficulty with their supervisor, for instance—and many did—we would check back in the following month if they had any updates for us. Since emotional labor is relational and relationships frequently change, the longitudinal, qualitative approach enabled us to see how the relationships evolved over the course of the year and, consequently, how emotional labor itself changed. Additionally, with monthly check-ins, we could better understand if a task a participant was feeling excited or angry about in one month was even on their mind the next. In this way, multiple interviews with the same participants allowed us to correct for an atypical bad day or good day when our goal was to paint a picture of a more typical day. Having multiple points of data for each participant gave us context and perspective for understanding the significance *for the participant* of the emotions on the job or emotional labor.

PROJECT TWO: THE SURVEY

We did not anticipate emotional labor factoring so decisively in directors' roles because there simply was no previous research on directors' emotional labor. We also did not anticipate that our study would point us to a potentially troubling trend: new writing center directors leaving their positions or leaving the profession. But it did. By the end of our study year, three of the nine case study participants had told us they would not be returning to their positions the following year. One stepped down, one moved to another state and took a different academic position, and one completed the two-year term of her position. Now, six years later, only three of the original nine are in the positions they held during the study year.[1] This finding spurred our next project and research questions: *Why do writing center administrators leave their jobs or the profession?* and *What role, if any, does emotional labor play in this decision?*

To begin to answer why writing center administrators leave, we looked more broadly at the existing research about why employees leave jobs in general, since little research exists on writing center administrators specifically.[2] The existing general research is extensive—researchers have peered into nearly every sector, including education and higher education. We read widely and deeply, and eventually landed on four salient, related terms: job satisfaction and burnout, both of which are closely connected to emotions and forms of emotional labor (Grandey and Gabriel); turnover or turnover intention (leaving a job or intending to leave a job); and flight (leaving a profession). Job satisfaction, for example, is related to a number of factors, including one's perceptions and feelings about the labor, workplace, coworkers, and supervisors. Burnout can happen if one reaches emotional exhaustion, as when unceasing emotional labor leaves one tapped out. From our case study and review of literature on turnover and flight, we came to understand that while emotions and emotional labor might be able to be separated from studies of work, they ought not be. Put simply, there is no work without emotions and emotional labor. A good study should be able to describe emotions and emotional labor and the effect they have on employee well-being, turnover, and flight. Said another way, our research keeps pointing us to the *effect* of emotion and emotional labor on writing center work.

---

1. One other has remained in writing center work, but at a different institution.

2. One exception is Healy, who seeks attitudinal data on writing center administrators in his study.

Though we noticed in our case study that there seemed to be a connection between how our participants were feeling at and about their work and their decision to stay at their jobs, with only nine participants, it was impossible to say what we saw was widespread. We knew we would want more participants when we launched our new study, the survey project. We also knew that most administrators who take a new job or leave the profession complete the academic year; in essence, that means there is one period of turnover and flight per year. We decided our study needed to be longer than one year to capture more than one period. We concluded we would aim to recruit at least one-hundred writing center administrators as survey participants who would agree to participate (i.e., retake the survey) for five years. Our hope was that we could learn how participants are feeling in their work in aggregate, and we could also track individual participants from year to year to see if we could identify factors that correlated with turnover or leaving.

The original case study project illustrated for us the importance of sticking with participants over several data collection periods. Thus, while we will not "know" the participants in the same ways we grew to know the case study participants—surveys are anonymous—we will be able to see how one survey participant responds to the same questions over the five-year period. By doing so, we might be able to see factors, including emotional labor, that influence turnover or flight even years before a participant takes a new job or leaves the profession.

Further, several researchers have shown that employees do not leave a job or profession for one reason (Ryan et al.; Gmelch et al.). People will not typically *only* leave a job or profession because of emotions and emotional labor, thus motivating us to look at many factors in the same survey and suss out later in analysis which were most pertinent to our participants. This is how we put the study of emotion and emotional labor in context. For example, researchers have found that age, location, salary, and prestige of an institution affects whether or not faculty stay in a job, so we wanted to make sure we captured so-called individual factors like gender and race, job-specific factors like time at an institution and teaching load, and job satisfaction factors like stress, level of autonomy, and decision fatigue. To do so, we drafted our own questions and drew from existing survey instruments, including Paul Spector's Job Satisfaction Survey and Christina Maslach et al.'s Maslach Burnout Inventory: Educators Survey, but we adapted them to writing center administrators. Doing so allowed us to see, to some degree, how writing center administrators as a whole compare to other professionals who have been studied under the existing surveys. Moreover, it gave us context that allows for us to put emotions and emotional labor in perspective for our participants. If we were to learn that twelve percent of participants leave the profession over the five years because of "emotional exhaustion," we could report that; but, if we also knew how many participants leave the profession because of a life change or because of geography, we could put that number in better perspective.

With the instrument drafted, tested, and approved by our IRBs, we recruited over one-hundred writing center administrators for the study cohort. Now, two years into the project, 119 of the cohort completed the Year One (Y1) survey and 126 of the cohort completed the Year Two (Y2) survey.[3] The majority of our participants have been on the job for less than five years (74% in Y1), identify as female (86% in Y1), are white (92% in Y1), and work at a four-year college or university (81% in Y1). They hold different types of writing center administrative positions–but most report at least half of their job is directing the writing center—and 60% of Y1 participants also teach. Most make between $41,000–$70,000 a year. Though we will continue to collect data for three more years, here we share a couple initial impressions from parts of the data collection related to how participants' emotions at work and emotional labor impact their decisions to stay at or leave their jobs and how our methodological decisions helped us to see this.

Job Satisfaction. General job satisfaction is an indication of how people feel about their job. We have one section in our survey that specifically probes participants' job satisfaction, and this section has forty-one statements—adapted from the Spector and Maslach surveys— participants respond to by selecting strongly agree, agree, neutral, disagree, or strongly disagree. Statements in this section address factors that previous research showed influenced how "satisfied" a person was at their place of work. Some of these statements get directly at the emotions on the job. For instance, "I often feel that my colleagues are upset with me or working against me," or "On most days, I look forward to my work and feel excited to start the day." Other statements tell us something about

---

3. We had more than 130 people agree to be participants. We sent the survey to those people in Y1 and Y2; we had seven more participants in Y1 than Y2, but for the sake of analysis, we consider them all the same cohort. We also recruited a second (much smaller) new cohort in Y2 who we will follow for four years. We do not report on the findings from this cohort in this chapter.

the emotional labor participants engage in. For instance, "I get along with my colleagues and supervisors," or "I feel emotional exhaustion in my work as writing center administrator."

Again, we did not want to presume from the start that strong emotions on the job or too much emotional labor was the singular reason that participants would be satisfied with the work or would leave. We consciously built the survey to cast a wide net and ask about a lot of factors, and we would advise other researchers to think about doing this, too. Sure, we had our suppositions and our own lived experiences, but qualitative research asks for inductive reasoning—to not decide *a priori* what participants would show us.

At this stage, we can speak to the overall job satisfaction for our participants—we have not yet disaggregated the data by participant or looked for correlations of factors that connect with job satisfaction or dissatisfaction. Thus, what we can say is that there is more indication of job satisfaction from our participants than not. To state the obvious: this is a good thing! For the most part, writing center administrators in our study are satisfied with their work, colleagues, and institutions. Specifically, what our survey results show so far, is that participants largely

- feel supported by their colleagues
- get along with their colleagues
- have autonomy
- feel recognized and accomplished
- feel their work is fulfilling and meaningful
- feel they are a good fit with their schools
- feel a sense of community on the job.

Participants decisively fell into the category of "satisfied" with the work and the impact they perceived they made doing the work. For example,

31.27 **I feel my work as writing center administrator is personally fulfilling.**

- Y1: 91% (agree + strongly agree)
- Y2: 84% (agree + strongly agree)

31.37 **When I consider the bigger picture, I'm not sure what the point of my work is.**

- Y1: 84% (disagree + strongly disagree)

- Y2: 86% (disagree + strongly disagree)

In his study, Dave Healy found similar results; the positive dimensions expressed by writing center administrators in his survey were "emotional rewards, satisfying relationships, and the feeling that they are making a difference in people's lives" (33). Though it is early in the study to say for certain, we suspect and hope that our findings will suggest narratives of the frazzled, put-out, long-suffering writing center administrator are, at least, complicated by the high level of job satisfaction that our participants report.

That said, there were ten statements in which participants' responses point to areas of job dissatisfaction across the board. The majority of participants in our study

- feel undercompensated, under-resourced, and misunderstood
- feel some degree of work-related stress and emotional exhaustion
- have decision fatigue
- have some difficulty turning off work.

Again, our results align with Healy who concluded from his survey that "writing center directors are generally satisfied with their jobs, with the exception of how much money they make" (33). One interesting distinction that came up was that our participants feel supported by *people* but not necessarily by their *circumstances*. There was a clear difference in statements that asked participants if they feel supported by or belonging with colleagues and those that explored whether they thought they were resourced or paid enough. While we are disappointed to see this discrepancy, we are not entirely surprised by it given the long history of writing center directors fighting for resources and given the new age of austerity in schools and universities.

Turnover & Turnover Intent. Another section of our survey asks participants about their own movement from one job to another, turnover; their turnover intent. a decision to leave a job and look for alternatives; and their reasons for both. Overall, responses to turnover and turnover intent appear to align with overall responses to job satisfaction discussed earlier. For example, Y1 and Y2 data show that roughly 75% of writing center directors did *not* apply for different internal or external jobs during the study year. Likewise, Y1 and Y2 responses indicate that the majority of participants consider it "highly unlikely" they will leave their positions before the start of the next year—although the percentage of "highly unlikely" drops from 64 % in Y1 to 53% in Y2 and the percentage of "somewhat unlikely" increases from 16% in Y1 to 21% in Y2. Overall, however, the turnover and turnover intention data correspond to one of our early findings that respondents are generally satisfied with their work, colleagues, and institutions.

The last two survey questions ask participants to identify factors that influenced their decision to apply for different jobs during a given year and why they might leave their current jobs in a future, five-year time frame. These factors include

- compensation
- general dissatisfaction with current position, colleagues, and institution
- partner and family
- location
- position more closely aligns with academic background
- promotion
- job opportunity in another field
- position will dissolve
- graduation
- retirement
- other

Survey data thus far shows that participants leave or intend to leave for each of the reasons above, although the top four reasons given for both Y1 and Y2 are

- compensation
- general dissatisfaction with current position/colleagues/institution
- partner **and** family
- location

We are not surprised to see compensation as one of the primary reasons participants gave for leaving or intending to leave a job. As we noted earlier, the majority of participants in our study indicated that a primary source of their job dissatisfaction had to do with feeling undercompensated, under-resourced, and misunderstood. Likewise, participants' general dissatisfaction with position, colleagues, and institution might be mapped onto the three specific sources of job dissatisfaction participants identified: some degree of work-related stress and emotional exhaustion, decision fatigue, and some difficulty turning off work. In this collection, Luke Iantorno reports on similar results from his survey research on emotional labor among writing center staff. When asked about their emotions, several participants noted that they had felt emotional exhaustion and burnout during their time in the writing center. Genie Giaimo, whose work also appears in this collection, observes that many writing centers have embraced wellness programs to address the emotional realities of writing center work. Importantly, however, she urges us to "interrogate where the sudden explosion of interest about wellness and self-care comes from" so as not to "ignore or normalize toxic work environments, structural exploitation, or occupational hazards."

For our participants thus far, turnover and turnover intention appear connected to a variety of factors, including feelings on the job, feelings about the job, and emotional labor. A longitudinal, contextual survey design allows us to see these patterns as they emerge over time and with a larger group of participants. Put another way, survey research offers a broad view of participants' working lives and the emotions, labors, satisfactions, disappointments, and movement that attend these lives. Purposefully not looking too narrowly at only emotions and emotional labor allow us to put the effect of emotions and emotional labor into perspective.

CONCLUSION

In writing center studies, even after the emotional turn, empirical research on emotion and emotional labor is still in its infancy. One of our aims in this chapter is to nudge this research along by offering our own methodological musings for studying emotion and emotional labor. We believe it is important to define our terms carefully, situate them in the literature, and then study them in ways that take us beyond the anecdotal or through a one-time measurement. Likewise, as we have argued here, taking a longitudinal, contextual approach gives us insight into and perspective on the residual effect of emotions and emotional labor at work.

Another objective of this chapter is to show how research evolves—one study leading to insights that prompt another study that, more than likely, takes an entirely different methodological approach. For us, the study of emotional labor emerged from a much larger qualitative case study on writing center directors' working lives, broadly construed. We had not set out to study emotional labor, and yet, there it was—work that we puzzled over and needed to account for in some way. Our insights into emotional labor then merged with a related finding from that initial study about job satisfaction and turnover among writing center administrators. This created an exigence for our current descriptive study of the potential impact of emotions and emotional labor on job satisfaction, turnover, and turnover intent.

Studying emotions and emotional labor from various methodological vantage points is important work. Emotional labor is central to writing center administration and is often that part of the job that writing center administrators most enjoy. Yet, emotional labor is also poorly understood and undervalued, often rendered invisible, and, in some cases, the source of emotional exhaustion that may impact how writing center administrators experience their jobs and whether or not they stay or leave. We hope this chapter helps sustain conversation about emotional labor and the multiple ways it might be studied.

Works Cited

Adams Wooten, Courtney, et al. *The Things We Carry: Strategies for Recognizing and Negotiating Emotional Labor in Writing Program Administration.* Utah State UP, 2020.

Babb, Jacob, and Steven Corbett. "From Zero to Sixty: A Survey of College Writing Teachers' Grading Practices and the Affect of Failed Performance." *Composition Forum*, vol. 34, 2016.

Brand, Alice. "The Why of Cognition: Emotion and the Writing Process." *College Composition and Communication*, vol. 38, no. 4, 1987, pp. 436–43.

—. *The Psychology of Writing: The Affective Experience.* Greenwood, 1989.

Caswell, Nicole I. "Affective Tensions in Response." *Journal of Response to Writing*, vol. 4, no. 2, 2018, pp. 69–98.

—. "Dynamic Patterns: Emotional Episodes within Teachers' Response Practices." *The Journal of Writing Assessment*, vol. 7 no. 1, 2014.

—, et al. *The Working Lives of New Writing Center Directors.* Utah State UP, 2016.

—. "Writing Assessment: Emotions, Feeling, and Teachers." *CEA Forum*, vol. 40, no. 1, 2011, pp. 57–70.

Chandler, Sally. "Fear, Teaching Composition, and Students' Discursive Choices: Re-Thinking Connections between Emotions and College Student Writing." *Composition Studies*, vol. 35, no. 2, 2007, pp. 53–70.

Composition Forum. Special issue on emotions, *Composition Forum*, 34, 2016.

Geller, Anne Ellen, and Harry Denny. "Of Ladybugs, Low Status, and Loving the Job: Writing Center Professionals Navigating Their Careers." *The Writing Center Journal*, vol. 33, no. 1, 2013, pp. 96–129.

Gmelch, Walter, et al. "Dimensions of Stress Among University Faculty: Factor-analytic Results from a National Study." *Research in Higher Education*, vol. 24, no. 3, 1986, pp. 266–86.

Grandey, Alicia A., and Allison S. Gabriel. "Emotional Labor at a Crossroads: Where Do We Go from Here?" *Annual Review of Organizational Psychology and Organizational Behavior*, vol. 2, 2015, pp. 323–49.

Haen, Mike. "The Affective Dimension of Writing Center Talk: Insights from Conversation Analysis." *WLN: A Journal of Writing Center Scholarship*, vol. 42, no. 9–10, 2018, pp. 2–9.

Healy, Dave. "Writing Center Directors: An Emerging Portrait of the Profession." *WPA: Writing Program Administration Journal*, vol. 18, no. 3, 1995, pp. 26–43.

Hochschild, Arlie Russell. "Emotion Work, Feeling Rules, and Social Structure." *American Journal of Sociology*, vol. 85, no. 3, 1979, pp. 551–75.

—. *The Managed Heart: Commercialization of Human Feeling.* U of California P, 1983.

Holt, Mara, et al. "Making Emotion Work Visible in Writing Program Administration." *A Way to Move: Rhetorics of Emotion & Composition Studies*, edited by Dale Jacobs and Laura Micciche. Heinemann, 2003. pp. 147–60.

Hudson, Tracy. "Head 'Em Off at the Pass: Strategies for Handling Emotionalism in the Writing Center." *Writing Lab Newsletter*, vol. 25, no. 5, 2001, pp. 10–12.

Lindquist, Julie. "Class Affects, Classroom Affectations: Working through the Paradoxes of Strategic Empathy." *College English*, vol. 67, no. 2, 2004, pp. 187–209.

Maslach, Christina, et al. "Maslach Burnout Inventory (MBI): Educators Survey." *Mind Garden*, 1996, www.mindgarden.com/316-mbi-educators-survey.

McLeod, Susan. *Notes on the Heart: Affective Issues in the Writing Classroom.* Southern Illinois UP, 1996.

Micciche, Laura R. *Doing Emotion: Rhetoric, Writing, Teaching.* Heinemann, 2007.

—. "More than a Feeling: Disappointment and WPA Work." *College English*, vol. 64, no. 4, 2002, pp. 432–58.

Mihut, Ligia. "Literacy Brokers and the Emotional Work of Mediation." *Literacy in Composition Studies*, vol. 2, no. 1, 2014, pp. 57–79.

Nicklay, Jennifer. "Got Guilt? Consultant Guilt in the Writing Center Community." *The Writing Center Journal*, vol 32, no. 1, 2012, pp. 14–27.

Perry, Alison. "Training for Triggers: Helping Writing Center Consultants Navigate Emotional Sessions." *Composition Forum*, vol. 34, 2016.

Richmond, Kia. "Repositioning Emotions in Composition Studies." *Composition Studies*, vol. 30, no. 1, 2002, pp. 67–82.

Ritter, Kelly. "'What Would Happen If Everybody Behaved as I do?': May Bush, Randall Jarrell, and the Historical 'Disappointment' of Women WPAs." *Composition Studies*, vol. 39, no. 1, 2011, pp. 13–39.

Robillard Amy. "We Won't Get Fooled Again: On the Absence of Angry Responses to Plagiarism in Composition Studies." *College English*, vol. 70, no. 1, 2007, pp. 10–31.

Ryan, John, et al. "Oh, Won't You Stay? Predictors of Faculty Intent to Leave a Public Research University." *Higher Education*, vol. 63, no. 4, 2012, pp. 421–37.

Saleem, Muhammad Khurram. "The Languages in Which We Converse: Emotional Labor in the Writing Center and Our Everyday Lives." *The Peer Review*, vol. 2, no. 1, 2018.

Spector, Paul. "Job Satisfaction Survey (JSS)." 1985. Statistic Solutions, 2021, www.statisticsolutions.com/job-satisfaction-survey-jss/.

Tsang, Kwok Kuen. "Emotional Labor of Teaching." *Educational Research*, vol. 2, no. 8, 2011, pp. 1312–16.

Winans, Amy. "Cultivating Critical Emotional Literacy: Cognitive and Contemplative Approaches to Engaging Difference." *College English*, vol. 75, no. 2, 2012, pp. 150–70.

WLN. Special issue on the affective dimensions of writing center work, *WLN: A Journal of Writing Center Scholarship*, vol. 42, no. 9–10, 2018.

Worsham, Lynn. "Going Postal: Pedagogic Violence and the Schooling of Emotion." *JAC: A Journal of Composition Theory*, vol. 18, no. 2, 1998, pp. 213–45.

2 EMOTIONAL AND EMBODIED RELATIONALITY IN WRITING CENTER ADMINISTRATION: ATTENDING TO INSTITUTIONAL STATUS, IN-BETWEENNESS, AND THE (RE)MAKING OF COMMUNITY

Kelin Hull and Marilee Brooks-Gillies

Writing Center Administrators often story writing centers as communities—homogenous, comfortable places—but within each writing center, individuals have different attachments to the center: institutional statuses, disciplinary backgrounds and leanings, and social identities. This is certainly true for us—an Assistant Director, Kelin, and Director, Marilee, writing center administrative team. We have different credentials, experiences, and expertise. We have different time commitments to the University Writing Center (UWC) we direct. Although we may be part of the same community, we experience that community differently than other members of the community. Like Michelle Gibson et al., we recognize "[t]he narratives told about social institutions are embedded in or with the narratives of individuals" (72) and that "our practices inform our theories, which inform our practices, which inform our theories in an ongoing dynamic process" (Greenfield 141).

As we consider how we continually make and remake our community, we see the centrality of our relationships with and among each other and members of our staff to the everyday work of the Center. In addition, it has become clear to us that those relationships are informed by institutional status, disciplinary credentials, lived experiences in and outside of the writing center, social identities, material and embodied realities, and emotion. As we continually negotiate relationships with and among one another and UWC stakeholders, we acknowledge that emotional labor is a significant part of our work as writing center administrators and for writing consultants in our Center. Like Laura Micciche, we understand that "emotion is central to what makes something thinkable" (47), is produced through "collisions of contact" (50), and is highly "variable" (109). In our chapter, we use story as methodology and theorize from lived experience to name and make visible the value and importance of emotional, embodied, relational work writing center administrators engage in to make and remake community. We argue that recognizing our work as relational and naming it as explicitly emotional and embodied makes these essential practices visible for ourselves, other writing center administrators, and our stakeholders.

Our different institutional and social identities must be recognized as relevant to our work and our communities. For this reason, we advocate for a cultural rhetorics approach to writing center administration that values the lived experiences and stories of writing center administrators and other members of our writing center communities. Andrea Riley-Mukavetz writes that a cultural rhetorics approach

> rejects the idea that "everything is a text" to be read and instead engages with the material, embodied, and relational aspects of research and scholarly production. One engages with texts, bodies, materials, ideas, or space knowing that these subjects are interconnected to the universe and belong to a cultural community with its own intellectual tradition and history. (109)

The work we do is in relation to other people, places, objects, ideas, texts, and material realities. Our relationships are made and remade through our lived experiences and the stories we tell about those experiences. We must account for the ways these relationships create openings, limit opportunities, and impact the overall sense of belonging and community consultants and administrators share across a writing center.

In our chapter, we attend to how relationships are formed and maintained. By considering places, identities, bodies, emotions, etc., we can begin to see how typically "unseen labor is crucial to how projects are organized, sustained, and analyzed. It lets us make the unseen and dif-

ficult to articulate visible and intellectual" (Riley-Mukavetz 121). Jackie
Grutsch McKinney reminds us that we tell stories as a way to belong to
a community—a point she uses to critique the pervasive story of writing
centers as "*comfortable, iconoclastic places where all students go to get one-
to-one tutoring on their writing*" (3, emphasis original). To interrogate
writing center grand narratives, we must constellate multiple stories of
lived experience and ask ourselves: "Why do we tell only one history of
the discipline? Why do we claim some ancestors and not others?" (Powell
et al.).

To embrace multiple stories of writing centers and disrupt the grand
narrative, we need to consider how the story we currently tell limits the
way we understand the possibilities of our work and our relationships
to our work and among members of our writing center communities,
local and disciplinary. To this end, we employ a cultural rhetorics framework to develop a lens of emotional and embodied relationality, which
allows us to "examine the sociopolitical contexts continually reshaping
who we are, how we come together, and what we do" (Greenfield 127).
Like Lauren Brentnell et al. outline in this collection, we see the value
of using stories to recognize the pervasiveness of emotions and affect in
writing center work. In our chapter, we focus primarily on stories of our
own practices and experiences as writing center administrators, positing
that emotional, embodied relationality provides a way to understand and
attend to our own experiences and the experiences of others within our
writing center community and colleagues within the discipline.

EMOTIONAL AND EMBODIED RELATIONALITY
IN WRITING CENTER ADMINISTRATION

Part of interrogating the grand narrative of writing centers is questioning the notion of community. Community is ubiquitous in writing centers, framed as a thing we can build. However, Elizabeth H. Boquet,
in writing of the potlucks and social gatherings she organizes to create
community in her writing center, realizes that these efforts do not "create community," they "*emerge from* one" (*Noise* 26, emphasis original).
Community is a set of actions, behaviors, and feelings we embody and
perform in, around, and with one another; these activities rely on our
relationships and our shared understandings of the community itself.

An important aspect of community in writing center administration is recognizing how we experience the world. Our work is connected

to our bodies, which allows us to orient "to how relationships between things and concepts are meaningful instead of the things themselves" (Riley-Mukavetz 113). As Trixie Smith et al. write, "Embodiment offers the understanding that instantiations of bodies are rhetorically and culturally situated in relation to institutions and discourses" (46). In recognizing that our work is embodied and relational, we see how our work has affective implications for us and for the people we come into contact with. Micciche explains that our simplistic view of emotion as singularly experienced and insular often causes us to "fail to grapple with their performative and embodied aspects" (51). She furthermore contends that "the extralinguistic quality of emotion leads to messier, harder-to-clutch meanings that circulate around and through texts, people, classroom, and cultures. . ." (51). We feel with our bodies and often react, respond, and perform emotions in embodied ways—long before our conscious brains catch-up—and what we do in relation to one another ripples out, around, and through, impacting the community.

By recognizing the ways our bodies and emotions are connected to larger contexts, we are enacting relationality. Riley-Mukavetz uses relationality to contend that "things and concepts do not exist in reality without relationships" (113). Reality is pieced together by each of our experiences and must be negotiated among bodies, emotions, ideas, places, texts, and things. Emphasizing the importance of relationships in writing center administration may feel tangential to the actual work of leading writing centers, but without knowledge of how our interactions and relationships impact our community, trust, and knowledge of each other, we cannot work together to make and remake writing center spaces. We need to learn how to work together and negotiate our roles, which means that attending to the ways that our work is embodied, emotional, and relational is an integral part of the work of writing center administrators.

We apply the lens of emotional relationality by sharing stories of our lived experiences in our writing center. Like Christina Cedillo and Phil Bratta, we value how "story as a guiding practice—in self-positioning and in constellating ourselves within networks of meanings—reminds us that epistemology is not ontology; our situated perspectives cannot tell a whole story except through exchange with others" (235). First, Marilee writes about the unexpected emotional labor of reconciling her institutional status with the larger university and disciplinary communities she has belonged to. Then, Kelin writes about the complications of inhabiting a liminal space as a graduate consultant turned graduate administrator turned assistant director and explores how titles, roles, and identities influence belonging in a community. In each story, we foreground the ways emotional, embodied relationality is present in the work of writing center administration and how recognizing it can help us articulate the nature of our work more clearly to ourselves, our centers, our institutional stakeholders, and our discipline.

EMOTIONAL RELATIONALITY AND INSTITUTIONAL STATUS

Marilee Brooks-Gillies. Before stepping into a tenure-track writing center administrator position at my current institution, I served as a staff writing center administrator at a different writing center with almost all of my everyday labor devoted to directing the writing center. In my current tenure-track role, only twenty-five percent of my everyday labor is allocated to directing the UWC. Navigating this shift and seeing the ways different institutions name and mark writing center administrator labor "reveals not just what it takes to be a writing center director but how, in a reciprocal move, a system uses a writing center director—what part of the load the writing center director carries, what personal worth a director finds in their work, and what worth the system places on the director's work" (Caswell et al. 4). As I began the transition into the tenure-track position, I also began a complex negotiation of identity with the continuing assistant directors. This negotiation did not feel good as our attachments to particular kinds of labor were linked to our identities, our senses of our Center, and affected our daily lives.

I am the first tenure-track writing center administrator to direct the UWC on my campus. The longtime, non-tenure-track, director advocated for a tenure-track writing center administrator for much of her career, recognizing how her institutional status limited the visibility and perceived importance of the Center—similar to the challenges I encountered in my staff writing center administrator position. Although the new position was supported by the college and the existing UWC leadership, the transition required making changes to the entire UWC administrative structure, leading to frustration and dismay from all of us. In my first year, the UWC was supported by two assistant directors who held non-tenure-track faculty positions. The assistant directors had two course reallocations to work in the UWC each semester and conceived of their roles as primarily consulting. They saw the administrative component as helping the director by taking on tasks that were delegated on an as-needed basis. This model was unfamiliar to me and concerned me since my administrative labor, which had been the bulk of my staff writing center administrator position, was now limited to one course reallocation each semester. I worried that if their approach to the positions did not change, we would spend fewer administrative hours across three positions than I spent directing my previous, and much smaller, writing center alone. What seemed like a straightforward concern about division of labor was connected to difficult relationship-building and emotion work around disciplinary labor, institutional status, and institutional histories.

The assistant directors had long histories in the institution and understood the work of writing centers primarily in relation to their work at this particular UWC and its place in the larger institutional structure—similar to Melissa Ianetta et al.'s "Local Professional" model of writing center administration. I, however, fell more under Ianetta et al.'s "Universal Professional" model and understood the work of writing centers as anchored to my disciplinary training in Rhetoric and Writing and my experiences in four different writing center communities. Because of these different experiences and orientations to the UWC, we framed the writing center's purpose and its core work differently. We clashed over how often to hold staff meetings and on whether all consultants needed to attend them, how or if to share information about sessions with faculty, and what our relationship with the writing program and other units on campus should be. These clashes came out of our differing personal and emotional investments in and relationships with the institution, the history of this writing center's operations, and our affiliation—or lack thereof—with the larger disciplinary communities of Writing Center Studies and Rhetoric and Writing. We were having a hard time trusting each other, even though we knew that we all had the best interests of the writing center in mind. We were also having difficulty dividing the administrative labor because we did not have a shared idea of what the writing center was—who it served, what it did, and why it did what it did. We did, though, have a lot of feelings, anchored in our own lived experiences and attached to institutional and disciplinary belongings, about the purpose and future of the writing center. As Caswell et al. note, emotions are "part of a complex web of behaviors and activities that characterizes and often motivates labor of all sorts" (26).

When I raised concerns that we could not possibly complete all the required administrative labor of the UWC with the current structure, the assistant directors responded with concern and frustration. Their work must be understood as teaching for it to count for them institutionally.[1] I saw much writing center administrative work as teaching. For example, mentoring consultants on consulting strategies and research projects and leading professional development workshops would easily fall in the teaching category. Alternatively, consulting one-to-one with student writers was much easier to classify as teaching and quantify through the number of sessions and the student demographics in those sessions. I was frustrated and fearful, too, because I knew I could not do all the administrative labor the writing center required while still having an active—and required—research agenda. This fear was anchored not just to a clear-cut question about administrative labor but in the emotional and embodied work of identity; the ways that we each saw ourselves as scholars, teachers, and members of disciplinary communities; our sense of the purpose of writing centers generally; and the specific mission and vision of our own writing center.

My hire and the shift in institutional status for the role of director—from non-tenure-track to tenure-track—had an immediate impact on the assistant directors and their relationship to the writing center. Not only was I a different person with different writing center education and experience than the former director, but I was also in a role that was new to our writing center—one that would require them to shift their identities more heavily toward administration within the writing center to accommodate my more limited appointment. While I am most rewarded for research-focused labor, and they are most rewarded for teaching-focused labor, none of us are particularly lauded professionally for service- or administratively-focused labor. The logic of collaboratively dividing up and completing tasks in a way that suited our course reallocations was deeply imbued with emotional labor of how those tasks felt to us and how they marked us personally and professionally. While we were each committed to working collaboratively, we could not agree on what felt like an equitable division of administrative labor because of our different institutional statuses, disciplinary identities, and sense of the

---

1. As a TT faculty member, the most important metric for promotion and tenure is scholarly production. Lecturers in my department, however, are seen primarily as teachers, and all promotion guidelines for them are anchored to excellence in teaching.

UWC's purpose. By ignoring our emotions about these differences, we reinforced them. Ultimately, both assistant directors left their positions in the UWC within my first two years as the director.

Directing a writing center requires collaboration and negotiating relationships with many other people, including members of the writing center community; unit supervisors like department chairs, college deans, etc.; faculty and staff; as well as college and university structures and institutional policies. I had thought that moving to a tenure-track position would make these negotiations easier since my title would provide greater institutional buy-in and respect from university stakeholders. What I failed to realize was that my limited time in the UWC itself—and my need to share its administration—meant that I would be spending far more time and energy negotiating relationships and boundaries within the UWC as opposed to alongside it. Whereas, before my entire institutional status had been identified with the writing center I directed, in this new role, I was primarily responsible for the UWC. However, I now had much more limited daily interactions with the community, making leading it difficult, especially since negotiating relationships among its other leaders felt impossible. My professional reputation and my own personal sense of self and success was—in more ways than ever—reliant on negotiating productive relationships with other writing center administrators.

The challenges I faced were replicated among a wider community of graduate student administrators when the former assistant directors left, and I worked with department leaders to create teaching assistantships for graduate assistants to take on some UWC administration. I knew that additional labor was necessary to run the UWC and also knew that supporting graduate administrators would be time-consuming. It was my job to make expectations clear while also supporting each graduate student administrator as they learned about themselves in relation to the discipline. This work was complicated by my maternity leave during the spring semester of the first year these positions were implemented. In addition, I did not realize how intensely their own relationships with each other would come to define their work, notions of success and failure within those roles, sense of fairness and equity across their roles, and overall feelings of community within the UWC. As Sara Ahmed explains, "feelings not only *heighten tension,* they are also *in tension*" (10, emphasis original).

Emotional Relationality: Between Becoming and Belonging

Kelin Hull. So much of my life in recent years has been trying to reorient my expectations to allow for the messiness of emotional relationality. During my first year in the UWC, I felt as if my body had moved me from one place to a new place without clear borders—my body seemingly everywhere, all at once. The lack of borders felt uncomfortable and confusing as my identities struggled and even competed to orient me into a new and different situation. I had moved from a consultant role to a new graduate student administrator role in the UWC. But what does that even mean? Definitions are not fixed. Differing definitions complicated the way I, along with other graduate students, worked to understand our own emotional, embodied versions of the graduate student administrator role.

Each graduate student administrator had our own set of expectations for the role, just as we each had our own definition of the role and ourselves within it. To complicate matters even more, each consultant had our own expectations and definitions about our role in the UWC. There was tension over what leadership styles to inhabit, what tasks among our shared labor were valuable, and what level of authority our graduate student administrator roles possessed. The labor within the boundary of the shared graduate student administrator title was intended to be equitable, and yet, not all labor feels equal to everyone and is often "undercut by the titles we bear" (Harrington et al. 58). This lack of "fixedness," as Laura Greenfield calls it, creates tension in relationships as we grapple with the expectations we have that likely do not neatly align with the expectations of others (108).

In a writing center, all of this uncertainty—the tension between boundaries and our relationships within and among ourselves, one another, and the writing center itself—can amplify and then multiply as emotions circulate and relationships ebb and flow throughout the community. The entry to my role as a graduate student administrator was complicated, similar to the way Melissa Nicolas identifies the "complex set of political, educational, and institutional circumstances" that marks the "betwixt and between" space of graduate administrators (3). We often consider ourselves and others in terms of defined roles with rigid boundaries because it is clearer. In the story writing center administrators tell ourselves, the writing center is a space that should feel and perform a certain way. As a result, we often try to draw boundaries, clarify with titles, and carve a niche of administrative tasks to help us understand and perform the shared labor of the center.

The graduate student administrators had to attend to the material aspects of our positions while also negotiating a relationship that crossed identities between friends, graduate students, and women, as well as writing center scholars and co-administrators at our writing center. The collaboration between us was eased and yet complicated by these entanglements. Harry Denny writes that,

> All of who we are commingles and spurs each of our identities in parallel and divergent ways. For faculty, administration, or tutors in writing centers, we too are growing and being shaped by multiple forces within, outside, and across us. Who we are is an amalgam of past, present, and future. There forces are critical, yet we rarely have the language or occasion to speak into and interrogate them. (120)

Not only are our identities complex and layered, but as Nicolas examines, a graduate student administrator in a writing center is predisposed to a blurring and melding of identities and roles (2). As the academic year progressed, this negotiation felt heavier and more complicated, each graduate student administrator retreating further away from one another as we held tight to the expectations and definitions we each had about our roles. Our disconnection and lack of unity caused disruption among the consultants, destabilizing the community.

While I cannot speak for how others in the community felt, I can tell you that I was carefully managing my emotions in order to manage the emotions of others (Caswell et al. 113). It felt awful and completely exhausting. Yet, my fellow graduate student administrators and I did not talk about what was happening to each of us or to the community until it was over, after it was too late to help us all feel connected and valued in the community. As is the habit in so many professional environments, we had failed to acknowledge our emotions as relevant to our work, unwittingly amplifying them (Fosslien and Duffy 4), similar to Marilee's experience. Our stories mirror one another in the ways the negotiations of emotional relationality felt and impacted us and the community.

After the upheaval of that first year in the Center, the graduate student administrators who had been with me left, each for their own reasons and in pursuit of new goals. There was now insufficient administrative labor—leaving just my assistantship and Marilee's single course reallocation each semester—and consultants expressed anxiety, bitterness, and even suspicion of one another and of leadership in our community. I became the acting Assistant Director while in my second year of graduate school. Like the previous year, I was still in a liminal space, the uncertain and uncomfortable "betwixt and between" (Nicolas 3). My relationships to everyone had to shift, often from minute to minute, depending on the role I needed to embody in that moment. Marilee was my partner, my friend, my peer—we are the same age—my boss, and also my thesis director. To other graduate students in the writing center, I was a friend, peer, and fellow student, and yet, also an authority figure who enacted disciplinary and administrative expertise. To the rest of campus, I was both or neither, depending on who you asked. My very existence caused disruption and conversations about who was good enough to have my job. In a school in the middle of a tough financial situation, was I really worth it? Could they not get someone better than me?

I graduated and was offered a visiting lecturer line in English with a full-time appointment to co-administer the UWC. I happily accepted. To me, shifting to a visiting lecturer line and shedding my graduate student identity would help me move out of liminality. I would finally be one thing that people could understand and value: the Assistant Director. Except, just like with any definition, people do not know what that position means to me, to Marilee, or the UWC. It means something different to different people, just as my graduate student administrator role did two years ago. To some, I am Marilee's assistant, there to "help" Marilee in whatever she needs. To others, I am not doing enough—I do not teach in a classroom but receive eight course reallocations[2] for my work in the writing center. I see what I do with consultants as teaching, but there are no course-driven deliverables or grades, so others do not. I am classified as faculty, but I do not feel as if I have colleagues in my department. I simply do not fit everyone's definition of visiting lecturer, and yet, I am still beholden to the demarcation of it, excluding me from eligibility for a stipend to work in the UWC over the summer—as if for ten months out of the year, I am valuable and indispensable, but for two months out of the year, Marilee can do both my job and hers.

---

2. Lecturers on our campus have a 4/4 teaching load. My one-hundred percent appointment in the UWC means that none of my teaching takes place in a conventional classroom.

The betweenness I experience feels ongoing and never-ending. At times, it feels like I do not belong; like I am an impostor. Other times, during those moments of communal highs in the writing center, it feels like it does not matter; I know I do a good job. Through this experience, I continue to pursue what Donna Haraway describes as "the tension of holding incompatible things together because both or all are necessary and true" (117). I see the necessity and power of the middle space. I recognize I can be both as well as neither at the same time; it does not have to break-down into a right and wrong binary. In the "betwixt and between" (Nicolas 3), performances of "right" and "wrong" coalesce, the binary deconstructing as we invoke our feelings and hold space for our partial—and sometimes even competing— identities. Communities, especially writing center communities, are about learning to live within this middle space, to live within and with difference (Ahmed and Fortier 255–56). Communities are not a static vessel of unity but a shared practice of re-making.

Concluding Thoughts: Making and Remaking Community through Emotional, Embodied Relationality

In the consistently uncertain environment of writing centers, practicing emotional, embodied relationality requires a "comfort in unknowingness" where "writing center praxis is not a utopian future but an immediate, love-inspired, reflective action we commit to again and again and again" (Greenfield 172). It is only by leaving a definition open can we draw attention to the embodied experiences of ourselves and the others in our stories. Instead of logical beings bound to an absolute truth that we are in opposition to, we become emotional and embodied—the relationships and identities, past and present, we negotiate and experience.

Understanding the making and remaking of our writing center communities is dependent upon writing center administrators, consultants, and writers in relationship together, which reinforces the importance of community while pricking at its instability. Unity, contends Haraway, is not natural; it is a possibility rooted in social relations and based on activity within those relations (125). In other words, difference exists as a constant in communities. Ahmed writes that "emotion is not always about the past, and how it sticks. Emotions also open up futures, in the ways they involve different orientations to others" (202). We as writing center administrators must understand and attend to communities as sites of emotional relationality, sites that we recognize are "never fully achieved" (Ahmed and Fortier 257). Community is an activity, and one that we as leaders in the community must model.

However, we acknowledge that relational work writing center administrators engage in to sustain the writing center community may appear to be in opposition of the kind of labor the academy expects and values. As Geller and Denny explain "the very aspects of [writing center administrator's] positions that turn out to be the most important to their success and satisfaction are at tension with the academic cultural actions that feed disciplinary growth and could position [writing center administrators] as central agents in the discipline of English" (97). In other words, writing center administrators have long understood emotion work to be central to our positions and our writing center communities, but to support disciplinary growth, we need to participate in academic publishing, which our institutional positions may not easily allow for. In addition, the academy often values labor it can quantify, such as the number and impact factor of scholarly publications or the number of writing center sessions a center conducts. As a result, writing center administrators often share stories about our centers "in sterile or rosy terms" (Dixon), as places where literacy learning is supported by cheerful, knowledgeable student consultants who happily participate in community together without sharing details of the messy, necessary, complicated—often invisible—emotional, embodied relationality involved in our work. As Boquet cautions, "for all of our championing of process and collaboration, we have actually constructed writing centers that are all about the singular object, the 'thing' that we can point to" ("Our" 479). We need to stop pointing at community as the outcome or answer and instead view the work of our center and our work within it as a complex, dynamic set of practices and relationships that require a great deal of our time and labor.

By failing to recognize the emotional, embodied relationality necessary to make and sustain our communities, "we are teaching others—tutors, student writers, colleagues, our institutions, and our profession—what we value about our work and, correspondingly, what it is that others should value about our work" (Geller et al. 121). In other words, by skewing our narratives away from the messy, complicated reality of emotional and embodied relationality, we are complicit as writing center administrators in continuing the invisibility and marginalization of our labor. We embrace "the excessive institutional possibilities that the writing center represents. The way in which the writing center exceeds its space, despite the university's best efforts to contain it. . ." (Boquet, "Our" 478). As we see it, writing centers are fiercely relational in their everyday practices. They exist alongside classrooms, where learning and interaction can happen in ways unavailable to more streamlined, course-driven objectives. Here, the messy relationships across bodies, emotions, places, texts, and ideas are valued in ways that cannot be measured in traditional, grade-oriented ways, and our administrative labor cannot be quantified simply as service, teaching, or research because all are intertwined in writing center administrator labor.

Because we frame the work of the writing center as embodied, emotional, and relational, we can model and make space for a range of experiences and emotions in our community. With each other, we take time to share our feelings, including adding a column along a master calendar of recurring UWC events and tasks that indicates how we typically feel during that time of the semester and while completing each task. Adding this column helps us make visible and helps us prepare for tasks and times that create stress and create the need for extended emotional labor. We also discuss how our consultants are feeling and who might need accommodation or attention. We work to listen to consultants and each other, recognizing how our different embodied and social identities, as well as institutional statuses, impact our experiences. Sharing our own stories with each other makes it easier for us to model that practice to consultants, which can help consultants see us as "figure[s] *with*, rather than *of*, authority gained through both personal experience and academic learning" (Cedillo and Bratta 221). By sharing our stories, we can "build trust" (221) with one another as a community, and because we attend to our relationships in ways that honor embodied and emotional experiences, our community is better positioned to create programming that complicates definitions and interrogates relationships. Emotions are within, among, and between each of us, in every relationship and encounter. We must practice a form of relationality that makes space for different embodied experiences and emotions.

Our chapter reinforces the boundary negotiations between the delineation of identities in the writing center. As our stories illustrate, emotions are bound to identities, which are never singular, and to our bodies through activity, and therefore enter into relationships in complicated ways (Ahmed 10). Emotional labor—when thought through in this way—becomes more than labor that is focused on emotions; it becomes all labor. Sharing and theorizing from our own lived experiences has helped us shape how we approach writing center administration. If Grutsch McKinney encouraged us to see what is on the periphery, then it is our goal to move what has been on those margins to the center. When we move an emphasis on the emotional, embodied, and relational to the center, it stops being the obstacle in the way of the work and becomes the most important part of our work (Caswell et al. 73). By naming our work as explicitly focused on the emotional, embodied, and relational, we make it more visible to us and our stakeholders; it becomes what we do, instead of an obstacle to move past or through.

WORKS CITED

Ahmed, Sara. *The Cultural Politics of Emotion*. Routledge. 2004.

—, and Anne-Marie Fortier. "Re-imagining Communities." *International Journal of Cultural Studies*, vol. 6, no. 3, 2003, pp. 251–59.

Boquet, Elizabeth H. *Noise from the Writing Center*. Utah State UP, 2002.

—. "'Our Little Secret': A History of Writing Centers, Pre- to Post-Open Admissions." *College Composition and Communication*, vol. 50, no. 3, 1999, pp. 463–82.

Caswell, Nicole I., et al. *The Working Lives of New Writing Center Directors*. Utah State UP, 2016.

Cedillo, Christina V., and Phil Bratta. "Relating Our Experiences: The Practice of Positionality Stories in Student-Centered Pedagogy." *College Composition and Communication*, vol. 71, no. 2, 2019, pp. 215–40.

Denny, Harry. "Of Queers, Jeers, and Fears: Writing Center as (Im)Possible Safe Spaces." *Out in The Center: Public and Private Struggles*, edited by Harry Denny, et al., Utah State UP, 2018, pp. 117–25.

Dixon, Elise. "Uncomfortably Queer: Everyday Moments in the Writing Center." *The Peer Review*, vol. 1, no 2., 2017.

Fosslien, Liz, and Mollie West Duffy. *No Hard Feelings: Emotions at Work (and How They Help Us Succeed)*. Penguin, 2019.

Geller, Anne Ellen, et al. *The Everyday Writing Center: A Community of Practice*. Utah State UP, 2006.

—, and Harry Denny. "Of Ladybugs, Low Status, and Loving the Job: Writing Center Professionals Navigating Their Careers." *The Writing Center Journal*, vol. 33, no. 1, 2013, pp. 96–129.

Gibson, Michelle, et al. "Bi, Butch, and Bar Dyke: Pedagogical Performances of Class, Gender, and Sexuality." *College Composition and Communication*, vol. 52, no. 1, 2000, pp. 69–95.

Greenfield, Laura. *Radical Writing Center Praxis: A Paradigm for Ethical Political Engagement*. Utah State UP, 2019.

Grutsch McKinney, Jackie. *Peripheral Visions for Writing Centers*. Utah State UP, 2013.

Haraway, Donna. "A Cyborg Manifesto: Science, Technology, and Socialist-Feminism in the Late 20th Century." *The International Handbook of Virtual Learning Environments*, edited by Joel Weiss, et al., Springer Netherlands, 2006, pp. 117–158.

Harrington, Susanmarie, et al. "Power, Partnership, and Negotiations: The Limits of Collaboration." *WPA: Writing Program Administration*, vol. 21, no. 2/3, 1998, pp. 52–64.

Ianetta, Melissa, et al. "Polylog: Are Writing Center Directors Writing Program Administrators?" *Composition Studies*, vol. 34, no. 2, 2006, pp. 11–42.

Micciche, Laura R. *Doing Emotion: Rhetoric, Writing, Teaching*. Heinemann, 2007.

Nicolas, Melissa, editor. "(E)Merging Identities: Authority, Identity, and the Place In-Between." *(E)Merging Identities: Graduate Students in the Writing Center*. Fountainhead Press, 2008.

Powell, Malea, et al. "Our Story Begins Here: Constellating Cultural Rhetorics." *enculturation*, no. 18, 2014.

Riley-Mukavetz, Andrea. "Towards a Cultural Rhetorics Methodology: Making Research Matter with Multi-Generational Women from the Little Traverse Bay Band." *Rhetoric, Professional Communication, and Globalization*, vol. 5, no. 1, 2014, pp. 108–25.

Smith, Trixie, et al. "Reflections on/of Embodiment: Bringing Our Whole Selves to Class." *Feminist Teacher*, vol. 28, no. 1, 2017, pp. 45–63.

3 Tales of Becoming and Letting Go: The Emotional Labor and Identities of Writing Center Administrators in Transition

Kate Navickas, Kristi Murray Costello,
and Tabatha Simpson-Farrow

While becoming a new writing center administrator will always be an on-the-ground learning experience, we contend that there is a significant amount of emotional labor—what Navickas has termed *the emotional labor of becoming*—involved in this transition and throughout one's career (59). Emotional labor is often thought of in the context of our labors—the stress and emotions required to enact and do our everyday work, but what about the labor of entering into a new normal or *unbecoming* a writing center administrator?

While research on emotional labor has primarily been discussed as a result of supporting and navigating relationships—for example, emotion management—as has been described by Mary E. Guy et al., we are extending the concept to include internal struggles that emerge from conflicts between identities, actions, and perceptions (5–6). Through coding interviews with two exiting writing center administrators—referred to hereon with the pseudonyms Ruth and Lucy—conducted by their successors, we have determined that emotional labor relates to a writing center administrator's sense of their ideal identity as an administrator or who they want to be in this role. This claim complicates previous understandings by arguing that emotional labor is more than just the emotions tied to *the labor of the job* or "corresponding action," as has been defined by Caswell et al. (26). Throughout our research, we found that Ruth, Lucy, and their interviewers felt emotionally conflicted and weighed down when they had to act in ways that disconnected them from their ideal sense of who they were in these roles or when others' perceptions of their work challenged their sense of identities.

Jackson et al. conclude their *Composition Forum* article, "Writing Center Administration and/as Emotional Labor," by claiming that emotional labor either greases the wheels or weighs us down. We agree and extend this argument by adding that emotional labor makes our work feel easier or harder precisely because the work is so often tied to the pursuit of an *ideal writing center administrator identity.* All of the writing center administrators in this small study, and we expect others in the field, carry and pursue their sense of an ideal writing center administrator identity. As a result, the actions, perceptions, and connections that align with their ideal identities make the work more joyful, fulfilling, and easier. Meanwhile, actions, perceptions, and connections that disconnect us from our ideal identities weigh us down, stress us out, and make the work more challenging—even though such challenges are often outside of our control. Our interview data illustrates that emotional labor feels fraught or motivating precisely because writing center administrators see their actions and choices as directly tied to their identities, even when they are not.

Writing Center Work as an Identity

In Rhetorical Genre Studies (RGS), there has been a long-standing interest in how people's participation in genres and genre systems conflict with, support, and reaffirm identities. Anis Bawarshi, for instance, has argued that all genres, including classroom genres, like syllabi and assignments, carry values that writers must enact through their writing and subjectivities that writers are interpolated into in order to write "successful" essays (127, 130). In other words, through students' uptakes of these genres, they are becoming a certain kind of student—they must identify as a writer and agree, at least to a certain extent, with the values embedded in the prompt. *Naming What We Know,* Kevin Roozen's "Writing is Linked to Identity," and Heidi Estrem's "Disciplinary and Professional Identities are Constructed through Writing" offer broader strokes, summarizing some of the work that has come out of RGS on how participating and communicating within communities of practice leads to identification with those communities—to become one of them.

Charles Bazerman makes a similar point but offers a stronger sense of the emotional and personal aspects of situating communicative acts within larger contexts that suggest particular identities and ways of being. He writes,

> In perceiving an utterance as being of a certain kind or genre, we become caught up in a form of life, joining speakers and hearers, writers and readers, in particular relations of a familiar and intelligible sort. As participants orient towards this communicative social space they take on the mood, attitude, and actional possibilities of that place—they go to that place to do the kinds of things you do there, think the kinds of thoughts you think there, feel the kind of way you feel there, satisfy what you can satisfy there, be the kind of person you can become there (Bazerman, 1997, 1998) [. . .] You adopt a frame of mind, set your hopes, plan accordingly, and begin acting with that orientation. (13)

The point is, through our engagement with particular communities and spaces, writing center administrators begin to identify as people who belong in those communities and spaces. We share in similar ways of speaking and writing, but we also adopt certain values, perspectives, and ways of behaving that help us identify as belonging. In writing center work, as with all academic positions, professional identities are formed and solidified through the ongoing engagement with and repetition of such shared field values through regular communicative acts—conferences, publications, writing center administrator work communications. These professional identities may be challenged when writing center administrators transition into new institutional contexts which require understanding a new discourse community's values, language practices, and ways of engaging.

In writing center research, quite a lot of work has gone into defining different aspects of a writing center administrator's identity. There have been several studies of writing center administrator job status and its effect on job satisfaction (Geller and Denny; Caswell et al. 4–9). Sherry Wynn Perdue and Dana Lynn Driscoll have studied writing center administrators' *scholarly identities* and production of RAD research. More recently, Caswell et al.'s longitudinal study of nine directors takes into consideration a more complex understanding of directors' work and identities—including their emotional labor, everyday labor, and disciplinary labor (23–27). In this collection, Kelin Hull and Marilee Brooks-Gillies expand Caswell et al.'s research regarding writing center administrator emotional labor by exploring how their relationships were complicated by failing to address emotions. We see our work as an important bridge between Caswell et al., who focus on writing center administrators' identities and labors—emotional and otherwise—and Hull and Brooks-Gillies, who explore the relational consequences of not talking about work-related emotions. Hull and Brooks-Gillies reveal that in navigating their relationship, it was essential to consider their center's history, the relationships within it, and the emotions wrapped up in their own identities. In our chapter, we illustrate how interviews exploring our emotional labor, identities as writing center administrators, and our centers' histories can serve as a method for doing the work Hull and Brooks-Gillies advocate for. Further, this chapter extends the conversation around writing center administrator identities through exploring how writing center administrators' philosophies and administrative values affect their emotional labor and shape their identities.

Through our interviews, we found that the participants' *identities* as writing center administrators seemed to be defined by their development of their sense of an *ideal writing center administrator identity.* This ideal writing center administrator identity is an imagined and articulated sense each director has about who they want to be in the role. It represents a director's values and philosophies that are either enacted or not in their actions and practices as an administrator I We found that Lucy and Ruth had very similar ideal writing center administrator identities. They both believed that writing center administrators should collaborate; foster communities of tutors; be anti-hierarchical, open, friendly, and inviting; and work regularly with writers. Through disciplinary socialization, the idea of an ideal writing center administrator identity gathers certain clout and emotional attachments. In "Affective Economies," Sara Ahmed theorizes that affect—fear, in particular—"does not reside in a particular object," but "slide[s] across signs, and between bodies," and that affect's "stickiness" comes from histories of associations (127). She argues, "not that there is a psychic economy of fear that then becomes social and collective: rather, the individual subject comes into being through its very alignment with the collective" (128). For our purposes, Ahmed's work can help us to see how each writing center administrator's associations with an ideal writing center administrator identity—values they have built up over time—create affective economies and emotions that stick to this idea of an identity and shift in response to challenging contexts, comments, and perceptions. While the two writing center administrators in our study both attached positive emotions with an idealized writing center administrator identity, we have found that much of the emotional labor they experienced in their day-to-day work occurred when this identity was challenged—by tutors, faculty across campus, or actions they took in response to specific contexts. Conversely, they experienced positive emotional labor when their actions, their work with tutors or faculty, or other experiences affirmed their ideal identities.

SELF-ACTION INTERVIEW RESEARCH FOR EMOTIONAL LABOR: WHAT WE DID AND WHY

Our small study draws on the teacher researcher or practitioner researcher tradition. In "Revisiting Teacher Research," Lee Nickoson traces some of the methodological divisions among teacher researchers, noting that the overwhelming common ground is that teacher research develops out of a "teacher's questions, concerns, and/or curiosities" (104). She describes teacher research as action research that seeks to improve classroom practices. We conducted and coded two interviews that draw on this research tradition from a writing center administration perspective, hoping to demystify and improve the often emotionally fraught transitions into and out of administrative roles.[1]

Although we have given the interviewees—the exiting writing center administrators— the pseudonyms "Ruth" and "Lucy," all three authors are a part of the interview data. While this overlap in researcher and participant identity creates biases, we see our interviews as a form of practitioner action research that allows us to consider whether there are consistencies or differences across each writing center administrator's reflections on their emotions, emotional labor, and how they navigated that labor. Perhaps not surprisingly, the common ground and relationships among participants led to honest and vulnerable conversations— that is, the interviewers' and interviewees' understanding of the positions and institutional contexts allowed for more productive interactions.

---

1. Ruth's interview was conducted in December 2016 as the interviewer, her successor, completed her first semester as a new writing center administrator. Lucy's interview was conducted by her successor in December 2018, as the interviewer was transitioning into her role as the new writing center administrator.

In terms of interviewing methods, both interviews were conversational in nature,[2] using the interview questions as a touchpoint while also allowing for natural follow-up questions and interviewer reflections and reactions, which were also coded.[3] Once both interviews were fully transcribed, we conducted two rounds of open and axial coding that were informed by grounded theory methods (Charmaz) and used descriptive codes (Saldaña) (see Appendix B for coding charts). We used grounded theory as a coding method in order to allow our findings to emerge more organically from the interview data. In this chapter, we detail our findings that resulted from the following coding subcategories: self-expectations and values; reflections on becoming; the emotional labor of others' expectations, attitudes, and actions; and the emotional labor of one's relationship to different communities.[4] Through our analysis of the codes, the connection between emotional labor and writing center administrator identity emerged as a significant focal point.

This project developed as a way to extend Navickas's initial study and findings. The method, which Navickas described as, "*centering* interviews on emotional labor" (62) was replicated in the second interview by using the same interview questions (see Appendix A). We replicated her initial interview because a similar situation arose—one writing center administrator was leaving and helping to support the incoming writing

---

2. In line with an approach detailed by Kathryn Roulston, ours follows "constructionist work that views research interviews as socially situated events in which how accounts are co-constructed by interviewers and interviewees may be either the focus of analysis, or of equal importance to topical analyses" (2-3). In Kathryn Roulston's list of theoretical backdrops for interviews, ours follows "constructionist work that views research interviews as socially situated events in which how accounts are co-constructed by interviewers and interviewees may be either the focus of analysis, or of equal importance to topical analyses" (298).

3. While the interviews primarily focus on the exiting writing center administrator's emotional labor, following our understanding of the interview as a collaboration and co-constructed exchange, we opted to code the transcripts in their entirety—including interruptions and impromptu conversation—because our experience suggests that valuable moments of vulnerability and introspection can evolve when we allow ourselves to talk about our emotions and emotional labor.

4. While all of our analysis comes from these coded categories, to better coincide with the organic and conversational style of the interviews, we have avoided using the coding terminology too heavily throughout.

center administrator—that we hoped would lead to both a meaningful transition experience for the writing center administrators and a better understanding of the emotional labor of transitioning. While Costello and Navickas had previously been studying emotional labor, the opportunity for this project came, as is often the case with action research, from a deep desire to make transitioning into and out of a writing center administrator position easier and less emotionally fraught. Of course, we recognize that the emotions or emotional labor of one writing center administrator will be necessarily different from another due to cultural location,[5] context, and a wealth of other factors. We also recognize, as Anne Ellen Geller and Harry Denny point out, that "the lived experiences of writing center directors are not as different as their position configurations might suggest" (101). Though we do not presume that the experiences of two exiting writing center administrators and two incoming writing center administrators will be universal, we anticipate that there will be relatable elements, moments, and sentiments, and we believe this method—interviews centered on emotional labor—will be of value.

THE IDENTITIES AND EMOTIONAL LABOR OF TWO TRANSITIONING WRITING CENTER ADMINISTRATORS

Across the experiences and stories of these two female writing center administrators from very different institutional contexts, what perhaps stands out most about their emotional labor is the extent that the joy, connections, and warmth of working with communities of tutors and writers sustain them—especially the exiting writing center administrators—despite the emotional labor from others' attitudes and expectations, their specific contexts, and the at-first overwhelming nature of the work. Whenever a director was able to make choices or act in ways that aligned with her ideal sense of identity as a writing center administrator—enacting her values and philosophy—she experienced the "relational work" that "greases the wheel and makes other tasks easier, lighter, and faster" (Jackson et al.). However, whenever a director was presented with challenging institutional contexts or problems, negative reactions

---

5. Cultural location is a term used by Krista Ratcliffe and Rebecca Rickly in *Performing Feminism and Administration in Rhetoric and Composition Studies* to describe race, ethnicity, social class, disability, gender, age, and sexual orientation (viii).

and comments from others, or decisions that disconnected them from their sense of identity as a writing center director, they experienced "the exhaustion of emotion work" that is stressful, draining, time-consuming, and otherwise perceived as negative (Jackson et al.). Thus, the interviews illustrated that identity-based alignments and disconnects came from each writing center director's internal sense of identity, as well as from external factors, such as the attitudes of others and our relationship to disciplinary communities.

In our coding, we developed two categories that highlight how one's sense of self and identity as a writing center administrator cause emotional labor: *self-expectations and values* and *reflections on becoming* (see Appendix B, Table 1). Together, these codes represent the emotional labor derived from the interviewees' internalized sense of who they are as directors and how they feel about their loss of identity in leaving this role. Passages coded as *self-expectations and values* include statements about the writing center administrators' values and goals that they had for their position, which we argue coincide with who they want to be in the position. Their hopes for their writing center to feel like a community and to be collaborative, for example, are self-expectations and values that foster positive emotional labor; enacting these values creates alignment with their ideal identities. However, both interviews also illustrate the negative emotional labor that can result from self-expectations and values conflicting with local contexts, attitudes, and other constraints. Such conflicts require administrators to reprioritize and redefine what their values are and how they can be enacted, which can cause shifts in their writing center administrator identities. Also relating to an individual's sense of self is the second category, *emotional labor of becoming*, which includes statements about transitioning in and out of a particular position, reflections on one's identity in relationship to being a writing center administrator, and realizations and retrospectives about the emotional labor of the work.

Both Ruth and Lucy made statements about their early expectations and hopes when they first entered their positions. These statements tended to be about positive emotions, values, and the writing center philosophies that they hoped to enact in their writing centers. Indeed, these statements suggest why they do the work. For example, Lucy noted, "I wanted a collaborative program. I want everybody to work together, and I want everybody to feel like [we] have a community." Similarly, Ruth discussed her expectation that tutors would have similar desires for community. She noted, "I expected them [tutors] to want to go on retreats." We see these expectations and desires for community as examples of *self-expectations and values* that motivate the choices the writing center administrators made and the kinds of larger visions they had for their writing centers. The desires for a collaborative community and tutors who go on retreats are values that positively define and reinforce their identities as writing center directors. While these statements are both examples of positive emotional labor that motivate the writing center administrators, the second quote shows how this type of value and self-expectation can also conflict with institutional realities. Ruth, who had envisioned a community of tutors who wanted to go on retreats, explained, "I had to reimagine my expectations for tutors, what I could reasonably ask of them." She reflected on how some of the tutors at her new institution did share her vision, but she also had to learn to value those tutors who were more independent or saw tutoring simply as a job. In this case, the generally positive emotions that motivate grander visions and ambitions can also cause reconsiderations and stress when local contexts make them challenging or impossible to enact. By "reimagin[ing]. . .expectations for tutors," Ruth recalibrated her expectations about what a collaborative community of tutors looked like, which, in turn, redefined her identity as a writing center administrator who fostered that collaborative community.

As we have been suggesting, the position of a writing center administrator is an aspect of a person's identity; however, the reflections on the loss of writing center administrator identities shared by the interviewees suggest that they each have a different relationship to their identities as directors. Ruth noted a variety of feelings regarding her movement away from the role. She said, "I'm nervous, I'm anxious, I feel sad [pauses]. It has been so much a part of my identity, for such a long time [pauses] that it's weird." While she felt the loss, she also described feeling ready to move on and support writers around campus in different ways. She appeared to feel conflicted, though in ways that we might naturally expect from an exiting administrator moving on from a program. Meanwhile, Lucy explained, "If I were just leaving and had no idea who is going to take over and they were going to do a national search and the people on the committee were not going to understand writing centers, I would have to just walk away from the whole thing." Lucy's reflection on her successor suggested an emotional labor tied to her sense of identity as a writing center administrator—she believed so strongly that an ideal writing center administrator needed to enact and hold certain writing center values that the idea of someone not sharing specific philosophical tenets caused her emotional labor. This moment also represented how hard it could be to let go of a program that helped professionally and institutionally define one's identity.

Lucy reflected more broadly on how her identity became overly identified with her work—a problem that seemed to exacerbate the emotional labor of the position:

> so much of my life has become work and about work and realizing that when the work that you do is very deeply entrenched in emotional labor and that the job is way too big—when it takes up a large part of your life, it's hard not to take things personal. And so if work isn't going well right then it feels like your life isn't going well, and I realized that [the university] never asked me to do that. They didn't put me in that position. I did.

Although Lucy was taking steps to remedy this imbalance by taking a new job at a new institution, her choice to leave her position from burnout and a lack of work and life balance echoes the research on job turnover reported by Grutsch McKinney et al. within this collection. Although burnout and work and life balance are referenced as two of many reasons related to emotions and emotional labor for leaving a position, we argue that such emotional labor is intensified precisely because writing center administrators start to see the job as a primary identity, and thus, as Lucy explains, even more "personal." These *reflections on becoming* illustrate not only the emotional labor of being in a position, but also the intensified stress and emotions involved in leaving or taking on a new role—changes we identify as having the potential to feel synonymous with becoming someone different. As Colin Charlton et al. suggest, our work as writing center administrators can go beyond the "position[s] that we might hold" to become instead "a way of being" (66). When a writing center administrator's identity blurs the line between work and life, these separate identities can become entangled to the extent that rather than "holding" a position of writing center administrator, one *becomes* a writing center administrator.

We also identified statements about emotional labor that come from sources external to the writing center administrator—specifically the emotional labor of others' expectations, attitudes, and actions and the emotional labor of one's relationship to different communities (see Appendix B, Table 1). Others—whether individuals or communities—help define our identities, too, either through affirming that we are enacting roles they attribute to our institutional identity or by triggering doubts and imparting negative responses to our institutional roles. The stories told by Lucy and Ruth illustrate how our relationships with individuals and campus communities can create both positive and negative emotional labor. WCAs experience positive emotional labor when we establish meaningful connections that reaffirm our sense of our ideal identities, and we experience negative emotional labor when these relationships lead us to doubt or defend our identities as WCAs or leave us feeling like outsiders.

Perhaps not surprisingly, both writing center administrators had stories of specific negative comments that colleagues had said to them—often early in their positions—that still stuck with them. We believe that the emotional labor that results from such comments is, at least in part, due to the way we tend to understand critiques as attacks on or misunderstandings of our identity, as well as the oppositional roles we may take on in response. Lucy noted, "we knew the more that we asked for the more they'd [upper administration] think we were being greedy." Lucy, who had successfully fought for writing center resources and a permanent space, shared several stories of negative attitudes towards her and the writing center's progress. She shared about a fellow faculty member who previously held the role of writing center administrator: "He was trying to be supportive but he was also incredibly resentful of the resources and support that I was being given." She continued, "I would find myself kind of competing with him. 'You know, I didn't have a budget for the first three years either, but I've been finding grants.'" Ruth shared a similar anecdote from her interview, saying, "In fact, [specific person] had said to me that there was no place for comp-rhet at [X university and in Y program]." While these two examples reflect different kinds of oppositional attitudes, both of them suggest how such interactions stayed with the interviewees for a long time. Through the carrying around of these moments—an example of what Sara Ahmed calls the stickiness of emotions (119)—these writing center administrators inhabited roles contrary to the collaborative and inclusive values that shape their ideal writing center administrator identities. In contrast with her goal of working alongside her department colleagues, the first example positioned Lucy in a more adversarial role, which resulted in emotional labor that challenged her sense of self. For Ruth, however, the comment was intended to suggest that because of her disciplinary identifications, she did not belong at this new institution; this moment resulted in emotional labor as she understood her options as either moving away from her disciplinary identifications in order to fit in or remaining an outsider. The interviewees' responses show how even small moments of opposition can have the potential to challenge their writing center administrator identities.

The interviews further illustrated how longer-term factors, such as the writing center administrators' relationships to campus and professional communities, could impact their identities and result in emotional labor. Ruth described two campus environments—one at a previous institution and one in her current position—where she felt isolated from the larger campus community because she was the sole rhetoric and composition faculty member. She described, "I felt very much like an outsider. And, alone in my work. [pauses] I never felt understood. People were very happy to let me do—be free to do what I wanted to do—but, there was never really an enthusiastic interest in what I did. And that is OK. I'm a grown up. But, it was hard to not have people to talk to about what was happening and what was going on." Ruth said about her current campus, "people on our campus don't know how to talk to us. They don't know how to understand us." As these two examples of isolation from a campus community suggest, there are feelings of disconnection and loneliness in the emotional labor of feeling like an outsider. Ruth's identification with her communities in rhetoric and composition and in writing center work connected her to the broader professional communities but created disciplinary identity dissonance on her campus. Meanwhile, Lucy offered an example of disciplinary harmony, noting how taking her graduate student tutors to a conference bonded them as a community. She described the positive impact of "being professionals in the discipline and being there together as a cohort." This example illustrated the ways that attending a conference strengthens the writing center values and creates a shared identity that tutors and the writing center administrator bring back to the center, lessening the emotional labor of the disciplinary isolation often felt on campus.

How Writing Center Administrators
Become Who They Want to Be: Strategies
for Negotiating Emotional Labor

During the interviews, the exiting writing center administrators were asked about how they negotiated the above emotional labor in real time, how they managed stressful situations, and how their identities were challenged or reinforced as a result. The strategies offered were small forms of self-care the writing center administrators used to protect themselves and advice they gave to incoming writing center administrators about being healthy and whole in administrative work (see Appendix B, Table 2). Like Genie Giaimo's chapter in this collection, we agree that material and structural support for administration is necessary for healthy and ethical writing center work, although many of these small self-care strategies were moments of considering how to evaluate and say, "*this is enough.*" Through focusing on how emotional labor relates to writing center administrators' sense of identity, we found that both Ruth and Lucy are drawn to strategies that empower them as the writing center administrators they want to be—by enacting actions that align with their philosophy and values—and feel weighed down by those that disconnect them from the identity they see as ideal.

Though not immediately recognizable as a strategy, the exiting writing center administrators' views of writing centers as comfortable and therapeutic spaces help to solidify and extend their identities as writing center administrators who actively and intentionally maintain positive connections to writing center work and spaces. Both writing center administrators described their writing centers with terms like "home," "retreat," "comfort," and "healing." Ruth explained that she perceived the writing center as an escape from the day-to-day grind and stressors of the position. "It's like my comfort food," she explained, "Retreating to the writing center has always been the way that I've cared for myself." Thus, as a strategy, both directors sought out work that they loved and found meaningful—specifically, work that further aligned with their ideal identities as writing center administrators. For example, both writing center administrators saw working one-on-one with writers as the heart of writing center work—as opposed to emails with faculty, budgets, hiring and training, and other more administratively-oriented work—and as representative of the kind of work everyone *should be* directly connected with, including the director. The decision to tutor as the director is a strategy that reinforces what both Ruth and Lucy saw as ideal writing center administrator identities, enacting the values of helping struggling writers and creating anti-hierarchical workplaces.

The conversations also covered self-care strategies for creating boundaries. The first interview, for example, discussed a common self-care strategy in offices and how it made the interviewer question her writing center administrator identity. The exiting writing center administrator, Ruth, explained, "I am not a door closer;" however, in response to the interviewer's—the new writing center administrator—anxiety over needing to close her door for both getting work done and for having time alone, she encouragingly said to the new director, "I think that you did a great job of [closing] the door when you need[ed] to." Even though closing doors seems like a small issue, the interviewer described experiencing anxiety over the tension between her perceptions of the office's social expectations—openness, collaboration, community—and her need to close the door. This incoming writing center administrator's anxiety is directly related to her concern regarding how others will perceive her as a director. She was essentially worrying that a closed door would be an action that would result in others reading her as being a certain kind of administrator—one who is closed, hierarchical, and even unfriendly. Thus, either closing or opening a door, here, functions as a strategy for establishing boundaries and even self-care within the workplace. Lucy's boundary-setting self-care strategy is more retrospective. She describes a realization that she cannot treat the university as if it were a person. That is, she explains her need to depersonalize the work and her connection to it in order to preserve a healthier emotional and personal life balance—even though that meant, in her case, a change in institution. More specifically, she reflects on how her new knowledge of emotional labor has led her to the realization: "I needed to go into a position that was going to allow me to be good at my job and also have a life outside of my job, and I don't think I was ever going to be able to do that here."

Ultimately, the interviewers and new writing center administrators' responses illustrate that they believed that all actions—even positive, self-care choices like closing a door—were direct and negative reflections of their identities as directors; however, the interviewees'—both exiting writing center administrators—responses demonstrated that their self-care and preservation strategies were not challenges to, but instead essential and positive additions to, their identities as writing center administrators that made their work lives more manageable. Thus, the exiting writing center administrators offered advice for self-care strategies on negotiating emotional labor to the incoming writing center administrators regarding how to *become* someone they are happy with in such administrative positions. For example, Lucy asserted the importance of "staying with" and "trying to figure out the emotions" tied to our work. She went on to explain that there were scenarios that she wished she had handled differently, but encouraged her successor to, "learn or get a warning from them [mistakes] and move past them." Lucy attempted to alleviate the unspoken pressure of taking over a position with gusto and perfection that is often self-imposed or imagined, not so unlike the guilt over closing one's door. Lucy attempted to offer a new narrative for what it means to be a successful writing center administrator: one that understands and acknowledges emotions and allows for mistakes.

Another silent pressure of taking on an established program may be an expectation for the new director to meet the standards or styles of the person who came before them. However, Ruth explained that part of becoming a writing center administrator—and protecting oneself in the process—is learning to make a program of one's own. She provided an example from a colleague who was well-liked and respected but pointed out that his methods "succeeded and failed with different personality types." She went on to note how she began to develop her own administrative style:

> Part of what makes me better able to express myself and be myself now, professionally, is that I have other women who are a decade and two-decades older than me, having lived a slightly different version of our reality, in their own unique ways, reminding me that it's ok to figure out what it means for me to be [myself] as an administrator and to be a woman administrator today.

This example is a moment of mentorship intended to encourage the incoming writing center administrator to develop her own administrative style, feel confident being herself, and to figure out what that means for her. As this example of Ruth's journey toward developing her own administrative style illustrates, many of the strategies shared in the interviews were not framed as advice but instead emerged through stories of navigating administrative struggles. We see this further demonstrated in anecdotes that conclude with lessons learned by the previous WCAs, such as the need to establish boundaries and locate work that is healing. In these moments, Ruth and Lucy were encouraging the incoming WCAs to become administrators with more self-awareness and less identity-based conflicts within the role.

EVOLVING IDENTITIES AND THE VALUE OF DIALOGUE

While we have a great deal of coding work that we do not have the space to explore here, there are two additional trends in the data that stand out as worthy of mention (see Appendix B, Table 3 and Table 4). First, the writing center administrators seem to move toward more positive emotional labor related to identity as they become more confident and comfortable with their statuses and identities as writing center administrators and on campus. While they still face challenges that result in emotional labor, they are less daunting and adversity becomes less "sticky," in that the day-to-day decisions seem less tied to the writing center administrators' identities (Ahmed 119). Second, over time, both directors felt a decrease in the emotional labor and time spent worrying about how colleagues might respond to them—especially to low-stakes program and policy decisions—in part, because they had gained confidence in themselves as administrators but also because they had developed keener awareness of the terrains of their campuses. While we cannot yet make strong claims about the role of *unbecoming* writing center administrators,[6] both Ruth and Lucy reflected on the benefits of these open and honest dialogues focused on emotional labor.

Both Ruth and Lucy discussed how time and experience in their positions led to feelings of increased autonomy and confidence, better awareness of the local context and needs, and a clearer understanding of what the job entailed. Ruth explored a process of becoming that moved towards confidence and less identity-based emotional labor. She outlined her path:

> A big transition for me, of course, was when I was able to trust myself. I feel like I know enough about this environment, I know enough about tutoring, and I knew that about myself, but there's always that context. There's the asking permission phase. Then, there's the still kind of asking permission, but framing it

---

6. Though as Martha A. Townsend suggests, one's identity as a WPA can extend beyond the role itself. She explains that she has "never not been a WPA" (qtd. in Charlton et al.).

as asking questions for collaboration: "what do you think?" but, really wanting validation. To truly getting to the place where I was able to just say, "Gosh, here's this thing I struggle with. Let's think it through." And really knowing that I was, in my heart, trusting myself to ask the right questions, to know what were sincere and honest questions. To ask those, to take in the information, and to know that I and my colleagues alike trusted me to make the right decisions. And that was a big process.

Here, Ruth described acquiring confidence in her role and writing center administrator identity as involving gaining institutional and disciplinary knowledge as well as validation from others. While affirmation from others may help administrators gain confidence—that our questions, actions, and choices are successfully aligning with others' sense of our writing center administrator identities and roles—it is important to note that, at least for Ruth, real administrative confidence and agency moved beyond this stage to trust in oneself. That transition from confidence coming from others to coming from self-trust is especially significant since others' perceptions of our work may or may not align with thoughtful and informed administrative decisions writing center administrators need to make. Lucy noted, "The truth is, if somebody comes into the Writing Center ready to yell at somebody it's going to be us." We perceived such understanding of, perhaps even resignation to, conflict and emotion management as a typical part of the process of becoming a more experienced writing center administrator. Lucy's acknowledgement of her identity as the responsible party when issues arise suggested a kind of peace with this often difficult part of her identity as a writing center administrator. Thus, throughout both interviews, there were reflections on their evolution in the role—about how they had come to better understand their roles, become more confident in them, and feel more at peace in them.

In addition to their identities as writing center administrators evolving, both interviewees noted the value of discussing and reflecting on emotional labor. They said, in different ways, that staying with their emotions encouraged them to take time to celebrate "wins" and progress and opened the door for having public conversations about work-related emotional labor. Perhaps Lucy best summed up the diverse value of such work to one's professional and personal identity when she explained near the end of the interview, "Being more reflective about what emotional labor looks like and where it exists in our lives is a really important part of our personhood, scholarly, writerly. Everything." Both interviewees reflected on how staying with emotion and better understanding emotional labor helped them to fight burnout, set boundaries, minimize negative feelings like resentment, better acknowledge what was going well, and better recognize when they were not being adequately or appropriately valued or supported. Further, Lucy explained how the value of such conversations may go beyond the personal benefits to shape the profession: "The value is if we keep having these conversations maybe then we can get to a better place with including the emotional labor in the job description and being better able to articulate how emotional labor and support and mentorship actually factor into our job description and find ways to value it and incentivize it." The exiting writing center administrators evolved in their identities in ways that softened the emotional labor related to identity conflicts. Through the interviews, the incoming writing center administrators gained tangible strategies for negotiating emotional labor and a sense of how professional identities evolve in ways that are sustainable.

Concluding Thoughts on the Evolution and Visibility of Writing Center Administrators' Emotional Labor

We hope that acknowledging the ways that our sense of an ideal writing center administrator identity is tied to emotional labor through our actions, connections, and others' perceptions can help alleviate some of the emotional labor of transitioning writing center administrators. Since the more experienced writing center administrators, Lucy and Ruth, both traced an evolution in their relationship to their roles—one that resulted in less identity-based emotional labor—we suspect that the moment of transitioning, either into or out of, is a particularly fraught moment that may actually amplify conscious thinking about one's writing center administrator identity. As writing center administrators are entering new positions or exiting positions, they may be more likely to evaluate themselves and their work in relation to their sense of an ideal writing center administrator. While this idealized identity is sometimes motivating, we hope that in elucidating it in this chapter, we might encourage transitioning writing center administrators, in particular, to let go of this connection a bit more. We hope transitioning writing center administrators will learn, for instance, that while there may be a tendency to understand closing an office door as an extension of one's identity, this inaccurate belief can lead to unproductive and unnecessary negative emotional labor and identity-conflict.

We further believe that focusing on the relationship between writing center administrator identities and emotional labor offers us a better way to understand emotional labor. Laura Micciche has written that studying emotional labor can lead to "new insights and new visions of possibility, as well as different ways of seeing the work we do" (453). Hull and Brooks-Gillies remind us, too, that by ignoring the complicated narratives or reality of emotion work, writing center administrators aid in furthering the marginalization of that labor. Interviews centered on emotional labor, such as those detailed in this chapter, have the potential to reveal more accurate depictions of writing center work and, as Micciche suggests, offer transitioning writing center administrators opportunities for learning, reflection, and connection. Though our study is small and limited in its ability to be generalizable, we hope that it motivates further research into the more abstract and psychic ways that affect circulates and impacts administrative work identities. We also offer these findings to extend our understanding of the emotional labor of administrators and advocate not only for the visibility of emotional labor, but for the role of dialogue or interviews centered on emotional labor in negotiating said labor and transitioning both into and out of writing center administrator positions.

Works Cited

Ahmed, Sara. "Affective Economics." *Social Text 79*, vol. 22, no. 2, 2004, pp. 117–39.

Bawarshi, Anis. *Genre and the Invention of the Writer: Reconsidering the Place of Invention in Composition.* Utah State UP, 2003.

Bazerman, Charles. "Genre and Identity: Citizenship in the Age of the Internet and the Age of Global Capitalism." *The Rhetoric and Ideology of Genre: Strategies for Stability and Change,* edited by Richard Coe, et al., Hampton Press, Inc., 2002, pp. 13–38.

Caswell, Nicole I., et al. *The Working Lives of New Writing Center Directors.* UP of Colorado, 2016.

Charlton, Colin, et al. *GenAdmin: Theorizing WPA Identities in the Twenty-First Century.* Parlor Press, 2011.

Charmaz, Kathy. *Constructing Grounded Theory: A Practical Guide through Qualitative Analysis.* SAGE Publications, Ltd., 2006.

Estrem, Heidi. "Disciplinary and Professional Identities are Constructed Through Writing." *Naming What We Know: Threshold Concepts of Writing Studies*, edited by Linda Adler-Kassner and Elizabeth Wardle, Utah State UP, 2015, pp. 55–56.

Geller, Anne Ellen, and Harry Denny. "Of Ladybugs, Low Status, and Loving the Job: Writing Center Professionals Navigating Their Careers." *The Writing Center Journal*, vol. 33, no. 1, 2013, pp. 96–129.

Guy, Mary E., et al. *Emotional Labor: Putting the Service in Public Service*. Routledge, 2008.

Jackson, Rebecca, et al. "Writing Center Administration and/as Emotional Labor." *Composition Forum*, vol. 34, 2016.

Micciche, Laura R. "More than a Feeling: Disappointment and WPA Work." *College English*, vol. 64, no. 4, 2002, pp. 432–58.

Navickas, Kate. "The Emotional Labor of Becoming: Lessons from the Exiting Writing Center Director." *The Things We Carry: Strategies for Recognizing and Negotiating Emotional Labor in Writing Program Administration*, edited by Courtney Adams Wooten, et al., Utah State UP, 2020, pp. 56–74.

Nickoson, Lee. "Revisiting Teacher Research." *Writing Studies Research in Practice, Methods and Methodologies*, edited by Lee Nickoson and Mary Sheridan, Southern Illinois UP, 2012, pp. 101–12.

Ratcliffe, Krista, and Rebecca Rickly. Introduction. "Actions Un/Becoming a Feminist Administrator: Troubled Intersections of Feminist Principles and Administrative Practices." *Performing Feminism and Administration in Rhetoric and Composition Studies*, edited by Ratcliffe and Rickly, Hampton Press, 2010, pp. vii-xv.

Roozen, Kevin. "Writing is Linked to Identity." *Naming What We Know: Threshold Concepts of Writing Studies*, edited by Linda Adler-Kassner and Elizabeth Wardle, Utah State UP, 2015, pp. 50–52.

Roulston, Kathryn. "Analyzing Interviews." *The SAGE Handbook of Qualitative Data Analysis*, edited by Uwe Flick, SAGE Publications, Inc., 2014, pp. 297–312.

Saldaña, Johnny. "Coding and Analysis Strategies." *The Oxford Handbook of Qualitative Research*, edited by Patricia Leavy, Oxford UP, 2014, pp. 581–605.

Wynn Perdue, Sherry, and Dana Lynn Driscoll. "Context Matters: Centering Writing Center Administrators' Institutional Status and Scholarly Identity." *The Writing Center Journal*, vol. 36, no. 1, 2017, pp. 185–214.

Appendix A. Interview Questions

1. When you first came to this position, how did you understand the work? What were your initial emotions in response to getting hired and starting the position? Did you have any internal struggles regarding the job?

2. What were some of your early struggles or accomplishments in this position?

3. What are some of the emotional components of your work? Could you map out different emotions you attached to different parts of the work?

4. As you have transitioned to your new role, what emotions have you experienced? How would you describe transitioning in terms of emotional labor?

5. What do you think you are most proud of having done in this position? What would you want your legacy to be? And what emotions do you attach to that work?

6. In what ways has the emotional labor of the job changed for you?

7. How have you negotiated the emotional labor of your work?

8. What advice do you have for me, especially in terms of negotiating emotional labor?

9. What does it mean to acknowledge emotional labor for you? What does it mean to share the emotional labor of your work with me? With others publicly?

APPENDIX B. CODING CATEGORIES

Table 1. Coding categories and examples in response to, "What are the sources of emotional labor?"

Guiding Question: What are the sources of emotional labor?	
Category (# of codes): **Definition of category**	**Example Codes**
Self-Expectations and Values (1): Articulation of one's self-expectations and values when entering a position or task	−The want for others to not be resentful −The want for a collaborative program, a community of tutors −Expectations for the writing center to be a place of healing −The belief one is not doing enough −The sense of others' expectations for you as an influence on thinking and decisions
Emotional Labor of Becoming (22): Articulations of moments of transition, growth, and reflection; this is different than self-expectations as it is more about who you are in the job, as opposed to what you expect yourself to do	−The hardship and sense of loss with transitioning out of a writing center administrator position and leaving a writing center −Reflections on how one's identity is tied up with the work and being a writing center administrator −Realizations of the emotional labor of the position −Reflections on balancing work and life

Guiding Question: What are the sources of emotional labor?	
Category (# of codes): **Definition of category**	**Example Codes**
Others' Expectations (32): Articulations of one's understanding of others' expectations for a job or task and others' attitudes or actions; others' expectations come from actual statements and actions, as well as one's felt sense of how others feel about something	−Others' resentment at new resources and institutional support −Faculty expectations about writers −Faculty expectations about what writing centers should do to "fix" writers −Administrative pressures to develop and make change quickly −Faculty distrust of rhetoric and composition as a discipline −Writing center administrators' ability to meet outside expectations with concrete data
Community (21): Articulations of both positive and negative experiences and feelings that come from communities, including communities of tutors, departments, campus communities and disciplinary communities; codes both express positive emotions about connecting with communities and negative emotions due to isolation from a community	−The joy of fostering community with tutors −The challenge of not having a community with tutors −The challenge of taking a non-tenure-track job that isolates you from the rhetoric and composition community −The challenge of not having a disciplinary community on campus

Guiding Question: What are the sources of emotional labor?	
Category (# of codes): **Definition of category**	**Example Codes**
Writing Center Context (39): Articulations of larger institutional contexts, pressures, spaces and geography; the specific writing center context, space, constraints, and work; the specific model of writing center and its relationship to disciplinary expectations for writing centers	−Untrained and unsupervised tutors −Broken computers and printers, flickering lights, and a lack of offices and space −The fight for resources and space −Understanding of campus culture and needs −A lack of community at a new institutional writing center −Creation of a tutoring community −Comparison of current institutional writing center model to previous jobs' writing center models and field narratives of writing centers
The Job (26): Articulations of one's sense of the job and what the position entails; sense of overwhelm at the scope of the work or other aspects of "the job" as a general thing	−Feeling of overwhelm of the work ahead of you, of the job, or specific parts of the job −Feeling of overwhelm at the size of the campus −Specific job tasks (working the faculty across campus, emailing, fighting for resources) that are described in terms of the work or the job

Table 2. Coding categories and examples in response to, "How did the interviewee navigate and negotiate emotional labor in real time or retrospectively?"

Guiding Question: How did the interviewee navigate and negotiate emotional labor in real time or retrospectively?	
Category (# of codes): Definition of category	Example Codes
Internal Strategies: (21): Actions that occur in relative isolation, within the interviewee, and lend themselves to personal growth, protection, or work and life balance	−Further study of the field, self-care −Special projects whose purpose are distraction or easing of emotional labor −Journaling −Emotional indulgences
Community and Collaboration (9): Moments in which the speaker seeks out or is influenced by colleagues or university standards for the work or fosters community within the center	−Talking, listening, and observation of the culture of the university −Established connection to the campus community prior to implementing programmatic changes −Recognition of differing management styles and their strengths and weaknesses
Agency and Action (5): Instances in which the interviewee describes putting their pedagogies into action (praxis) and how they deal with the emotionally intensive way that this happens for new WPAs and WCDs at new institutions	−Personalization of the program and the space −Development of resources −Implementation of one's own pedagogies −Placement of expertise in action for change
Supervisory Expectations (4): Descriptions of working with GAs and Colleagues in which the speaker intentionally tempers their expectations of the behavior, needs, and emotions of others to protect the speaker from absorbing unnecessary tensions within those interactions	−Temperment of one's expectations for how GAs will want to interact −Development of an awareness for other's work styles −Strategic, often hands-off, management to foster functionality in the writing center and professional development GAs

Guiding Question: How did the interviewee navigate and negotiate emotional labor in real time or retrospectively?	
Category (# of codes): *Definition of category*	**Example Codes**
Mentoring in Action (11): The speaker is actively giving advice within the interview and talking about mentoring on the job	−Pointing to history to illustrate trial and error, overcoming difficult situations and interactions −Emphasis on a need to find one's unique identity within the job −Encouragement of the exploration of projects outside the realm of the work −Reassurance that perfection is not possible

Table 3. Coding categories and examples in response to, "Did the interviewee speak about the evolution of their understanding of their emotions and emotional labor?"

Guiding Question: Did the interviewee speak about the evolution of their understanding of their emotions and emotional labor?	
Category (# of codes): *Definition of category*	**Example Codes**
Experience and Maturation (10): The evolution of one's emotional labor over time and their understanding of themselves, their work, and the profession that is typical with experience on the job	−Increased autonomy and confidence felt with having a proper space for the writing center −More confidence in one's decision-making and prioritizing abilities −Understanding that dealing with conflict is part of the job −Recognition of the job and work as less daunting over time

Guiding Question: Did the interviewee speak about the evolution of their understanding of their emotions and emotional labor?	
Category (# of codes): **Definition of category**	**Example Codes**
Discussions And Understandings of Emotional Labor (20): The evolution of one's emotional labor over time and their understanding of themselves, their work, and the profession as a result of discussions about emotions and understanding of emotional labor	—Recognition of wins and positive aspects of the work, institution, and progress —Placement of the job and our own importance in perspective —Feeling of comfort managing one's expectations and moves toward progress in direct relation to time and resources —More trust that others will trust your leadership —Open to engaging in public conversations about the emotions and emotional labor of writing center work —Depersonalization of the actions of the institution --Reclaimed time and space for identity beyond work

Table 4. Coding categories and examples in response to, "Why is talking about and understanding emotions and emotional labor meaningful?"

Guiding Question: Why is talking about and understanding emotions and emotional labor meaningful?	
Category (# of codes): **Definition of category**	**Example Codes**
Value to Self (19): The value of discussing and understanding emotions and emotional labor to oneself	—Fighting off of burnout —Minimized feelings of resentment and insecurity —Progress reflection —Feelings of support, comfort, and not being alone —Better recognition ofwhen we are not being adequately or appropriately valued or supported —Understanding of when and how to depersonalize aspects of work and make work more pleasant and enjoyable —Better set boundaries and better feelings about those boundaries
Value to Program or University (9): The value of discussing and understanding emotions and emotional labor to one's program or university	—Set of and focus on priorities —Expanding ofcommunity and collaboration —Others learn it is okay to discuss, recognize, and support each other's emotions and emotional labor —Others recognize and put into perspective progress, wins, and areas of growth —Over time, reduction of the energy needed to train and guidance of colleagues and students toward being better to each other

Guiding Question: **Why is talking about and understanding emotions and emotional labor meaningful?**	
Category (# of codes): **Definition of category**	**Example Codes**
Value to Profession (9): The value of discussing and understanding emotions and emotional labor to the profession	−Set precedent for understanding writing center work as emotional and emotionally labor intensive −Writing center administrator and colleagues understand their emotions and emotional labor, while also contextualized, as normal and important −Establishment of better policies, practices, expectations, and safeguards to ensure current and future writing center administrators are supported and recognized for their emotion work

4 Navigating Emotions and Interpersonal Relations in Graduate Administrative Writing Center Work

Nicole Chavannes, Monique Cole, Jordan Guido, and Sabrina Louissaint

Graduate students in leadership positions bring a unique perspective to writing center scholarship. By working closely with administrators, faculty, and students, they provide different leadership advantages and perspectives for research, project implementation, and professional development. Being graduate students allows us to be more aware of student life on campus and to better understand some of the struggles our peers may be experiencing. However, being a student in a writing center leadership position leaves us vulnerable to feeling unsure about our authority or professional capabilities. Hierarchical lines can blur as we navigate our emotions and interpersonal relationships in the center. Andrea Theresa Gannon draws on Michael Mattison's work to emphasize the importance of acknowledging the balance among different positions in writing centers, saying, "It's not a matter of switching positions so much as acknowledging the multiplicity of positions and noticing the overlaps and connections—and disconnections" (Mattison 16, qtd. in Gannon). As Master's students who hold leadership roles in our writing center as graduate assistant coordinators, GACs, we tend to struggle with hierarchical and peer-based relations because we sometimes minimize the impact of interpersonal relations. Instead, we focus on negative emotions and are often preoccupied with leadership requirements and academic hurdles.

The failure to recognize our emotions can be detrimental to our relationships in our writing center as well as to our mental well-being. Acknowledging our emotions is important because writing center consultants work with students from multiple disciplines on a variety of writing assignments. Like Lauren Brentnell et al. acknowledge in their chapter in this collection, writing centers are unlike other spaces on campus because the work that students bring to us can be personal or emotional. With our professional roles constantly evolving and being rewritten to better accommodate the needs of our center and professional aspirations, we feel that it is necessary to recognize how our emotions influence our interpersonal relationships and our overall impact on the center, particularly with our daily performance as leaders and as consultants. Our interpersonal relationships provide us a heightened understanding of how emotional labor pertains to our work as writing center leaders when it comes to communicating with each other and developing as professionals.

Graduate students who work in writing centers must also conduct emotional labor as part of our daily responsibilities, since, as Kelin Hull and Marilee Brooks-Gillies outline in their chapter in this collection, relationship-building and writing center work are all emotional because of the individual identities and power structures involved. Emotional labor has been explored in relation to writing center directors (Jackson et al.) and consultants (Mundy and Sugerman), but an area of research that we elaborate on here is that of graduate student writing center administrators who work as both leaders and consultants. In our work, we find that emotional labor is often like being on a roller coaster, consisting of moments of highs and lows, due to the multiple expectations set by our administration, professors, staff, students, and the university. How we show our emotions is one thing, but we also tend to absorb the emotions that surround us, especially those of the students we help (Morris et al.). We work with stressed graduate students who are also worried about their coursework or theses, and this feeling can translate and, for some, "stick" throughout the day (Micciche 27).

Scholars have recognized the challenges graduate students in writing center leadership positions face by examining their preparation for such work (Rowan). While acknowledging that graduate students must actively learn administrative work, Karen Rowan recognizes the discrepancy that exists among writing center scholars, some of whom believe graduate students should be "explicitly prepar[ed]" for writing center administration, while others think the "potential risks of such administrative professional development, [. . .] outweigh their merits" (13). It is difficult to determine the best approach for preparing graduate students for writing center work. Our thinking aligns with Hull and Brooks-Gillies, who outline in their chapter in this collection that relationship-building and writing center work are all emotional because of the individual identities and power structures involved. The messiness of administrative work can put graduate students in uncomfortable positions, especially if they do not recognize their leadership ability or have poor interpersonal relationships with other members of the leadership team, writing center staff, or peers.

Graduate students in administrative positions can contribute to the messiness of managing conflicts and expectations. The tension between leadership, staff, and peers can be complicated by the graduate student administrators' own perception of the importance of writing center work to their post-graduate professions (Grouling and Buck). For example, duties, expectations, and personal motivations for an undergraduate tutor working in a writing center for a semester differ from those of graduate administrators who may choose writing center work for financial reasons or to further professional goals. In addition, Jennifer Grouling and Elisabeth Buck found "the amount of time that a tutor spent in the center affected the way they related to that space" (55), which is also evident in our experiences as GACs. While a GAC's position in our writing center typically lasts years, some of us were also involved in writing centers as undergraduate tutors, thus affecting our relationship to the space. Ultimately, how we view ourselves and roles within the center factors into our negotiation of expectations and boundaries related to communication and interpersonal relations.

We begin this chapter by defining three major themes under the umbrella of interpersonal relationships—emotional labor, burnout, and imposter syndrome—as we focus on analyzing how emotions within our interpersonal relationships with one another affect our experiences. We recognize that as GACs and students, we must navigate maintaining a healthy relationship with ourselves by cultivating both mental and physical well-being. In this chapter, we examine how emotional labor, burnout, and imposter syndrome can affect interpersonal relationships within graduate student administrative writing center work. Through personal narratives, we seek to better understand how to build healthy relationships as a leadership team and within ourselves while dealing with the strains of burnout and imposter syndrome. We then provide strategies based on our personal experiences in the hopes that they help future GACs navigate similar emotional challenges.

Interpersonal Relationships, Emotional Labor, Imposter Syndrome, and Burnout in Graduate Administrative Work

Emotions and affect impact interpersonal relationships and should be examined carefully because forming relationships within writing centers—whether with consultants, administrators, faculty, or other GACs—can help to foster a community of trust and unity. Interpersonal relationships, or "interpersonal bond[s] (uniting force or agreement) in which both individuals acknowledge that they are connected" (Miller 6), are unavoidable in writing centers. As both students and leaders, we face some challenges in maintaining healthy interpersonal relationships, including communicating effectively, working collectively, and trusting one another. Interpersonal relationships foster learning and have a significant impact on people in the workplace.

Communication is perhaps the most important attribute to foster among team members when navigating interpersonal relationships, particularly when the dynamics include varying relationships between members—friends, colleagues, classmates, mentors, and mentees. How we deal with certain situations can ultimately affect how we operate on a daily basis, both as leaders and graduate students, because it can contribute to how we trust and work with one another. On the clock, we are leaders and represent our writing center by acting in a professional manner to establish a productive and safe environment. We serve as mentors to consultants and strive to make sure they feel cared about and accounted for. However, off the clock, we become more focused on our personal and academic concerns while interacting with each other in a less professional manner, whether it be through close friendships or limited interactions outside the center. One way we seek to recognize the different roles we play is by identifying how our emotions affect our work and understanding how our interpersonal skills can help us navigate those relationships and work through differences. In an effort to mitigate the competing factors involved in maintaining productive interpersonal relationships, graduate students in writing center leadership positions often practice emotional labor.

Writing center director and tutor emotional labor is an integral part of writing center practice (Jackson et al.; Mundy and Sugerman). Emotional labor—or emotion work—as defined by Mara Holt et al. is the "responsive attention to the emotional aspects of social life, including attention to personal feelings, the emotional tenor of relationships, empathy, and encouragement, mediation of disputes, building emotional solidarity in groups, and using one's own or other's *outlaw emotions* to interrogate structures" (147). Rebecca Jackson et al. found in their study of writing center directors that emotional labor can take shape when "mentoring, advising, making small talk, putting on a friendly face, resolving conflicts, and making connections;" along with "delegating tasks . . . working in teams . . . gaining trust, and creating a positive workplace." While Jackson et al.'s study focuses specifically on writing center directors, we find that these same components of emotional labor also apply to graduate students in writing center leadership roles. Each instance of emotional labor requires additional care and support, and available solutions are often based on our social groupings—mentors, consultants, and fellow GACs. Therefore, we must consider how we show our emotions, as "the emotions that we experience dwell, potentially affecting those around us" (Morris et al. 48). As GACs, we are competing with many different social expectations across a single day and often find ourselves fatigued from performing long stretches of emotional labor alongside our administrative duties.

Our emotions manifest through our interpersonal relationships, which can influence how we interact with one another when performing different roles in the writing center. In shifting through our social spheres—classroom, writing center, program, social gatherings, and more—the overextension of emotional labor can contribute to feelings of burnout, leaving little space for graduate students to conduct their disciplinary labor or pursue professional development opportunities. Working as a GAC is often an opportunity for exponential professional growth, where we develop strong interpersonal relationships. These positive relationships can alleviate negative feelings, such as burnout. Arnold Bakker and Patrícia Costa define burnout as "a syndrome characterized by chronic exhaustion, cynicism, and a lack of personal accomplishment" (113). As they write, burnout can encompass emotional exhaustion, which is the "central strain dimension of burnout, described as feelings of being emotionally drained by one's work" (113). In writing center administration, burnout might come from working on too many projects, trying to organize tasks within work hours, and tackling unexpected situations.

Adding to the cause of burnout, some graduate students in writing center leadership positions might quickly find themselves immersed in their work or take on multiple competing tasks before officially settling in. Anne Ellen Geller and Harry Denny examine writing center professionals and how they navigate their roles, finding that participants "expressed the desire to embrace just about every new initiative presented to them—or that they themselves came up with—sometimes because they were excited about the initiative and sometimes because they felt pressure to take it on" (110). While writing center leadership can enhance professional growth, it can also stunt emotional and mental well-being because the excitement and pressure to take on initiatives, coupled with the emotional labor of navigating our various roles, can become too overwhelming and lead to burnout. Burnout can prove detrimental to both the graduate student in the writing center leadership position and to the advancement of the writing center. Individuals who become burned out can end up distancing themselves "emotionally and cognitively from their work activities" (Bakker and Costa 113). Due to this distancing, employees can experience a reduction in their work performance by engaging more in "counterproductive work behaviors" (Bakker and Costa 114). For example, a graduate student in a writing center leadership position who feels burnout might be less likely to collaborate with other members of the leadership team. Long-term burnout can be detrimental for GACs because "burned out individuals seem to fail to satisfy their basic psychological needs," leading to poor mental and physical well-being (Bakker and Costa 117).

As graduate students in writing center leadership positions, we are prone to imposter syndrome as we negotiate our academic identities and professional growth. We think it is important to acknowledge our tendency to feel inadequate because of our lack of authority, experience, or lack of complete control within the writing center. David Knights and Caroline Clarke highlight the insecurities attributed to imposter syndrome as "a mixed blessing because while they can be debilitating, they are also a driving force of our productive power that help generate high standards and pride in our work" (349). We find their assessment of the dual nature of imposter syndrome to be true; while it has motivated us in many ways to do our best and show both ourselves and our colleagues that we belong, it has also at times been mentally debilitating, as we become discouraged at the prospect of simply not being good enough. If we do not feel good enough, our execution of writing center work might not be the most effective, or we might become stunted in our professional growth. We find that new GACs can be at a higher risk of imposter syndrome because individuals entering a new workplace can experience "identity conflicts," which "are natural when individuals negotiate the relationship between one identity and their various other communities" (Grouling and Buck 55).

NARRATIVES

Being a GAC can be an emotional rollercoaster, and the GAC title itself illustrates dual roles: "graduate assistant" and "coordinator," which involve unique emotional challenges. To expand on these challenges, we complicate how imposter syndrome, burnout, and emotional labor play a role in our experiences and interpersonal relationships. In addition, we navigate how our backgrounds and identities have prepared us to understand our feelings, imposter syndrome, burnout, and emotional labor. By uncovering how our diverse backgrounds, educational upbringings, leadership experiences, and identities intersect, we illuminate the importance of acknowledging interpersonal relationships and emotion within graduate-level administrative work.

Jordan. Promptly starting my role as a GAC at the Writing and Communication Center (WCC), I jumped head-first into the throws of graduate school. I welcomed the challenge of expanding my skill sets; however, the realities of imposter syndrome, administrative office politics, and the emotional ups anddowns of graduate coursework left me feeling uncertain about my positioning in the center as a leader. My previous writing center had a majority-minority staff ratio, allowing for a space engaged in discourse surrounding race, gender, nationality, sexual orientation, and socioeconomic status. I had grown used to feeling supported and appreciated for my identities; when shifting into this new culture, I felt a loss more deeply than I anticipated as establishing social connections was a challenge. I found myself unable to find others who expressed my values and cultural understanding as the community surrounding the center seemed to promote white-cis ways of envisioning our work. In an effort to address the hegemony of the space, a fellow GAC and I conducted diversity and inclusion workshops for WCC consultants and administration. The efforts were well-received yet proved to be ineffective and harder to implement than originally thought, resulting in the lessening of their importance throughout the remainder of the semester.

Feeling I was not a "right" cultural fit for the WCC created echoes of imposter syndrome throughout my shifts. Imposter syndrome washed over many interactions in the WCC moving forward with consultants and GACs alike. During my formative months in the center, I felt overwhelmed with the amount of knowledge that I did not know for my position—scheduling times, appointment procedures, and general clerical tasks to more nuanced social-cultural rules. The feeling of being overwhelmed physically manifested itself as fear, headaches, and butterflies in my stomach before every shift. As Rowan suggests, I had come to feel underprepared and overwhelmed by the lack of ties to the center, personally culminating for me in my distanced interactions with my fellow GAC-mates. I often found myself confused as to how I should present myself in social situations with the same group of individuals—as friends? co-workers? peers? In my previous writing center experience, I never had these questions as my leadership position was always negotiable. If I did not want to lead, I could elect not to; if I felt burned out, I could refrain from adding more to my workload. As a graduate and professional attempting to position myself as approachable and knowledgeable, I felt I had no choice but to lean into a distanced professional identity to achieve a sense of balance. By leaning into a professional identity, I was able to bypass these feelings of imposter syndrome by fronting a facade of false confidence.

The tension only grew as my fellow GACs and I were also part of the same graduate studies program and saw each other semi-frequently. The lines between these groups began to merge and offered a space to engage in conversations that aligned with my values. In making these connections and approaching them with a sense of curiosity instead of my forced "professionalism," I came to learn my peers were also battling with many of the same emotions I was. Through learning that others also felt the pressure to perform in the WCC, I began to remove aspects of my "professional" facade and show an authentic version of myself as a leader. In creating an open dialogue about my concerns by showing up as myself to my role, I began to make connections to others in more meaningful ways. Through leaving my comfort zone, I was able to step into space as a member of the writing center community, as a student, and as a leader.

Monique. Before becoming a GAC, I worked at the WCC for three years, serving as an undergraduate peer consultant and student coordinator. To an extent, my experiences helped prepare me for my new adventure of becoming a GAC. However, when I entered the GAC role, I quickly found myself overwhelmed. While I was staying within the same working environment, I was taking on two new identities that consisted of additional responsibilities and expectations, along with working with new individuals from various backgrounds and writing center experiences. My relationships with these individuals played a role in my day-to-day writing center practices and collaboration on center initiatives. The strength of these relationships had the power to transform my professional identity to new heights, while simultaneously putting me at risk for burnout.

James Kouzes and Barry Posner talk about a "climate of trust" that focuses on leaders fostering a community of trust for *others* (200). When leaders generate a "climate of trust" they "create an environment that allows people to contribute freely and to innovate" (200). Trust is not innate but is a key component of communication and the development of healthy relationships. Trust, for me, is something that is not easily given and quick to lose, especially when I care deeply about some of the projects I work on. For example, one of the largest changes for me was the growth of the WCC social media and marketing team. When I began as a GAC, the team consisted of myself and one other person and later transformed into two teams containing multiple people who were eager to change protocol and style of posting. With the increase of people interested in marketing and social media, my chance to really have full control over creative marketing projects declined.

I felt empowered by my writing center director to take on projects that interested me, which boosted my confidence. However, my sense of empowerment also led to distrust, due to the heightened expectations I had developed for my fellow colleagues and myself. I felt empowered by my writing center director to take on projects that interested me, which boosted my confidence. However, I sometimes felt like a child let loose in a candy store with multiple opportunities to participate in scholarship or to develop new initiatives for the center. The lingering thought of trying to build up my CV for advancement after graduation coupled with my genuine interest in the research we were conducting contributed to my desire to try and do everything. I had that mentality that saying "no," might reduce the expectations from a fellow peer or faculty member. I was surrounded by multiple projects with varying deadlines, which caused me to ask myself, "where do I begin?" If I felt like I was spending too much on a project, I would feel disappointment for my failure to concentrate on just one thing. Being a full-time graduate student added to the pressure, especially during midterms and finals week, where my brain felt like it was going into overdrive.

To prevent feelings of burnout, I had to constantly remind myself that I could not always do everything, or at least not alone. I felt emotionally drained and uncomfortable seeing new people enter on projects I started. However, as a leader, I learned to be collaborative and let other people shine. I realized I could not control everything. If I failed to empower or trust other team members to succeed, it reduced my level of productivity and increased my chances of burnout. The most magical thing that has happened—by becoming more mindful of my feelings of burnout and strengthening my interpersonal relationships with my team members—is the heightened feeling of community and support. That support fosters the feeling that everything is going to be okay for me, my team, and members of the WCC. It makes me excited instead of feeling burned out because I can finally take a step back, breathe, and focus on what needs to be done and I can trust that others will help me along the way.

Sabrina. Having been in leadership roles in the past, without prior writing center experience, I found myself intrigued by the many different facets WCC work had to offer. I felt like I had to find myself all over again. My identity as a Black, Haitian-American woman was to be shaped in a brand new place, with brand new people.

Only a week after I graduated, I began my Master's program and started working at the WCC as a GAC in the summer, which was, thankfully, a slow period. I did a lot of work that summer developing training materials for consultants. I will say, in the beginning, it was strange working on materials for a position I, myself, had no experience in. That is where the imposter syndrome started to come out. Nevertheless, we managed to complete training modules and I learned a lot about writing center work. It is safe to say I started in the calm before the storm. By Fall, GACs went through training and learned about different policies and procedures, and I tried to envision what the center would look like in full capacity. Once the mass of consultants started working and students swept in, that is when the storm began. The staff functioned so well, and everything was fast-paced and organized. I recall a brief moment, staring in amazement as everyone began working at the top of the hour and just reflecting on everything I learned.

I agree with Jackie Grutsch McKinney that "writing center work is complex, although the storying of it often is not" (20). Everyone's experience is different; however, as GACs, our roles include many tasks and no easy way to communicate the work that we do, as we mostly learn in the process. In the beginning, I felt like I could not handle everything, but I remained optimistic. I was also adjusting to two graduate classes, which brought an extra layer of stress. I was excited to work on different projects and teams, like social media and planning professional development workshops. I figured, if I am going to be here for two years, I have to make the most out of it, despite feeling burned out.

When I felt like I had too much on my plate, I looked to some of my peers who were battling the same tasks as me and remembered that we were all in this together. Along with the behind-the-scenes functions to keep the center running smoothly, there were so many things I was involved in. If I was asked to do something else beyond these commitments, I felt like I could not say "no," even when it was not required of me. The feeling of being overwhelmed swept in and, oddly enough, I sought comfort in keeping myself busy to avoid having a meltdown. When I felt like I was easing into the transition, the reality was that I was in a room full of seasoned veterans. There was the imposter syndrome, again. I often thought whether or not I belonged there or if I was doing enough; this was partly due to lack of experience in the field. I went through a rollercoaster of emotions—ranging from uncertainty to hopefulness. This would occur all in one shift. Like Talinn Phillips et al., I questioned if the problems I faced were "part of the territory of [a graduate student's] WPA work" (43). At times, I did not feel equipped to tell others what to do or not do. I found myself gaining more problem solving and multitasking skills. I started thinking creatively, and—I have to say—it was all worth it.

I experienced a lot of growth in one semester. By navigating my role and coming to terms with my identity in the space, I found that the relationships I gained from the center grounded me. The executive director and faculty coordinators helped me find my niche within the center, and that has been my motivation ever since. There are still times when I feel the overwhelming pressures to be "perfect," but that is my own cognitive perspective. I know that I am surrounded by support and, most importantly, I feel accepted.

Nicole. Like my colleagues, I was riddled with insecurities and imposter syndrome when I first began graduate studies and work as a GAC. I had trouble understanding readings for class—looking back at old notes now, I chuckle—and I felt uncertain as a figure of authority in the writing center. While I had worked at the WCC as an undergraduate, I had taken a year-long break just as the center moved spaces and the dynamic shifted. I felt that younger consultants knew more than me, so I was not sure how to conduct myself and be genuinely helpful. I was torn between wanting to be trusted and feeling that I could not be. As a woman, I watched other women in my program and position who had been navigating it longer than I had and seemed so capable and self-assured. I felt I did not measure up and was, therefore, inadequate. Logically, I knew I would get there, with time and experience. Emotionally, however, I struggled with feelings of anxiety, depression, and frustration. As Shauna Morimoto and Song Yang suggest, "graduate students are vulnerable, and must rely on their advisors and departments for support, resources, and their ultimate success. . ." (103). As such, I relied heavily on the friendships I had made and faculty I had grown to know in undergrad.

Despite my background with the department's faculty and the WCC, I did struggle with imposter syndrome, particularly in my first semester. The expectations of grad school were daunting, especially as I struggled with navigating the various spheres of my life—an outside job, family and friends, and relationships within the center. While everyone was welcoming, I struggled to ask for help from the previous cohort of GACs—many of whom were in their final year, in the throes of their theses, and facilitating the transition of newer GACs into the role while coping with the demands of the growing center. Ultimately, I engaged in the emotionally laborious "fake it 'til you make it" attitude, which seemed to hold me over until I felt truly confident in my role as a GAC. In hindsight, I recognize this attitude was detrimental to my mental health. Eventually, I developed close relationships with the other GACs—owed in large part to our being in the same program and thus experiencing many of the same expectations—and felt more comfortable voicing when I was stressed or overwhelmed to both my peers and upper leadership.

Watching my male coworkers, I could not help but feel envious of the ease with which they seemed to cultivate relationships with leadership and of their calm demeanors as deadlines neared and the center became busier. This is not to say that any of my coworkers were ever unwelcoming—they were infinitely supportive and helpful. However, it was not until I began truly opening up about my feelings to my peers around me that I found we all seemed to be struggling with feelings of inadequacy brought on by imposter syndrome. Even the GACs that had been working in the writing center for several semesters longer than I had still struggled with similar feelings, and we quickly bonded over our shared experiences. I found, like Morimoto and Yang, that "relationships with others in the same graduate program are an important form of social support" (100), especially within the WCC. With time, I began to trust myself and the knowledge I had accumulated and felt truly capable within the space. I have not forgotten, however, the deterioration of my mental health brought on by grad school and, ultimately, the pressures I had placed on *myself* to perform and be liked.

It is because I remembered acutely how unsure of myself I felt when beginning my work as a GAC that I tried to be welcoming and helpful when new GACs joined our leadership team a few semesters later. However, I think like Monique and others, I was reluctant to trust newer GACs upon their arrival—not because I doubted their abilities, but because I became attached to the work I performed. As a result, I think I played a hand in creating mutual resentment among the leadership team, which—while minor and treated with professionalism—created a tense work environment. It seems that my distrust of others reflected a larger distrust within myself and my experiences with imposter syndrome.

CONCLUDING THOUGHTS AND STRATEGIES

Our stories show how our work as graduate student writing center leaders mingle with emotions from the start of our transition period into our graduate endeavors. Ultimately, we have discovered that we have all suffered from similar emotional burdens during our time as GACs and graduate students, and many of them have been self-imposed, situational, or largely out of our control—as we have struggled with imposter syndrome, burnout, emotional labor, and the stressors that most grad students face. We recognize that many of our failures to communicate as a team have exacerbated these emotions, sometimes creating a tense work environment unnecessarily, but by acknowledging our emotions, our interpersonal relationships can improve. Each GAC will negotiate their role differently but may find it helpful to know that they are not alone in their struggles. While each writing center operates differently, we have developed the following strategies for future graduate students working as writing center leaders. While emotions have a powerful role in our work, we find these four strategies can act as a foundation for navigating emotional situations in writing centers. The four main strategies are:

Communicate. Professional and emotional communication are both important in fostering productive interpersonal relationships. In addition, a failure to communicate can result in a loss of trust and willingness to collaborate. To improve communication and awareness of each other's concerns, roles and tasks should be clearly outlined and understood by all parties in a statement of mutual expectation (Adams Wooten and Babb 11–12).

Empathize. Realize that everyone on the leadership team is human and going through their own emotional struggles. If someone fails to meet an expectation, do not be quick to judge; instead, use it as a moment of learning and reflection, as "self-awareness can positively impact the relationships we have with others" (Concannon et al. 15). As a team, schedule time to debrief both on professional and personal objectives to reach a holistic sense of the team's well-being and performance attitude.

Reflect. When confronting feelings of inadequacy or uncertainty, provide spaces and times for reflecting on both difficulties and successes. Creating a dialogue to allow others to bridge gaps in collective experiences can nurture self-esteem and ensure everyone in the leadership team feels in control (Kouzes and Posner 108).

Maintain boundaries. Respect both individual and collective boundaries and avoid placing too much pressure on yourself to perform. We all grow at different speeds. It is okay to say "no." Prioritize what is important and do not commit to something you will not follow through with. As Kouzes and Posner point out, "Words don't just give voice to one's mindset and beliefs; they also evoke images of what people hope to create with others and how they expect people to behave" (79). As such, realize that words and actions matter.

Even when drawing on existing writing center research and training resources, it is not easy to understand all that graduate students in writing center leadership positions undergo, mentally or emotionally. In our experience, however, by cultivating interpersonal relationships and working in areas we are passionate about, opportunities and emotional rewards have naturally unfolded. We value our experiences as GACs. We have tried to foster productive working relationships by practicing the above strategies, which we hope to continue developing and improving moving forward. In recognizing imposter syndrome, burnout, and emotional labor as difficult factors within our roles, we have been able to identify our common stressors. By giving ourselves this foundational language, we are better equipped as administrators to address recurring emotional challenges. We acknowledge the different perspectives in our writing center, and that to successfully integrate into this space and role, we must adjust to one another accordingly.

WORKS CITED

Adams Wooten, Courtney, et al. Introduction. "Travels, Transition, and Leadership." *WPAs in Transition: Navigating Educational Leadership Positions*, edited by Courtney Adams Wooten and Jacob Babb, Utah State UP, 2018, pp. 3–22.

Bakker, Arnold B., and Patrica L. Costa. "Chronic Job Burnout and Daily Functioning: A Theoretical Analysis." *Burnout Research*, vol. 1, 2014, pp. 112–19.

Concannon, Kelly, et al. "Cultivating Emotional Wellness and Self-Care through Mindful Mentorship in the Writing Center." *WLN: A Journal of Writing Center Scholarship*, vol. 44, no. 5–6, 2020, pp. 10–17.

Gannon, Theresa Andrea. "The Undergraduate as Administration: Recollections and Lessons of a Graduating Senior." *Praxis: A Writing Center Journal*, vol. 10, no. 2, 2013.

Geller, Anne Ellen, and Harry Denny. "Of Ladybugs, Low Status, and Loving the Job: Writing Center Professionals Navigating Their Careers." *The Writing Center Journal*, vol. 33, no. 1, 2013, pp. 96–129.

Grouling, Jennifer, and Elisabeth H. Buck. "Colleagues, Classmates, and Friends: Graduate versus Undergraduate Tutor Identities and Professionalization." *Praxis: A Writing Center Journal*, vol. 14, no. 2, 2017, pp. 50–60.

Grutsch McKinney, Jackie. *Peripheral Visions for Writing Centers*. Utah State UP, 2013.

Holt, Mara, et al. "Making Emotion Work Visible in Writing Program Administration." *A Way to Move: Rhetorics of Emotion and Composi-

tion Studies, edited by Dale Jacobs and Laura Micciche, Heinemann, 2003, pp.147–60.

Jackson, Rebecca, et al. "Writing Center Administration and/as Emotion Work." *Composition Forum*, vol. 34, 2016.

Knights, David, and Caroline A. Clarke. "It's a Bittersweet Symphony, this Life: Fragile Academic Selves and Insecure Identities at Work." *Organization Studies*, vol. 35, no.3, 2014, pp. 335–57.

Kouzes, James M., and Barry Z. Posner. *The Leadership Challenge: How to Make Extraordinary Things Happen in Organizations.* 6th ed., Wiley, 2014.

Mattison, Michael. *Centered: A Year in the Life of a Writing Center Director.* Lulu, 2008.

Micciche, Laura R. *Doing Emotion: Rhetoric, Writing, Teaching.* Heinemann, 2007.

Miller, Sheila J. "Conceptualizing Interpersonal Relationships." *Generations: Journal of the American Society on Aging*, vol. 10, no. 4, 1986, pp. 6–9.

Morimoto, Shauna, and Song Yang. "What Friendship Entails: An Empirical Analysis of Graduate Students' Social Networks." *Sociological Spectrum*, vol. 33, no. 2, 2013, pp. 99–116.

Morris, Janine, et al. "Keeping a Clear Head: Enhancing Graduate Student Wellness through Meditation and Journaling in the Writing Center." *SDC: A Journal of Multiliteracy and Innovation*, vol. 23, no. 1, 2019, pp. 47–55.

Mundy, Robert, and Rachel Sugerman. "'What Can You Possibly Know About My Experience?': Toward a Practice of Self-Reflection and Multicultural Competence." *The Peer Review*, vol. 1, no. 2, 2017.

Phillips, Talinn, et al. "Thinking Liminally: Exploring the (com)Promising Positions of the Liminal WPA." *WPA: Writing Program Administration*, vol. 38, no. 1, 2014, pp. 42–64.

Rowan, Karen. "All the Best Intentions: Graduate Student Administrative Professional Development in Practice." *The Writing Center Journal*, vol. 29, no. 1, 2009, pp. 11–48.

PART II: TUTORING AND TRAINING

5 MIXED EMOTIONS AND BLENDED CLASSED POSITIONS: CIRCULATING AFFECT IN THE WRITING CENTER

Anna Rita Napoleone

I poked my head in to say "hello" to a new tutor, Miles,[1] just after he had finished a tutoring session. I asked how he was doing, and we spoke a bit about his semester. I then asked him about his hours for next semester. He said that he was thinking of not returning at all. He was working extra hours at another job and he did not think he could do both jobs. I said, "Okay, but we pay a competitive wage;" I knew we paid as well as his other job. He said, "Yeah, but the other thing is that I don't feel like I belong." He said that the other tutors seemed to have it together, but that he did not. I asked him to elaborate; this sounded all too familiar to me, as this is what I often hear from my working-class students. He said he could not—he just thought he was not as good as the other tutors. He saw the shock on my face as he said that. I had heard from some of his peers and from the assistant directors that he was very reflective and present when tutoring. I told him so. I told him he was great and that he most certainly belonged in the writing center. I let him know that I respected his decision, but that I would love to have him come tutor at the writing center next semester, even if for just a few hours every week. I told him he should stay connected to us because his work and insights are valuable. He had taken a tutoring class with me, and we had had plenty of conversations about how social class and specific ideas of literacy clash in writing centers.

---

1. All tutors named in this chapter are given pseudonyms.

During our conversation, Miles spoke of his class background—he was from a white working-class neighborhood that was in close proximity to a more affluent neighborhood—impacting how he understood his relationship to school. He said his experiences and feelings did not coincide with what other students seemed to be experiencing. He did not see his experience, the ways he approached writing, or his relationship to writing as being consistent with the qualities one needed to be a tutor. He was, indeed, perfectly able to critically discuss literacies, class, and the stratification of education. For example, he noted how many cultural references in the texts we discussed in our class were consistent with white middle-class monolingualism. When those experiences were his experiences—as he is a white male—he connected them to larger systems.

Miles's feelings and reactions towards being a tutor at the writing center reminded me of the feelings, tension, and reactions I myself have had, and continue to have, in academic spaces. These reactions echo those of other working-class academics whom I have read. Long after getting their degrees and good university jobs, many working-class academics—myself included—continue to experience imposter syndrome, despite their ability to function well in the classroom, in faculty meetings, and at conferences. That tells me how deeply class lines work. It is also why affect became of such interest to me. I wonder: What gives rise to such affective feelings in relation to the academic space? How do these feelings implicate the bodies in the space and the choices one sees available in the space? How do our encounters and social structures inform how we think we can *be* in academic spaces and in writing centers?

Emotions inform relationships and reflect social tensions, revealing how discourse and power structures are felt. As such, tutors and writing center directors cannot operate only at the level of critiquing academic literacy norms but must also work at an emotional level by considering the affective dimensions of the kinds of literacy work done in their spaces. Emotion is understood as an experience that can be defined, coherent, and understood; whereas, affect "is something that is *before* emotions" and is seen as a bodily reaction or a direct response that is prior to consciousness (Åhäll 39). Although these are useful definitions, Sara Ahmed states that just because "we can separate [affect and emotion] does not mean they are separate" (qtd. in Åhäll 39). As Anu Koivunen explains, some scholars—André Green, Teresa Brennan, and Sara Ahmed in *The Cultural Politics of Emotion*—use "emotion and affect interchangeably to highlight the fluidity of the conceptual boundaries" (10). Ahmed highlights this fluidity by stating that direct bodily responses, understood as affect, "actually evoke past histories, and that this process bypasses consciousness, through bodily memories" ("Collective" 39). In other words, the body remembers even when the mind does not. We live in our bodies, and our bodies encounter and have relations with other bodies and objects. Therefore, when using these terms, I acknowledge their fluidity and how they are imbued in socio-political contexts and past histories.

Julie Lindquist states that "we understand class as a problem of distribution of resources, but we experience it affectively, as an *emotional* process" (192). Class identity, as defined by Julie Bettie, "is not to be understood as a politicized identity (class-for-itself) but as a sense of one's place(s) in a cultural economy of meaning—that is, a sense of place or difference that may or may not contain a feeling of opposition or antagonism and that may or may not (more often the latter) be commonly named and known as 'class'" (43). Bettie's distinction between a politicized identity and class identity is an important one because one's sense of place and difference is affective and does not claim a class consciousness. Therefore, moments that connect to class difference are understood as personal feelings, values, and beliefs that either coincide or not within structures and institutions. As Ahmed notes, "the disappearance of the surface is instructive: in feelings of comfort, bodies extend into spaces, and spaces extend into bodies. The sinking feeling involves a seamless space, or a space where you can't see the 'stitches' between bodies" (*Cultural* 148). Ahmed's understanding of the seamlessness of bodies in a space as telling highlights Bettie's definition of class identity "not as a politicized identity," but rather as a sense of belonging. These two insights reveal that we feel class individually but always in relation to space—in this case, academic space. Although in this chapter I focus on white, working-class tutors, I believe understandings of affect and performance highlight the interconnectedness of the identities we hold and the social space where we enact those identities. A focus on difference in terms of class can bring to light the same feelings that white, working-class folks experience in the academic space because of their whiteness. In this chapter, I reflect on the role of affect in relation to the class identities of tutors and students in academic space, as well as its impact on how one performs in the space. Throughout, I also discuss how understanding emotion differently, as a product of social space and performance or performativity, rather than the attribute of an individual, can reveal the systemic and social nature of affect and its impact on writing center practice. Bettie notes the distinction between performance and performativity in terms of class. Performance means deliberate acts of middle-class actions and expressions of cultural capital. Such performance "refers to agency and a conscious attempt at passing" (Bettie 52). Performativity, in terms of class, "refers to the fact that class subjects are the effects of the social structure of class inequality, caught in unconscious displays of cultural capital that are a consequence of class origin or habitus" (52).

The social nature of affect provides a window into how administrators can better critically reflect on our social worlds (Hemmings). Ahmed describes the stickiness and accumulative effects of affect through the circulation of objects and signs (*Cultural* 10–11). In addition, as noted by Carolyn Pedwell and Anne Whitehead, emotions can be understood "as one important (embodied) circuit through which power is felt, imagined, mediated, negotiated and/or contested" (120). This understanding reveals how structures and bodies interact—the socialness of affect. Understanding the role of affect provides insight into how we might analyze feelings around working-class performances in order to better understand how, as Ahmed states, "feelings might be how structures get under our skin" ("Feminist Hurt/Feminism Hurts"). We feel structures and boundaries as much as we live in them. We need to better understand the feelings that are consequences of those structures if we are to understand how class inflects academic discourse and if we are to better address the needs of working-class students.

In addition to engaging scholarship centered on affect, I also place myself in dialogue with writing center scholars who have long recognized the political and transformative aspects of writing center work, particularly those read against issues of identity—and working-class identity specifically (Boquet; Denny; Denny and Towle; Denny et al.; N. S. Green; Salem). I do this as a way to further examine how performances coincide or collide with the "proper or ideal" affect inscribed by writing center spaces and how working-class performances and bodies are, and become, marked or blurred. I then look towards translingualism scholarship (Blazer; Lorimer Leonard) to consider the transformative impact of diverse literacies in writing center practice. I conclude that more critical awareness of affect can provide insight into the classed aspects of our tutoring practices, as well as provide suggestions for critically reflecting on the role of affect in writing center spaces.

FEELING THE BOUNDARY

Many working-class scholars in rhetoric and composition have demon-strated how class manifests itself in academic settings and intersects with other identities. They have shown how class is affective, as well as per-formed, produced, and enacted (Denny; Denny and Towle; LeCourt; Lindquist; McLaren; Micciche; Peckham; Rose; Trainor). Harry Denny and Beth Towle provide insight into the complicated relationship that working-class tutors and students have with academia. They note that "[t]he style by which we signify our class position is always already dis-cursive and performed. Just as other codes imprint us with our class positions, our very ways of arguing, of advocating, represent 'classed' ways of doing rhetoric." Donna LeCourt explains that class is marked when difference in cultural capital is made apparent, and in that mark of difference, class identity is understood as fixed. LeCourt states that, "if class is the cause, then class identity must also be understood as fixed, as part of identity that is being performed inappropriately" (40). I argue that the sense of one's place in academia reveals the affective functions of spaces. I suggest that the demarcation is not just one of literacy or value but also one of affect. Ahmed says that "emotions play a crucial role in the 'surfacing' of individual and collective bodies through the way in which emotions circulate between bodies and signs . . . It suggests that emotions are not simply 'within' or 'without' but that they create the very effect of the surfaces or boundaries of bodies and worlds" ("Affec-tive" 117).

What Ahmed notes here is the relationship of emotion to the produc-tion of boundaries. To my mind, Miles's reasons for wanting to leave the writing center and work his other job reflect a specific understanding of who and how a tutor should be. His reasons also reflect the ways he has experienced schooling, in that he must perform a middle-class body, lan-guage, and way of being. Miles was confronting and straddling multiple worlds that enacted class and was making choices that reflected and, at the same time, enacted class themselves. In other words, his place in the space brought about a feeling of difference—of divisions created—and he was choosing one side of the line. Those experiences produced affec-tive understandings of who does or does not belong in academic spaces and hence informed the choices that he saw available to him. As Ahmed argues, "assimilation and transgression are not choices that are available to individuals, but are effects of how subjects can and cannot inhabit social norms and ideals" (*Cultural* 153). Miles did not see assimilation as a choice, nor did he see any agency of transgression. The academic space in which he found himself would not accommodate alternative ways of being—assimilation into the middle-class monolingual norms or confrontation followed by departure were the only two choices presented to him.

In "Tell Me Exactly What It Was That I Was Doing that Was So Bad," Denny et al. conducted cross-institutional interviews to show the voices of working-class students and their experiences in writing centers. Although the focus was on working-class students, the interviewees varied in age, race, ethnicity, language, gender, and discipline. According to Denny et. al, working-class students visiting our writing centers want more direct tutoring than we offer. The authors propose guidelines for how to better support working-class students. Looking closely at these interviews can reveal the affective dimensions of class. The interviews offer a window into how students understand their relationship to academia through a deficit model. The question in Denny et al.'s chapter's title, "Tell me exactly what it was that I was doing that was so bad?" already implies that students do not feel they belong. After all, their sense of what is bad is only understood as a personal deficit. They did not go to the right schools. Their writing is bad. Their literacy norms and ways of being are suspect. A situation is set up whereby students perceive their options to be limited by an academic discourse and working-class discourse binary. This boundary is primarily made visible to them affectively.

In the interviews, Denny et al. show awareness of this affective dimension when they note that simply equipping the tutees with the skills explicitly demanded by academia does not obviate their urgent quest for the type of performance that they feel and know is most welcome in the academic space: "Critically, even as [undergraduate tutees'] confidence and writerly experience grew, our interviewees did not change their overall view of the importance of grammar. To them, *'sounding right'* was still an essential requirement for belonging at the university; they just became more confident about their ability to achieve it" (Denny et al. 82; emphasis added). "Sounding right" and "belonging" speak to an understanding of the divisions and tensions that they have come to understand exist between academic and working-class discourses. For working-class students, "sounding right" is an attempt at passing—at belonging—because of the discomfort that they feel in the space. In other words, students are feeling the boundary, and they feel that they must choose one side or the other. The affective component informs the choices they see as available. These emotions are not just individual senses of self; they are circulated and regulated in academic social spaces. As a result, their need to perform particular skills and possess specific resources speaks to how understanding and performing appropriateness are never neutral processes but are rather classed. The sense of what they need is as political as the marking of difference from where that need is articulated.

In academic spaces, specifically, "sounding right" means performing and aligning with middle-class practices. Working-class students learn to avoid situations that produce discomfort because it is they who are uncomfortable and, therefore, they who need to find ways to blend in. The onus continues to be on the working-class students to change, as it is with other markers of difference. What Denny et al.'s interviews reveal is that students feel those boundaries. They live those boundaries. This speaks to more than just aligning academia's literacy demands to the literacies of working-class students; it also speaks to students' realization that they discursively and affectively should align with academic discourse because the discourses they bring to campus are not seen as legitimate. Hence, as writing centers, we must be careful that in our quest to meet the needs of our students, we do not end up promoting an assimilationist model of literacy.

QUESTIONING THE BOUNDARY: AFFECT, PERFORMANCE, AND CHOICE

Choice is more than a performed, "rationalized," deliberate individual act in the consciousness of those who are seemingly choosing to align or disalign themselves with white, middle-class, monolingual values that permeate academic spaces. The affective components of the choices available or unavailable speaks to who feels difference in that space. As Lori Salem notes, educational choices are made via our environment even if they are felt as personal. She explains that, "educational decisions are also influenced by implicit social beliefs about what certain people—girls, boys, African-Americans, Asians—are supposed to want from education, and are supposed to be good at. Such beliefs are pervasive. We all contend with them, and they affect all of us, even, or perhaps especially, when we are unaware of them" (148). Choices reveal our affective investments or divestments in academia. Choices are embodied and guide how one interprets and negotiates social spaces. Examining the feelings and the performances in a local moment shows how the choice between different kinds of classed performances can lead administrators, tutors, and tutees to think about how class is enacted in academia spaces and more specifically, in writing centers.

In the wake of one of the staff meetings in our writing center where we discussed class and classed literacies, a veteran tutor, Melinda, told me that she had rarely thought about class, especially in terms of identity, and did not think of class as embodied or felt. She then proceeded to say that she made sure to pronounce certain words in such a way as to hide her working-class background. She noted how at home her accent came back, but her parents reacted to that by saying that she went to college,was "educated," and should not sound that way. When she made certain arguments, they said school was changing her. That, Melinda said, made her feel bad and disconnected from her family.

Melinda's understanding of what gets valued is linked to how she experiences language and schooling. Ahmed notes that emotions stick and slide and that "[w]hat moves us, what makes us feel, is also that which holds us in place, or gives us a dwelling place" (*Cultural* 10–11). What Ahmed offers is a way to better understand how emotions are always in relation to our surroundings and, therefore, inform our choices. What Melinda's narrative reveals is how identities are seen as fixed, rather than fluid. Her comments reveal how social spaces encourage and coerce her to enact and perform specific identities, including class-based ones. Whereas she saw potential for fluidity in that she could be both "educated" *and* working-class and enact it all at home, she did not see that same possibility in the writing center. In other words, at home, she was blending her positions and her discourse communities, but that did not seem like a choice she had in the writing center and in school, generally. Her feelings are constructed by—and constructing—her identity, revealing how specific social spaces encourage us to perform specific identities, including class-based ones. This means that we have to understand academic spaces in different ways than we do now, in terms of how they impact classed actions and reactions.

Melinda understood the first shift—from the working-class tenor to the "academic" way of speaking—as an instance of performance and as a conscious act of "passing" and "performing middle-class expressions" (Bettie 52). And she saw the second shift—back to the working-class "accent" that she associated with family and home—as a return to authenticity. Her parents' negative reaction and her own feelings at their reaction speak to the importance of a person's *emotional attachments* to certain markers of class positions, such as ways of speaking.

Melinda recognizes difference and experiences it, in Bettie's terms, as performativity (52). It impacts the way she acts but is not necessarily an enactment of agency. Her performing in school as someone who does not have an accent is seen as an individualistic choice, which obviates the larger structural and symbolic capital that is present in the space and is embodied. Feelings, when seen as individualistic, miss the moments when power and capital are working in academic spaces. Melinda has come to understand in specific moments how to *perform* so that she can fit in academic spaces. However, how she has come to understand the hierarchies of identities determined by power relations is a process that is embodied and felt. How one feels about specific moments varies because of one's interpretation of a classed position. Therefore, understanding class as both performed and performative—as both an identity and a re-action to the space—means that we have to understand academic spaces in different ways than we do now, in terms of how they impact classed actions and reactions, and how our everyday movements and practices are informed by the choices that we see available in the space. Furthermore, the choices we enact are not free of the affective investments and divestments actively produced in social spaces but rather show the relationship between them. Class is not experienced or enacted as an inherent aspect of self; instead, it makes itself known in our actions and interactions with various social spaces and with other bodies.

In reflecting on this moment, Melinda began to question the divisions of class and her performance of class both on and off campus. Class is expressed, performed, and created, rather than fixed. Ironically, it is these very performances that recreate seemingly fixed classed identities; hence the need to be deliberate in reflecting critically on such performances and the affective states that are present in those performances and social spaces.

Thinking about affect and performance in terms of class and other identities that are seen outside of the "norm" but are, in fact, *the* norm, can lead tutors to rethink their practice and their own experiences and look at the spaces where such feelings of difference and sameness occur. For example, Melinda revealed that she had not thought of class as an identity but solely as an economic situation. Such discussions presented possibilities for her to rethink her own positioning in academia, her own tutoring practices, and how others were positioning her,.

Affectively, Melinda had come to examine those feelings also internally and in relation to the space, particularly in the writing center. These moments of feeling inform how and what she believes her actions to be, how she should perform, and also show the ways that affect functions on and through her in the space—how it circulates and accrues value. Later on, in an informal meeting with me in the writing center, Melinda reflected on how she did not make space in the writing center for other identities, including her working-class identity, and what that meant for how she conducted her tutoring sessions. It also provided room to extend the space by making apparent that difference is the norm, even in a predominately-white institution like the one we were in. In critically reflecting, Melinda began to reorient what she believed could happen in the space and in her tutoring sessions. Discussions like this one on class occur monthly at our staff meetings, where we spend an hour critically reflecting on literacies, identities, and power. These are not one-off discussions but rather discussions that we refer back to—whether it is with directors sitting in the writing center talking with tutors; during other staff meetings; at presentations at regional conferences; or through tutor reflections where we engage with various readings and tutoring sessions. This kind of reflective and affective practice is key to moving towards a more socially just space.

Confronting the Writing Center's Production of Boundaries

One's sense of place and difference is, in part, affective, and does not necessarily come with class consciousness. That, of course, greatly complicates the quest to properly assess working-class students' needs and to devise ways to meet those needs in writing centers. In other words, we must be careful of that fine line between giving students what they want—that is, the right "voice," the grammar and the self-confidence that would grant them access to academic spaces—and perpetuating the very structures that exclude them in the first place. Such feelings cannot be assessed solely as individual feelings but rather always in relation to the larger ideological, structural, and neoliberal policies in place. Noting that affect accrues value in these spaces can better help us understand how affect, as a form of capital in universities, regulates and constructs needs and expectations.

If we do not address the structural dimension of the feelings that our students come into writing centers with, the interactions in the centers will be seen as transactional only. Writing centers themselves will be seen as places where value is tied to producing middle-class bodies, and will, therefore, produce and contribute to an assimilationist—and neoliberal—model. We need to critically reflect on how such a model might lead to a flattening and a dismissal of inequities. As Randall Monty notes in "Undergirding Writing Center Responses to the Neoliberal Academy":

> It is necessary to recognize how writing centers are culpable in perpetuating myths of upward mobility, access through standardized language/academic performance, and of an idealized "middle-class identity" that is often uncritically coded as white, standard English speaking, and heteronormative (Denny and Towle). Unless critically examined, writing centers risk designating those identifications as invisible or immaterial to their objectives and practices. (40)

Writing centers should continue paying attention to ideologies, how they circulate in their institutions, and how they affect the larger political landscape and its connections to the bodies and affective possibilities and impossibilities in those spaces. The market logic of universities proposes a transaction model where value is tied to producing white, middle-class bodies as the only understanding of upward mobility and of standards that contribute to the reification of structures of power and privilege. If we do not examine the codes and performances that award and value white, middle-class, heteronormative ways of being, we risk perpetuating the oppressive structures that give rise to such understandings and feelings.

Writing centers must examine their own affective orientations alongside students and examine how institutionally, locally, and individually, they have come to understand those needs and expectations. These analyses can allow for a better understanding of how we fix and fixate on certain ways of being. According to Ahmed, "emotions may involve 'being moved' for some precisely by 'fixing' others as 'having' certain characteristics" ("Collective" 28). In terms of class, the flattening of inequities as well as the "fixing" of others are also noted in Denny et al.'s article. As the authors explain, the interviewees saw their success as individual and happenstance: "Thus, even as [the interviewees] took justifiable credit for their own hard work, our *interviewees became less able to see* the barriers to education that face other working-class students" (85; emphasis added). This flattening of difference is seen as a personal choice and not as a systemic effect. In fact, "this narrative also led our interviewees to question, and in some cases to explicitly judge, their own family members who had not gone to college" (Denny et al. 85). What can be noted—and should be avoided—is perpetuating individuality at the expense of recognizing systemic inequities. Furthermore, the students' explicit judgement of their family members shows the seductive and affective nature of neoliberalism. Affectively, the interviewees were seeing their family and communities as deficient, rather than noting the oppressive structures at play. The focus and the feelings became so individualized that the larger systemic issues were put to the side.

Writing centers must work against the neoliberal logic that utilizes affect as a tool. This, for me, makes evident that writing centers must use critical reflection as something that is always on-going and must look for moments where we can confront the boundaries that are reconstructed again and again in academic spaces. Performing difference only when acceptable in such spaces does not confront the inequities here. How might writing centers, as semi-formalized spaces, affectively reorient themselves? How might writing centers move away from "just wanting to belong" and, therefore, performing the white, middle-class identity as the only possible identity? How might writing centers work towards expanding the space so that students who are not white, middle-class, cisgender, and able-bodied can see themselves as part of the academy? How might these students see "where they come from" not as something to exclude but something to leverage? Also, how might identifying and affectively reorienting ourselves to difference allow us to intervene in the space and see difference as something more than the norm? How might doing so allow us to identify the inequities and power dynamics at play in that site of difference? If we do not confront difference, we risk flattening difference and perpetuating the ways in which difference operates in neoliberal universities. I believe that a reflective practice that uses affect as a site of inquiry is crucial in moving towards this understanding.

Sarah Blazer highlights the importance of leveraging the ways of being that students bring to the academy to enact more translingual approaches. She calls on the work of such scholars as Suresh Canagarajah, Min-Zhan Lu, and Bruce Horner; and Horner et al. to make clear the "diversity-as-norm perspective" (Blazer 22). Also, Blazer, referencing Rosina Lippi-Green, states that language variation is the norm among US

English speakers. Blazer argues that "viewing diversity or difference this way is a fundamental and necessary shift in perspective regarding the writing and writers we see" (21). As mentioned above, one way to shift the narrative is thinking more about the reflective and affective practice in ongoing staff meetings, and such work "represents an opportunity to intervene *at the site of difference*, within the moments at which difference is being produced" (LeCourt 47). Academic spaces are where the politics of language are not only spoken but also felt, and writing centers have always seen themselves as spaces that generate possibilities and push boundaries. Now, we must do so by making visible the ways in which neoliberal policies push difference but enact conformity.

These shifts in orientation and perspective towards a translingual model are for the writers coming to writing centers but also for tutors, administrators, and directors. I have been a writing center director for only a short time, and the imposter syndrome is still strong. The expectation that you should, and could, sink into the space for those with a white, working-class body, like mine, is how the flattening of difference and divisiveness works. In a sense, the assumption is that despite identity, you too can sink into the space, and if you do not, it is your decision and not an effect of systemic inequities. Yet, boundaries are not only material but also discursive and affective, and the coercion to pass in whatever way possible—the "fake it till you make it" mantra—comes on strong. This is why we must all engage in critical and affective reflection at all levels.

Feeling like you do not belong speaks to the social and systemic ways that class functions on the self. It is in the relationship and proximity to school and school experiences that such feelings emerge, and they should be discussed in that context. After all, this feeling of difference—of not belonging—speaks to how academia, while attempting to be classless, is indeed classed and "actively *produce*[s] class divisions" (LeCourt 34). Writing centers are not there to simply ameliorate feelings of inadequacy in literacy; they can also be spaces to confront their own production of difference by inquiring into how affect informs bodily boundary negotiations in writing centers.

Critical and affective reflection can provide moments where boundaries are confronted and offer different choices and orientations to the space, thereby expanding it. Such an experience of extending the space and seeing possibilities happened to me recently. I am a participant in a grant that looks at language diversity. Several faculty and administrators meet monthly to discuss, read, and present on language diversity, and we discuss ways to put in place policy that takes into consideration the language diversity on our campus. After one of our meetings, several of us from different academic units began discussing our experiences with language diversity—our own and on campus. I said to the three people that remained that I get nervous when speaking, and being in a director position has seemed to increase this nervousness, anxiety, and feeling of imposter syndrome. One of the participants—a person who said that she comes from a white, working-poor background—said she heard my voice shake when I was discussing my experiences with faculty from across campus on language diversity. I looked at her and the others and asked, "You did?" I was really trying to keep it under control. The other person in the room—a person of color and first-gen student who knows me outside of the university—looked at me and said she thought it was odd since I am usually pretty talkative. We discussed the ways we perform in these spaces, and that even though we are indeed navigating the space, the feeling of being an imposter—of not belonging—continues to be strong. We talked about how that comes about in interactions across campus and in our writing. The third person in the group—an administrator from another academic unit—said that these experiences are very similar to those of the students in her academic unit. This moment for me provided an instance of critical reflection I recognized that in this new director position, I continue to struggle with academic expectations as much as I am a part of academia.

Classed literacies travel in a similar way to Rebecca Lorimer Leonard's findings with multilingual writers. She recognized that the practices she captured can point backward to "social structures encountered" (33), and to extend her point, experienced affectively. We bring the past—power relations, social relations, locations, and more—with us to particular social spaces. With such travels and encounters with social structures, there is affective work being done.

Although this is not a macro change, these kinds of moments and these kinds of porous spaces do provide opportunity for change. Making class and affect visible, and looking at the ways that educational discourse lines up with the affective attachments that are a result of class, might help us recognize moments and opportunities for dialogue that are not solely couched in middle-class norms. Bringing class and affect into view is important for understanding how we are negotiating, fighting against, or accommodating middle-class norms. As I think of the working-class tutors in the writing center where I am the director, of my own experiences that I have had in academia and in writing centers (Napoleone), and of the interviews that Denny et al. discuss, I see that merely choosing one side of the binary is not enough.

WORKS CITED

Åhäll, Linda. "Affect as Methodology: Feminism and the Politics of Emotion." *International Political Sociology*, vol. 12, 2018, pp. 36–52.

Ahmed, Sara. *The Cultural Politics of Emotion*. Routledge, 2004.

—. "Affective Economies." *Social Text 79*, vol. 22, no. 2, 2004, pp. 117–39.

—. "Collective Feelings: Or, The Impressions Left by Others." *Theory, Culture and Society*, vol. 21, no. 2, 2004, pp. 25–42.

—. "Feminist Hurt/Feminism Hurts." *feministkilljoys: Killing Joy as a World Making Project*, 21 July 2014, feministkilljoys.com/2014/07/21/feminist-hurtfeminism-hurts/. Accessed 30 July 2020.

Bettie, Julie. *Women Without Class: Girls, Race, and Identity*. U of California Press, 2003.

Blazer, Sarah. "Twenty-First Century Writing Center Staff Education: Teaching and Learning towards Inclusive and Productive Everyday Practice." *The Writing Center Journal*, vol. 35, no. 1, pp. 17–55.

Boquet, Elizabeth H. "'Our Little Secret:' A History of Writing Centers, Pre- to Post-Open Admissions." *College Composition and Communication*, vol. 50, no. 3, Feb. 1999, pp. 463–82.

Brennan, Teresa. *The Transmission of Affect*. Cornell UP, 2004.

Canagarajah, Suresh A. Introduction. *Literacy as Translingual Practice: Between Communities and Classrooms*, edited by Canagarajah, Routledge, 2013, pp. 1–10.

Denny, Harry. *Facing the Center: Toward an Identity Politics of One-to-One Mentoring*. Utah State UP, 2010.

—, and Beth Towle. "Braving the Waters of Class: Performance, Intersectionality, and the Policing of Working-Class Identity in Everyday Writing Centers." *The Peer Review*, vol. 1, no. 2, Fall 2017. https://thepeerreview-iwca.org/issues/braver-spaces/braving-the-waters-of-class-performance-intersectionality-and-the-policing-of-working-class-identity-in-everyday-writing-centers/. Accessed 30 July 2020.

—, et al. "'Tell me exactly what it was that I was doing that was so bad': Understanding the Needs and Expectations of Working-Class Students in Writing Centers." *The Writing Center Journal*, vol. 37, no. 1, 2018, pp. 67–100.

Green, Neisha-Anne S. "The Re-Education of Neisha-Anne S. Green: A Close Look at the Damaging Effects of 'A Standard Approach,' the Benefits of Code-Meshing, and the Role Allies Play in this Work." *Praxis: A Writing Center Journal*, vol. 14, no. 1, 2016.

Green, André. *The Fabric of Affect in Psychoanalytic Discourse.* Translated by Alan Sheridan, Routledge, 1999.

Hemmings, Clare. "Invoking Affect: Cultural Theory and the Ontological Turn." *Cultural Studies*, vol. 19, no. 5, Sep. 2005, pp. 548–67.

Horner, Bruce et al. "Opinion: Language Difference in Writing: Toward a Translingual Approach." *College English*, vol. 73, no. 3, 2011, pp. 303–21.

Koivunen, Anu. "An Affective Turn? Reimagining the Subject of Feminist Theory." *Working with Affect in Feminist Readings: Disturbing Differences*, edited by Marianne Liljeström and Susanna Paasonen, Routledge, 2010, pp. 8–28.

LeCourt, Donna. "Performing Working-Class Identity in Composition: Toward a Pedagogy of Textual Practice." *College English*, vol. 69, no. 1, Sep. 2006, pp. 30–51.

Lindquist, Julie. "Class Affects, Classroom Affectations: Working through the Paradoxes of Strategic Empathy." *College English*, vol. 67, no. 2, 2004, pp. 187–209.

Lippi-Green, Rosina. *English with an Accent: Language, Ideology, and Discrimination in the United States.* 2nd ed., Routledge, 2012.

Lorimer Leonard, Rebecca. "Traveling Literacies: Multilingual Writing on the Move." *Research in the Teaching of English*, vol. 48, no. 1, 2013, pp. 13–39.

Lu, Min-Zhan, and Bruce Horner. "Translingual Literacy, Language Difference, and Matters of Agency." *College English*, vol. 75, no. 6, 2013, pp. 582–607.

McLaren, Peter. "Schooling the Postmodern Body: Critical Pedagogy and the Politics of Enfleshment." *Journal of Education*, vol. 170, no. 3, 1988, pp. 53–83.

Micciche, Laura R. *Doing Emotion: Rhetoric, Writing, Teaching.* Heinemann, 2007.

Monty, Randall. "Undergirding Writing Centers' Responses to the Neoliberal Academy." *Praxis: A Writing Center Journal*, vol. 16, no. 3,

2019, pp. 37–47. http://www.praxisuwc.com/163-monty-et-al. Accessed 30 July 2021.

Napoleone, Anna Rita. "Class Divisions, Class Affect, and the Role of the Writing Center in Literacy Practices." *Out in the Center: Public Controversies and Private Struggles,* edited by Harry Denny, et al., Utah State UP, 2018, pp. 203–11.

Peckham, Irvin. *Going North, Thinking West: The Intersections of Social Class, Critical Thinking, and Politicized Writing Instruction.* Utah State UP, 2010.

Pedwell, Carolyn, and Anne Whitehead. "Affecting Feminism: Questions of Feeling in Feminist Theory." *Feminist Theory,* vol. 13, no. 2, 2012, pp. 115–29.

Rose, Mike. *Lives on the Boundary: A Moving Account of the Struggles and Achievements of America's Educationally Underprepared.* Penguin Books, 1999.

Salem, Lori. "Decisions . . . Decisions: Who Chooses to Use the Writing Center?" *The Writing Center Journal,* vol. 35, no. 2, 2016, pp. 147–71.

Trainor, Jennifer Seibel. *Rethinking Racism: Emotion, Persuasion, and Literacy Education in an All-White High School.* Southern Illinois UP, 2008.

6 "Could You Please Tell Me How?": Listening, Questioning, and Emotional Knowledge Making in Online Synchronous Writing Center Conferences

Neal Lerner and Kyle Oddis

In this chapter, we turn to text-based, online synchronous writing center sessions to better understand how to observe and describe listening and emotional expression without the possibility for face-to-face interaction. We see online tutoring as particularly important, given that nearly 30% of our writing center's sessions were held online in the fall 2018 term—an increase of 124% since the fall 2012 term—and a consistent figure since then. Of course, in the current context of a coronavirus pandemic, 100% of our consulting is now online. The growth of online consulting—and its future as a standard writing center service—calls for increased understanding of its possibilities and practices, rather than simply a lamentation of its shortcomings compared to face-to-face consulting.

An initial question driving our research was to ask what "listening" looks like in online synchronous tutoring. Listening has been framed as a hallmark of one-to-one tutorials (Feibush). Kathryn Valentine points out, however, that although listening frequently appears in writing center training manuals as an important practice to cultivate, it is still not well-defined in the field (91). Developing consultants' listening skills to offer students more emotional support has also been emphasized (Lawson; Effinger Wilson and Fitzgerald; Haen; Thompson). Empathetic listening and responding can help to "1) find a balance between acknowledging students' emotions and supporting their writing and 2) develop listening and responding strategies that support nondirective efforts that honor student agency" (McBride et al.). If empathetic listening is indeed important for creating safe and productive tutoring spaces—and we believe it is—what does it look like in the absence of many of the familiar cues we have come to identify as markers of "effective" listening in face-to-face tutoring? How do we train consultants to listen and respond effectively in the absence of these cues, particularly when staff feel that emotion is expressed "barely, if at all" in online, text-only spaces,[1] as one consultant offered in a recent survey?

Our curiosity about the relationship of listening and emotion in online synchronous text-only tutorials led us to examine the role of questions for consultants and clients. Question-asking practices are frequently touted as central to writing center pedagogy (Calle-Arango; Ashton-Jones; Thompson and Mackiewicz; cf. Johnson). As an exchange of discourse marked by clear interlocutor requests for response—whether simply yes and no questions or more open-ended varieties—we assumed consultant and client questions might be the most visible manifestation of listening in online writing center sessions. We also believed that consultants' questions would offer a window into expressions of "emotional knowledge," which, following Michalinos Zembylas, we define as "a teacher's [and tutor's] knowledge about/from his or her emotional experiences with respect to oneself, others (e.g. students, colleagues), and the wider social and political context in which teaching and learning takes place" (356). In these ways, emotional knowledge ties directly to Krista Ratcliffe's concept of "rhetorical listening," a practice that can ultimately be deeply relational and empathic:

> *Understanding* means more than simply listening *for* a speaker/writer's intent. It also means more than simply listening *for* our own self-interested intent. . .Instead, *understanding* means listening to discourse not for intent but *with* intent—with the intent to understand not just the claims, not just the cultural

---

1. While consultants in our center had the option of engaging voice and video for online tutorials, it was not a standard or required practice; the sessions we examine in this study, therefore, are text-only—consultants and student interactions were mediated by WCOnline's "chat" interface. In that context, consultants and students were challenged to perceive and respond to each other's emotions without the benefit of gestural, facial, and verbal cues.

logics within which the claims function, but the rhetorical negotiations of understanding as well. (205)

How might we prepare our consultants to listen *with* or *for* intent? How can we best prepare consultants to listen empathetically and to know when listening *with* rather than *for* is required? How might asking questions express these goals and values in online spaces?

DATA SELECTION, SAMPLING, AND CLEANING

The data for our IRB-approved study[2] comes from a private, medium-sized research-intensive institution in Boston, MA. Our data set consisted of the 377 online writing center sessions conducted during the fall 2018 semester. We had client permission to use any data generated for research purposes from an option clients chose or opted into on our intake form—"I permit the WC to use my data anonymously for research." From these 377 sessions, 365 were usable after removing responses that were missing demographic information or contained duplicate or incomplete responses to intake form questions. In order to achieve a 95% confidence-level—p=0.05 with a margin of error +/- 10— we chose a random, representative sample of seventy-seven sessions for our analysis, using a random sequence generator from www.random.org/sequences/.

For all writing center sessions, online and face-to-face, we used WCOnline—mywconline.com/—to make appointments, gather data, and conduct online sessions. For this study, we relied on an established intake form that all clients completed (see Appendix A), asking a variety of demographic questions, as well as asking about clients' goals for the session.[3]

The WCOnline synchronous tutoring platform consists of a "whiteboard" space for participants to post drafts and attachments and a "chat" space for a textual conversation (see Appendix B). We chose to focus only on the textual chat between clients and consultants, rather than also take into consideration clients' drafts and consultants' responses to those drafts conducted in the whiteboard space. Our reasoning was partially to minimize the variables that we were working with and to focus on the

---

2. Northeastern University IRB# 17-04-02.

3. We need to note that we did not create or alter the intake form for the purposes of this study—a potential shortcoming that we discuss later in this chapter.

textual language of interaction—he primary space in which consultants and clients can ask questions, offer answers, and demonstrate the rhetorical listening and expressions of emotion that we hoped to find.

QUANTITATIVE ANALYSIS

To look at the relationship between consultant and client questions and other affective and interpersonal dimensions in online sessions, we conducted statistical analysis on fifteen variables we identified from the WCOnline intake form data and chat transcripts. As shown in Table 1, these variables are primarily demographic data drawn from intake forms, but we also included "session agenda" and "genre," which were based on our reading of the chat transcripts. Using SPSS, we conducted chi-square tests for categorical variables and linear—multiple and single—regression for continuous variables to find out whether any significant relationships existed in the data, like a relationship between two or more of those fifteen variables could be attributed to something other than chance.

To gather question-asking instances in the seventy-seven sessions, we counted the questions and exclamations in each chat transcript, assuming that questions would be marked by question marks—as we indicated previously, could mark an instance of consultant or client "listening"—and that exclamations were a textual expression of emotion. In some cases, neither consultant nor client used punctuation when asking questions, so we also read through transcripts to identify questions based on the presence of constructs starting with "What," "How," "Why," and more. We determined "session agenda" by looking at a client's response to consultant questions like "What would you like to work on today?" In some cases, a client set the agenda before the consultant asked; in these cases, we determined the session agenda by looking for phrases toward the start of the session like "I also wanted to see if you could do X. . ."

Table 1. Frequencies of each categorical and ordinal variable

Variable (type)	Label (value)	Frequency (%)
Student/client status (ordinal)	Undergraduate (1)	44 (57.1%)
	Graduate (2)	32 (41.6%)
	Alumni (3)	1 (1.3%)
Home language (dichotomous)	Not English (0)	49 (63.6%)
	English (1)	28 (36.4%)
College (nominal)	Professional Studies	26 (33.8%)
	Arts, Media, and Design	10 (13%)
	Health Sciences	10 (13%)
	Science	9 (11.7%)
	Engineering	9 (11.7%)
	Social Sciences and Humanities	8 (10.4%)
	Business Administration	4 (5.2%)
	Computer and Information Sciences	1 (1.3%)
Returning student/client (dichotomous)	Yes (1)	52 (67.5%)
	No (0)	25 (32.5%)
Course mode of instruction (nominal)	Face-to-Face	54 (70.1%)
	Online	23 (29.9%)
Authorship (nominal)	Individual	73 (94.8%)
	Group	4 (5.2%)
Session agenda (dichotomous)	Higher Order Concerns (e.g., "ideas") (1)	47 (61%)
	Language Level Concerns (e.g., "grammar") (0)	30 (39%)
Genre (nominal)	Essay/Paper	39 (50.7%)
	Other (e.g., personal statement, literature review, mixed genre, proposal, discussion post, resume/CV, or reflection)	38 (49.3%)

QUANTITATIVE RESULTS

Within our seventy-seven session sample, consultants most frequently asked between 6–10 questions per session—39% of sessions fell in this range—and clients most frequently asked 0–5 questions per session—54.5% of sessions fell in this range. Consultants averaged eight questions per session while clients averaged six questions per session. In addition to asking more questions per session, consultants also used more exclamations: 59.8% of sessions saw consultants using between 6–20 exclamations while 59.7% of sessions saw clients using between 0–5 exclamations. Consultants averaged ten exclamations per session, and clients averaged five exclamations per session. The most frequent word count range for sessions was 41.6%, which fell between 751–1500 words. On average, less than one emoticon was used by consultants or clients per session.[4]

The correlations among variables (see Appendix C, "Correlations Table") highlighted several points:

- There is not a significant relationship between number of questions consultants ask and a "grammar" agenda,[5] but there *is* a significant relationship between the grammar agenda and the number of questions clients ask.
- There is a significant relationship, .031, between the number of questions consultants ask and the client's home language. We noted also that the two instances in which a consultant asked more than twenty questions were both sessions where the agenda set by the client was not "grammar." When the client set a "grammar" agenda, instances of consultants asking 6–10 questions decreased by half. Twenty sessions with non-grammar agendas saw consultants ask between 6–10 questions; only ten saw the same

---

4. We need to note that the WCOnline's synchronous tutoring environment does not have emoticons pre-built into the system as most current chat platforms might; consultant or client would need to use ASCII characters to form "old-school" emoticons like :(.

5. We determined whether the session agenda was focused on "ideas" and higher-order concerns or "grammar" and language-level concerns by examining the words students used to describe their needs at the start of the session—usually in response to a tutor's prompt along the lines of "What would you like to work on today?"

count of questions from consultants in sessions with a set grammar agenda.

• We observed that clients use more exclamation marks with a
"grammar" agenda—perhaps expressions of thanks or "ok!"

We also conducted several single- and multiple-regression analyses in
SPSS, which led to observations that complicate our understanding of
how listening and emotion function in online sessions. As shown in
Model Summary 1 in Appendix C, there is a statistically significant
relationship, .005, between the number of questions consultants asked
and the number of exclamations they used—more questions meant more
exclamations. In Model Summary 2 in Appendix C, we see that use
of "emotive" punctuation including both emoticons and exclamation
marks is significant in terms of relationship to the number of questions
asked during sessions. We can see that the combined effect of all independent variables in Model Summary 2 is significant at .027 when
p=0.05; in other words, we can be 95% confident that more "emotive"
punctuation use—like emoticons and exclamation marks—is correlated
with more questions asked during a session. This finding would suggest
that a more "emotive" consultant or client might ask more questions
during a session.

These models suggest there *is* a relationship between the number of
questions asked during online sessions and the level of emotional expressiveness between client and consultant when affective indicators are
defined as exclamations and emoticons. These models, while suggesting
a connection between emotions and questioning, do not tell us whether
questioning is indicative of rhetorical listening, or whether the presence
of emotional knowledge— as expressed through indicators like exclamation marks or emoticons—demonstrates listening or understanding. To
gain more insight into this, we turned to qualitative analysis.

QUALITATIVE ANALYSIS

For qualitative analysis, we chose, from our set of seventy-seven sessions,
ones that represented both median or "average" examples and examples
that contained the largest percent of questions to total words or sessions in which questions were particularly frequent. More specifically,
we chose to analyze the following six sessions as a window into our data
set as a whole. These sessions represented:

- the median for mean percent of total questions to total words
- the median for total consultant questions to total words
- the median for total client questions to total words
- the greatest percent of total questions to total words
- the greatest percent of consultant questions to total words
- the greatest percent of client questions to total words

We developed the following coding scheme to analyze questions asked by both consultants and clients in these six sessions:

- questions referring to the agenda, like "What would you like to work on today?"
- questions referring to the text, like "What would be a better way to phrase this?"
- questions referring to the consultant-client relationship, like "How are you?"
- questions referring to the context, like "Did your professor give you an example?"
- questions to clarify intent and gain understanding, like "What do you mean by. . . ?"
- questions to gain understanding about the technology, interface, and medium, like "How do I. . . ?"

QUALITATIVE RESULTS

As we noted above, our qualitative analysis involved coding the form and function of the questions that consultants and clients asked. Here are a few observations about these results:

- Consultants asked questions to create an agenda, and clients did not.
- For the sessions that were "average," #1–3, consultants asked questions much more frequently than did clients; T = 18, S = 12.
- The session with the greatest frequency of consultant questions, #5, was one in which the consultant attempted to clarify the client's meaning or intention.
- The session with the greatest frequency of client questions, #6, featured questions intended to elicit a consultant's response to the client's textual choices.

In the following excerpts, we hope to show what these patterns looked like.

Online Tutoring Excerpt 1. In Excerpt 1, the client's questions drive this passage, focusing on soliciting her consultant's advice on textual changes:

CONSULTANT 1. [15:09] As for the last section i underlined, I think it needs to be broken up a little more into a couple of sentences

CLIENT 1. [15:10] could you please tell me how?

CONSULTANT 1. [15:10] well, just looking at the last sentence, its very long

CONSULTANT 1. [15:10] i think you might have a comma where you need a period before "all in all"

CLIENT 1. [15:11] got it

CLIENT 1. [15:11] how about the flow?

CLIENT 1. [15:11] is it good?

CONSULTANT 1. [15:12] So one thing that I noticed, is that it seems like you're listing off a lot of experience (which is good) but to a reader, it can seem sort of like information overload

CLIENT 1. [15:13] ok

CLIENT 1. [15:13] which sentences do u think I should delete?

CONSULTANT 1. [15:13] the way that the essay is worded seems like you're answering the question of why you would be a good RA, but the essay prompt is asking you how being an RA will contribute to your personal development

CLIENT 1. [15:14] I don't really know how to expand on personal development

CLIENT 1. [15:15] I basically write all of the points that I can think of

CONSULTANT 1. [15:15] so really what the essay prompt is asking, is what can you learn by being an RA and what you've written is more about skills that you already have

CLIENT 1. [15:15] yeah, it is what I was worried about earlier

CONSULTANT 1. [15:16] So I think maybe you should try to add a sentence or two explaining how the experience of being an RA will add to your skills

CLIENT 1. [15:16] could you give me an example?

Online Tutoring Excerpt 2. In Excerpt 2, the consultant's questions are the driving force, seeking clarification on the context for the task and the student's intent:

CONSULTANT 2. [20:10] OK I just read the prompt. What exactly is O&M?

CLIENT 2. [20:10] It''s an advertising company call Ogilvy & Mather

CLIENT 2. [20:10] called

CONSULTANT 2. [20:10] And you learned about Beers' advisor's cultural exchange?

CONSULTANT 2. [20:11] In class?

CONSULTANT 2. [20:12] OK, that sounds cool. So you want to work on the campaign part for this session, right? Anything else?

CLIENT 2. [20:13] It's in the case study, she is the first female CEO of a multinational company around 1990

CONSULTANT 2. [20:13] Before we work on brainstorming for campaign ideas, can you give me a brief background of what went wrong with Beers' first attempt?

Online Tutoring Excerpt 3. Finally, in Excerpt 3—from the same session as Excerpt 1 above—consultant and client have a somewhat more equal share in question-asking and answering:

CLIENT 1. [20:43] Is it a advertising company where you work for coop?

CONSULTANT 1. [20:44] No, it's a publishing company which just launched a new campaign

CLIENT 1. [20:44] Thank you very much for the idea, I'll think about more details for this

CONSULTANT 1. [20:44] You can also do the blog posts alongside it. It's important to incorporate a timeline as well for the 6-month campaign. When do you want it to be at its peak?

CONSULTANT 1. [20:45] Do you have any other pressing questions/concerns? The session is just about done. I hope this brainstorming helped!

CLIENT 1. [20:45] what do you mean by at its peak?

CONSULTANT 1. [20:46] When do you want the most engagement by your employees, if that matters?

CLIENT 1. [20:46] I don't know

CLIENT 1. [20:47] how to measure the engagement

CLIENT 1. [20:47] like how many people are actively participated in the campaign?

CONSULTANT 1. [20:47] Depending on which platform you choose to post the videos, how many likes, clicks, comments did the video get?

CONSULTANT 1. [20:47] How many employees actually participated in the contest?

CLIENT 1. [20:48] 70%

DISCUSSION AND IMPLICATIONS

Perhaps what was most striking to us about these results was how infrequently questions occurred overall. For comparison, in their study of eleven face-to-face conferences, each of which ran for thirty minutes, Isabelle Thompson and Jo Mackiewicz report a total of 690 questions or sixty-three questions per conference. In our study of seventy-seven conferences, we saw a total of 1,090 question—or fourteen questions per conference—despite the fact that our conferences ran on average for forty-six minutes. Expressed another way, though our conferences were

53% longer than those in the Thompson and Mackiewicz study, questions occurred 78% less frequently.

One difference between our results and those of Thompson and Mackiewicz is that the share of questions that clients asked was higher in our study. More specifically, Thompson and Mackiewicz report that "tutors in our study asked most of the questions: 81% (562) of the total 690 questions, while clients asked 19% (128). Tutors averaged 51.1 questions per conference, and clients averaged 11.6 questions per conference" (45). For our seventy-seven sessions, consultant questions were 58% of the total, and clients asked 42% of the questions. Consultants averaged 8.2 questions per conference, while clients averaged 5.9 questions per conference.

We have no hard data to account for these differences. Perhaps it is the difference in institutional context between our study and Thompson and Mackiewicz's. Perhaps it is the nature of text-based synchronous writing consulting. Perhaps it is that question-asking is not a productive strategy to advance the conversation and meet one's goals in sessions of this type. We do not have data from face-to-face sessions in our center to conduct a comparison—though that is a goal for further research. What we can conclude is that question-asking was *not* a particularly frequent discourse strategy by clients and consultants in these online synchronous sessions and did not seem to contain the ideal features of rhetorical listening—listening not merely for intent but with intent (Ratcliffe). Consultant and client questions were primarily transactional—to solicit information about the text or the context—not necessarily to form social bonds, express emotion, or build empathy. Language to achieve those latter goals might be occurring, but we would need to look for them through other discourse markers.

That is not to say that emotion and listening never played a role in our data set. In the following three examples, we focus on one particular consultant who uses a mix of questions, exclamation marks, emoticons, and, simply, empathic language to express emotional knowledge and create relationships with her clients:

CONSULTANT 5: EXAMPLE 1.

> CONSULTANT 5. [10:09] Okay, I just wanted to clarify: are you asking for guidance in calculating the optimal number of hours or in creating and formatting your assignment memo?

CLIENT 4. [10:11] calculating the optimal number of hours.

CLIENT 4. [10:11] overall im not clear what assignment is asking

CONSULTANT 5. [10:14] Okay, I understand. Unfortunately, as a writing center tutor, my position is to help clients with the writing process incl. creating and formatting essays, memos, and other written pieces. If you are asking for help in your calculations and on course content, I'm afraid that I cannot help you today.

CONSULTANT 5. [10:14] What I can do is direct you to other tutoring resources at Northeastern, where I know they have econom ics tutors

CLIENT 4. [10:15] ok. I understand.

CONSULTANT 5. [10:15] I have pasted a link in the white board to the undergraduate peer tutoring website, if you need.

CLIENT 4. [10:15] Yes i got the link, I will contact them. Thanks E_____.

CONSULTANT 5. [10:16] Absolutely! No problem at all. If you have a concern about formatting the memo after your assignment calculations, I can help you with that in another appointment.

In a session where the client is actually asking for help with his mathematical calculations in his economics paper, Consultant 5 gently offers the intent of the writing center couched as an "I" statement with "my position is to help clients with the writing process incl. creating and formatting essays, memos, and other written pieces," expresses remorse for misunderstanding with "I'm afraid that I cannot help you today," but also directs the client to appropriate resources, for which the client thanks her. Consultant 5 thus acknowledges the client's needs as important, offers information on helpful resources, and finishes with encouragement for the ways the writing center might help in the future. Consultant 5 asks a question in only her first remark, but still demonstrates "listening" by showing the client that she "hears" his needs and directs him to where those needs might best be met.

CONSULTANT 5: EXAMPLE 2.

> CLIENT 5. [13:19] Well, we had a peer review in class on Thurs too, and my partner suggested that I needed to add a little more "so what" to it, which is what I've tried to do by tying it into my appreciation for translation stuff. However, I think the transitions aren't working too well right now since I sort of typed that up and smacked it to the bottom without too much thought . I also wanted to see if you could see any points for expansion still I probably still have room to make this a little deeper
>
> CLIENT 5. [13:20] Deeper as in like more fleshed out not like philosophical
>
> CONSULTANT 5. [13:20] Yeah, absolutely! You have some really great ideas about your own paper and it really creates a narrative. I completely agree with your own assessment and feel confident we can strike the right balance during this appointment.
>
> CONSULTANT 5. [13:21] So, let's jump in.
>
> CONSULTANT 5. [13:21] Do you see the section that I have in bold at the top of your project?
>
> CLIENT 5. [13:21] Yes, I see it
>
> CONSULTANT 5. [13:22] I feel like this is definitely a place you could expand on. You're script definitely creates a narrative and a personality that your listener and audience can relate to. It's funny in all the right places and flows well.
>
> CLIENT 5. [13:23] Thanks :) yeah, I think that's a place I can expand as well. It's sort of on its own up there and I never bring any of it up again

In this example, Consultant 5 starts with praise and then creates a shared understanding of the task ahead by saying "You have some really great ideas about your own paper and it really creates a narrative. I completely agree with your own assessment and feel confident we can strike the right balance during this appointment." While the comment that follows—"Do you see the section that I have in bold at the top of your project?"—is focused on the text itself, Consultant 5 is building on her relationship with the client and offering praise for the choices the writer made, while also indicating possible revision. The client responds with thanks and an emoticon, indicating the shared emotional connection.

CONSULTANT 5: EXAMPLE 3.

> CONSULTANT 5. [19:25] Is there anything in particular in your professional statement that you want to work on today?
>
> CLIENT 6. [19:26] I'm not sure what I have written is considered a professional statement.
>
> CLIENT 6. [19:28] I guess did I respond to the prompt correctly? did I use enough APA? Though I don't know how to copy from a book if it's a statement about my own work history.
>
> CONSULTANT 5. [19:29] Got it, I understand what you mean. I will finish reading through your statement and will send you a message when I'm all done! Should be no longer than 5 minutes.
>
> CLIENT 6. [19:31] no pblm.
>
> CONSULTANT 5. [19:41] Sorry I am a slow reader!
>
> CONSULTANT 5. [19:41] You've done lovely work, D____!!!
>
> CLIENT 6. [19:43] no worries. I'm fixing mistakes as I i read along. I too am a slow reader.
>
> CONSULTANT 5. [19:43] I think you have answered most of the prompt effectively. The one place that I think you should beef up is the conclusion—your "academic learning goals" could be a bit clearer.
>
> CLIENT 6. [19:44] Ya I felt the same way. though I don't know what I want to be when I grow up. So developing goals is difficult.
>
> CONSULTANT 5. [19:44] I totally understand your dilemma. Maybe you could talk about that; state that you aren't sure (as you have done) and then expand on the areas you want to explore

In this third example, Consultant 5 builds a relationship with the client by admitting a weakness—"Sorry I'm a slow reader!"—which the client responds to with an empathic identification: "I too am a slow reader."

These examples offer a variety of strategies and indications of rhetorical listening in online synchronous writing centers sessions, where conversations about the text are accompanied by attempts to build a relationship, offer emotional support, and show empathy. That these moves are made largely without the need to ask questions is perhaps the defining feature of online writing center sessions, at least in our data set.

IMPLICATIONS FOR PRACTICE AND FURTHER RESEARCH

We learned a great deal from this research—though not necessarily what we expected. Rather than see the rich potential of questions to express and share emotional knowledge and represent a form of rhetorical listening in synchronous online writing tutoring, we saw that questions were primarily meant to solicit information or a response about a text or its context. In other words, the text was the driving force in these sessions—a focus on the writing, not the writer, to draw on Stephen North's famous dictum. Questions did little to build the social relationship between consultant and client or scaffold one or both participants' emotional needs. However, as we show in our last examples, consultants used other forms of expression to perform that work.

Our research suggests we might need to rethink how we train consultants to use questions in an online setting if our goal is to practice rhetorical listening, no matter the tutoring modality. Alternatively, we might consider reframing online training in a way that does not place as much emphasis on asking questions as face-to-face training might. Lee-Ann Kastman Breuch and Sam Racine suggest that because "online writing centers occupy spaces different from face-to-face centers . . . *online tutors need training specific to online writing spaces*," and face-to-face training does not "translate easily to online writing centers" (247).

Our research hints that an approach specific to online contexts might be a useful path forward. We did observe generation of emotional knowledge, and we did observe expression and personality quirks that were apparent when reading transcripts. As is true for face-to-face sessions, emotions online do exist; we see this as an opportunity and invitation to learn how to perform and read them. In other words, rather than avoiding the difficult work of attending to emotions or abandoning questions in online consulting, we feel our work opens up space to look at language and consultant-client relationships in their many forms, not merely in question-asking and answering. Perhaps we need to work with staff to use questions productively to elicit and convey emotional knowledge that demonstrates rhetorical listening. Staff can learn to "perform" in online spaces or take on particular personae when it comes to expressions of emotion (see Iantorno in this collection on consultants' emotional labor). What we are describing is not necessarily inauthentic if we are asking consultants to take on particular personae; it might be necessary to support clients and get productive work done, as well as allow consultants' emotional lives outside of the center to co-exist with their work in the center (see Storey in this collection).

We return here to Ratcliffe's idea of "rhetorical listening" to point to the ways that writing center work in online synchronous environments might demonstrate the mutual learning that our field values. While we quoted part of Ratcliffe's definition earlier in this chapter, we point to the larger definition here:

> As I employ it, then, *understanding* means more than simply listening for a speaker/writer's intent. . .Instead, *understanding* means listening to discourse not *for* intent but *with* intent—with the intent to understand not just the claims, not just the cultural logics within which the claims function, but the rhetorical negotiations of understanding as well. To clarify this process of understanding, we might best invert the term and define *understanding* as *standing under*—consciously standing under discourses that surround us and others, while consciously acknowledging all our particular and fluid standpoints. Standing under discourses means letting discourses wash over, through, and around us and then letting them lie there to inform our politics and ethics. (205)

What, then, would online synchronous writing center tutoring look like when we are "letting discourses wash over, through, and around us and then letting them lie there to inform our politics and ethics" (205)? The challenge Ratcliffe poses for online synchronous writing center tutoring is what it would look like when we are "letting discourses wash over, through, and around us and then letting them lie there to inform our politics and ethics" (205). We maintain that such acts of listening and emotional attending are consistent with the client-centered ethos long associated with writing center work. Ideally, we offer clients help at *their* point of need; we respond to the client in front of us—whether virtually or physically—rather than the client we wish we were working with; we attend to the discursive and affective needs that clients feel comfortable expressing—a level of comfort that they might not often feel with classroom teachers. We ultimately see successful online consulting as steeped in such overt realizations of our and our clients' "fluid standpoints" (205).

Our study also points to long-standing conceptual conundrums in the practices of writing centers: How much is a center's work driven by the texts clients are eager, if not anxious, to improve, and how much is driven by the relational aspects of our work? Is this dichotomy too simplified, and are there ways that we might address the "whole writer," including the emotional and affective needs that all writers have, while also addressing the needs of writers' texts? How are these choices complicated when our tutoring is done in online, text-only spaces? Our study does not leave us with clear answers to these questions but instead a great deal of curiosity toward better understanding them. We look forward to exploring these questions—and others—in future research and sharing the results of our research with our writing center staff, all in an effort to better understand and refine the work of online writing consultation.

WORKS CITED

Ashton-Jones, Evelyn. "Asking the Right Questions: A Heuristic for Tutors." *The Writing Center Journal*, vol. 9, no. 1, 1988, pp. 29–36.

Calle-Arango, Lina. "Questioning in Writing Center Tutorials." Íkala, vol. 24, no. 1, 2019, pp. 137–152.

Effinger Wilson, Nancy, and Keri Fitzgerald. "Empathic Tutoring in the Third Space." *Writing Lab Newsletter*, vol. 37, no. 3–4, 2012, pp. 11–13.

Feibush, Laura. "Gestural Listening and the Writing Center's Virtual Boundaries." *Praxis: A Writing Center Journal*, vol. 15, no. 2, 2018.

Haen, Mike. "The Affective Dimension of Writing Center Talk: Insights from Conversation Analysis." *WLN: A Journal of Writing Center Scholarship*, vol. 42, no. 9–10, 2018, pp. 2–9.

Johnson, JoAnn B. "Reevaluation of the Question as a Teaching Tool." *Dynamics of the Writing Conference: Social and Cognitive Interaction,* edited by Thomas Flynn and Mary King, National Council of Teachers of English, 1993, pp. 34–40.

Kastman Breuch, Lee-Ann M., and Sam J. Racine. "Developing Sound Tutor Training for Online Writing Centers: Creating Productive Peer Reviewers." *Computers and Composition*, vol. 17, no. 3, 2000, pp. 245–63.

Lawson, Daniel. "Metaphors and Ambivalence: Affective Dimensions in Writing Center Studies." *WLN: A Journal of Writing Center Scholarship*, vol. 40, no. 3–4, 2015, pp. 20–27.

McBride, Maureen, et al. "Responding to the Whole Person: Using Empathic Listening and Responding in the Writing Center." *The Peer Review*, vol. 2, no. 2, 2018.

North, Stephen M. "The Idea of a Writing Center." *College English*, vol. 46, no. 5, 1984, pp. 433–46.

Ratcliffe, Krista. "Rhetorical Listening: A Trope for Interpretive Invention and a 'Code of Cross-Cultural Conduct.'" *College Composition and Communication*, vol. 51, no. 2, 1999, pp. 195–224.

Thompson, Isabelle. "Scaffolding in the Writing Center: A Microanalysis of an Experienced Tutor's Verbal and Nonverbal Tutoring Strategies." *Written Communication*, vol. 26, no. 4, 2009, pp. 417–53.

—, and Jo Mackiewicz. "Questioning in Writing Center Conferences." *The Writing Center Journal*, vol. 33, no. 2, 2014, pp. 37–70.

Valentine, Kathryn. "The Undercurrents of Listening: A Qualitative Content Analysis of Listening in Writing Center Tutor Guidebooks." *The Writing Center Journal*, vol. 36, no. 2, 2017, pp. 89–115.

Zembylas, Michalinos. "Emotional Ecology: The Intersection of Emotional Knowledge and Pedagogical Content Knowledge in Teaching." *Teaching and Teacher Education*, vol. 23, 2007, pp. 355–67.

APPENDIX A. WCONLINE INTAKE FORM QUESTIONS

- First Name
- Last Name
- Email Address
- Telephone Number (If we need to cancel your appointment for any reason—consultant illness, snow day—you will receive an email or phone call)
- Status
- Expected Graduation Year
- First or Home Language
- Major
- College
- Student ID
- I permit the WC to use my data anonymously for research.
- How did you hear about the NEU Writing Center?
- Have you been to the Writing Center before?
- Course Number and Title (Ex: ENGW 1111 First-Year Writing) (If applicable)
- Instructor Name (If applicable)
- Are you coming with work from an online course?
- Provide an overview of your assignment or writing project.
- Is this a group project or group essay?
- What SPECIFIC aspects of your writing would you like to work on today?
- What are your goals for the session and how can your consultant best help you achieve these goals?
- Assignment
- Was this session online or in person?

APPENDIX B. WCONLINE SYNCHRONOUS TUTORING ENVIRONMENT

The WCOnline synchronous tutoring platform consists of a "white-board" space for participants to post drafts and attachments and a "chat" space for a textual conversation; shown here is the first screen students encounter (see Figure 1).

Figure 1. Screenshot of WCOnline tutoring environment.

APPENDIX C. RESULTS OF QUANTITATIVE ANALYSIS

Correlations Table. This table shows Pearson correlations and two-tailed significance for the sample set of sessions—N=77. Highlighted and bolded cells show statistically significant relationships—when the *p*-value is ≤ 0.05—among variables that correspond to those discussed in this chapter, meaning there is equal to or less than five percent probability that the results are random. ** next to a number indicates that the correlation is significant at the 0.01 level, two-tailed, and * next to a number indicates that the correlation is significant at the 0.05 level, two-tailed. A negative or inverse correlation means that the variables—reflected in Table 1 in the chapter—move in opposite directions. For instance, in our data set, a move toward an "ideas" agenda correlates inversely with a move toward the client's home language being "English." Cells of duplicate data are left blank.

		home lang.	tutor-qs	client-qs	total-qs	tutor excl.	client excl.	total excl.	tutor-emoticon	client-emoticon	total-emoticon
agenda	Sig (2-tailed)	.000	.913	.029	.134	.605	.175	.384	.682	.031	.294
	Pearson Corr.	-.438**	-.013	-.249*	-.172	-.060	-.156	-.101	.047	-.246*	-.121
home lang.	Sig (2-tailed)		.031	.977	.106	.387	.061	.613	.945	.188	.418
	Pearson Corr.		-.245*	.003	-.186	-.100	.214	.058	-.008	.152	.094
tutor-qs	Sig (2-tailed)			.852	.000	.015	.818	.058	.203	.874	.231
	Pearson Corr.			-.022	.747**	.277*	.027	.217	-.147	.018	-.138
client-qs	Sig (2-tailed)				.000	.059	.038	.010	.308	.842	.372
	Pearson Corr.				.649**	.216	.237*	.293**	.118	.023	.103
total-qs	Sig (2-tailed)					.001	.116	.001	.768	.805	.746
	Pearson Corr.					.357**	.181	.364**	-.034	.029	-.037

Model Summary 1. This model shows relationships between total number of questions asked during sessions—constant and dependent variable—and the number of exclamations used by consultants and clients—quantitative variables and predictive "counts." We treated our discrete quantitative variable counts as continuous for the purposes of regression analysis. The model shows that there is a significant relationship—when the p-value is ≤ 0.05—between the total number of questions asked during sessions and the use of exclamations by consultants and clients; the R value shows that this is a moderate positive relationship.

Model 1	R	R Square	Adjusted R Square	Std. Error of the Estimate		
	.365	.133	.110	6.319		

ANOVA	Sum of Squares	df (degrees of frequency)	Mean Square	F		Sig.
Regression	453.757	2	226.879	5.681		.005
Residual	2955.048	74	39.933			
Total	3408.805	76				

Model Summary 2. This model shows relationships between total number of questions asked during sessions—constant and dependent variable—and the number of emoticons and exclamations used by consultants and clients—quantitative variables and predictive "counts." The model shows that there is a significant relationship—when the p-value is $\leq$ 0.05—between the total number of questions asked during sessions and the use of emoticons and exclamations by consultants and clients; the R value shows that this is a moderate positive relationship. This suggests that the presence of emotive indicators like emoticons and exclamations has a positive relationship to total number of questions asked—more emoticons and exclamations suggests more questions.

Model 2	R	R Square	Adjusted R Square	Std. Error of the Estimate		
	.373	.139	.091	6.384		

ANOVA	Sum of Squares	df (degrees of frequency)	Mean Square	F		Sig.
Regression	474.744	4	118.686	2.912		**.027**
Residual	2934.061	72	40.751			
Total	3408.805	76				

7 Relational and Affective Factors Mediating Learning Between Tutors and Multilingual Writers

Lisa Bell

Tutoring is complex cognitive and affective work. Within effective tutoring sessions, tutors and writers learn with and from each other while navigating and negotiating the boundaries of their individual and collective understanding and abilities. Tutors and writers define roles and relationships while dealing with the disconnects and discomforts that make learning and transforming possible. As tutors and writers interact as a way to learn and produce knowledge, these borders and boundaries matter. In fact, Nancy Grimm suggests, for writing centers to fully function as learning spaces and communities, boundaries are not to be managed or maintained but used as tools to inform the work of tutoring writers (*Good Intentions* xiii). Carol Severino furthers this idea by describing writing center work as boundary work designed to help students articulate the cultural and rhetorical similarities and differences they observe and confront; to help them "grapple with" or negotiate between and among intersecting and clashing cultures, languages, literacies, discourses, and disciplines; to help them decide when to follow organizational and stylistic conventions . . . and when to take risks and violate them—instead of being "violated" by them (2).

In writing center work, boundaries and differences must function as "potential learning resources rather than barriers," reinforcing the idea that "all learning involves boundaries" (Akkerman and Bakker 137, 132). Tutors and writers encounter the borders of new perspectives and practices, allowing them to rethink assumptions and reimagine possibilities for their work with writers and writing. In essence, the relational and boundary work that takes place between tutors and learners both facilitates collaborative, multi-directional learning and defines the purpose and scope of writing center work.

Given the interdisciplinary space writing centers inhabit and the rich relationships and interactions possible between tutors and writers, the role of writing tutors is often that of boundary crossers (Akkerman and Bakker 140), coordinators (Wenger 105), and expert-outsiders (Nowacek and Hughes 182). In this capacity, tutors continually shift between areas of expertise and unfamiliar territories as they work with individual writers to traverse new genres, writing concepts, levels of proficiency, cultural contexts, and educational systems or settings. This happens daily in writing centers—a tutor majoring in biology may assist a writer on a history paper, or a graduate writer may collaborate with an undergraduate tutor. These learning exchanges can be challenging, but—as scholars within writing center work and the larger landscape of literacy and learning attest—the challenges inherent in boundary work do not reside within learners or their identities; the challenges exist within the borders—the systems and institutions—being navigated and negotiated (Grimm, "Attending" 8; Gutiérrez et al. 218; Ahmed, *On Being* 26). Working in these boundary spaces, tutors must learn to see writers' experience and understanding of systems and structures as contextual, not deficit.

Unfortunately, writers whose linguistic, cultural experience and expertise are deemed outside the bounds of a dominant definition of "standard" English are often viewed as deficient, and interactions with them are framed as problematic. When writers are viewed as deficit or lacking knowledge or skills to bring to the learning exchange, such roles and perceived identities position tutors as established experts or "more capable peers" (Vygotsky 86), frustrating opportunities for dynamic and multidirectional identities, roles, relationships, and learning within tutorials. This deficit framing often reduces individual learners with unique language and learning experiences to a single group, like ESL. It reifies boundaries rather than encouraging tutorial participants to redefine, navigate, or negotiate them. These static, stagnant identities, roles, and relationships reduce sentence-level language learning to editing and frame writing and language choices to correct or incorrect, instead of contextual and cultural.

Framing multilingual writers as deficient and tutors as experts has often led to a focus on tutors learning *about* multilingual writers rather than *with* or *from* them. It has also reinforced the idea that challenges within tutorials are connected to a writer's identity rather than the systems and borders they are navigating. Tutors—framed as experts in relation to multilingual writers—are rarely trained to interact with multilingual writers and writing "beyond what comes naturally to an earnest, well-read, and verbal native speaker" (Rafoth 137). Rather than training tutors to address or even "anticipate what knowledge, information, and skills are needed in order to function in a multilingual context" (136–37), tutors are often left without a working understanding of the boundaries multilingual writers navigate or the expertise and experience they bring to tutorials.

To improve learning exchanges within tutorials, scholars have called for additional research into interactions between writing center tutors and multilingual writers (Mackiewicz and Thompson 58; Grimm, "Attending" 18; Kim 73). Understandably, since "the work of a writing center is a matter of being available mentally and emotionally to engage in the mutual construction of meaning with another" (Grimm, "Attending" 9), this body of research would include cognitive and affective realms. Writing center scholarship and practice often focus on how writers acquire and make use of new knowledge, but the affective and relational variables present in tutorials are not always recognized despite their impact on learning. For example, writers may feel motivated, relieved, or excited as they work with a tutor on a writing task. On the other hand, writers may also feel manipulated, self-conscious, or frustrated within a tutorial. Likewise, tutors experience a range of affects and emotions in their work with writers and writing, including feeling respected and supported as well as guilty and ashamed (Nicklay 26).

It is important to note that while tutors and writers may bring feelings into a tutorial, emotion and affect are present based on tutoring interactions and context. According to cultural critic, Eric Shouse, "[a] feeling is a sensation that has been checked against previous experiences and labelled." Conversely, "[a]n emotion is the projection/display of a feeling" and an affect "is the body's way of preparing itself for action in a given circumstance by adding a quantitative dimension of intensity to the quality of an experience." In short, "Feelings are *personal* and *biographical*, emotions are *social*, and affects are *prepersonal*," or contextual (Shouse). As Sara Ahmed further explains, "it is through emotions, or how we respond to objects and others, that surfaces or boundaries are made: the 'I' and the 'we' are shaped by, and even take the shape of, contact with others" (*Cultural* 10). Teresa Brennan adds to this idea, noting how "affects are not received or registered in a vacuum" but are influenced by and even transmitted among individuals (6). However, as Shouse suggests, "the transmission of affect does not mean that one person's feelings become another's. The transmission of affect is about the way that bodies affect one another . . . By resonating with the intensity of the contexts it infolds, the body attempts to ensure that it is prepared to respond appropriately to a given circumstance." Since tutors and writers bring with them identities and feelings that inform interactions within tutorials (Denny 8; see also Napoleone and Storey in this collection), the relational and affective work present in learning exchanges needs closer examination if writing centers are to more fully understand the work of tutoring.

In response to calls for additional research, this chapter examines the relational and affective variables mitigating learning and tutoring interactions between tutors and multilingual writers. Specifically, findings from this mixed-methods action research study identify participation, common ground, validation, and confidence as central relational and affective aspects of such interactions. Within this study, tutors and writers participated when initiating genuine dialogue, asking questions, or providing and inviting information or insight on a concept. Participants also sought common ground in shared language and experience to draw upon as part of their learning exchanges. Tutors and writers provided validation by confirming, understanding, or approving choices made about writing and learning processes or products. Finally, participants identified how their shared learning exchanges were influenced by their confidence, understood as self-efficacy or participants' "perceived capabilities for learning or performing actions at designated levels" (Schunk and DiBenedetto 515). Although tutoring is a complex series of interactions and relationships that cannot be reduced to individual or isolated variables, findings from this study indicate that participation, common ground, validation, and confidence informed tutors and multilingual writers opportunities for learning within tutorials.

METHODS

This interdisciplinary IRB-approved research was designed as a mixed-methods action research study. Action research, often referred to as teacher research, centers around an innovation or intervention designed to address a problem of practice. This type of research involves a systematic cycle of inquiry, reflection, collaboration, innovation, and evaluation (Creswell). Thus, the pre- and post-intervention data gathered from a range of stakeholders informs the next iteration of the intervention. While action research may contribute to a larger body of knowledge, its primary purpose is "the improvement of practice, the improvement of the understanding of practice, and the improvement of the situation in which the practice takes place" (Ivankova 29).

This action research study centered around a tutor training intervention designed to increase participatory scaffolding within tutoring sessions with multilingual writers. The intervention consisted of classroom training and experiential learning as part of mandatory ongoing tutor education. The classroom portion of the intervention consisted of three fifty-minute class periods. Each class focused on a different topic: scaffolding as a central tutoring strategy, explicit sentence-level language instruction, and cultural and disciplinary framing of writing and language, including shifting from deficit to contextual thinking about multilingual writers and writing. The experiential learning portion of the intervention followed the classroom modules and consisted of administrative and peer observations and post-observation discussions about structuring learning interactions and working with multilingual writers. In initial cycles of the action research, tutors and multilingual writers noted how participation, common ground, validation, and confidence mediated learning exchanges. Given the cyclical nature of action research, returning to the data was important for understanding and addressing these relational and affective factors and resulted in a final cycle of data collection and analysis reported here.

The research setting was a large—33,000+ students—private university in the western United States where the university's writing center conducted over 15,000 tutorials each year. When writers registered to use writing center services, they had the option to self-identify as having a first language other than English, and those who did were predominantly international students. In fall 2018, when this study took place, self-identified multilingual writers accounted for approximately eight percent of the writing center's clientele and fifteen percent of all tutorials.

Participants in this study included multilingual writers and mostly monolingual writing center tutors. The nineteen multilingual writers who participated were international students for whom English was an additional language. Participating writing tutors were undergraduate peer tutors who had completed a semester-long internship, had at least twenty-five hours of actual tutoring experience, and attended a weekly, ongoing tutor education class used for the intervention. Two tutors identified as bilingual, but most tutors—despite having learned other languages—functioned as monolingual English speakers. From the larger sample of twenty-one tutors, five tutors also participated in interviews and observations. This representative sample included two tutors who had just completed the internship, a bilingual tutor with multiple semesters of tutoring experience, and two tutors with multiple years of tutoring experience. All participants provided informed consent and engaged with the study voluntarily and anonymously.

Data was collected before and after the training intervention (see Table 1). Participating tutors completed anonymous pre- and post-intervention surveys. Representative tutors also provided pre- and post-intervention interviews. Participating multilingual writers attended focus groups, and tutors and multilingual writers were observed within ten audio-recorded tutorials.

Table 1. Data collection sources

Data Sources	Number of Participants (n=)	Qualitative Data Word Count
Post-intervention focus group with multilingual writers	9	15,744
Pre-intervention interviews	5	13,087
Post-intervention interviews	5	11,042
Post-intervention tutorial observations (10 sessions)	20	43,982
Pre-intervention surveys	19	1,978
Post-intervention surveys	21	1,491
Total		87324

Data analysis followed a convergent, mixed methods approach, with the qualitative and quantitative data being analyzed separately, prior to analysis of all data sets. Qualitative data were coded and analyzed thematically alongside *a priori* coding of common tutoring strategies and techniques developed by Jo Mackiewicz and Isabelle Thompson (65–66). Quantitative data from survey responses and observations were analyzed statistically. Frequency measurements—standard deviation, mean, mode—were applied to observed tutoring sessions with the understanding that this approach would not produce generalizable, quantitative outcomes about tutoring but would identify the presence of certain strategies within idiosyncratic sessions. A Cronbach's alpha score of 0.796 indicated a high level of internal reliability for the survey instrument, and—given the sample size and Likert-scale survey questions—Wilcoxon signed-rank testing, a nonparametric version of the more common paired samples t-test, was used to compare the median responses from survey data. The reliability and validity of the data collection and analysis processes were increased through the cyclical nature of the action research study, peer review, member checking with participating tutors, and the triangulation of data.

Results

The research findings connected to four main relational and affective variables influencing learning exchanges between writing tutors and multilingual writers: participation, common ground, validation, and confidence. The qualitative data were supported by quantitative findings, offering a mixed methods understanding of these mediating variables.

Participation. Participation within this study was understood as engagement within tutorials. Tutors and writers were seen as active participants when they facilitated learning exchanges by initiating conversation, asking authentic questions, or inviting and providing information on a topic. In pre-intervention survey and interview responses, tutors described themselves as knowledgeable and active participants within tutorials, but they often depicted multilingual writers as receivers of learning and deficient in language and literacy. Following tutor training on writing as cultural and contextual and multilingual writers as experienced and engaged language learners, tutors increasingly described tutoring relationships as participatory with an emphasis on multilingual writers as valued participants. Tutor responses shifted from speaking about applying scaffolding *to* multilingual writers to scaffolding *with* multilingual writers, describing a much more multidirectional version of this core tutoring strategy. In a pre-intervention interview, one tutor described scaffolding as asking a student questions "just a little bit above their level and then eventually they'll get it and get to where you want them to go." This response problematically positioned tutors as experts and multilingual writers as deficient followers. This depiction of tutoring provides a reductive learning model when tutors lead writers to determined destinations and avoid genuine dialogue and learning exchanges. This depiction of tutoring reduces learning to tutors leading writers to a destination determined by the tutor and avoiding questions that spark dialog or genuine learning exchanges.

Following the intervention, this same tutor explained scaffolding with a multilingual writer as much more participatory:

> And so with him, I think he wanted to focus on, like, organization and understanding of his piece. . .I think with him, just being involved and making it that way so that it wasn't just me telling him all the time "OK this is what's wrong with it. Fix it." It was "what do you feel about it? OK. How can we go about fixing it? This is what I got from it when I was reading through. Is that what you wanted to convey?" . . . And so, at the end of the session, he, I felt like he was really happy with his work . . . because we were so involved with it, because of the scaffoldings that we had done.

In this post-intervention interview response, the multilingual writer was seen as a valued participant. The learning interaction involved the participatory, relational work of negotiation and collaboration rather than the tutor simply transferring knowledge to the writer. Additionally, the tutor noted the importance of an emotional outcome—the student's satisfaction with his work—as a measure of effective tutoring.

Throughout post-intervention data, tutors and multilingual writers identified participants' willingness and ability to actively engage with each other as necessary to facilitate learning. In focus groups, multilingual writers spoke appreciatively of tutors who asked questions, provided reader responses, or modeled choices. They commiserated about having to work with tired, shy, or disinterested tutors whom they described as "slacking" or offering only "superficial" interactions. In interviews, tutors agreed, noting that being sick or at the end of a long shift caused them to be less engaged with writers. In survey responses, tutors were also asked questions such as "How do you help students who are not willing to engage in the discussion?" These questions reinforced the idea that the writer's participation also influenced learning interactions. Tutors also described how effective tutoring and collaborative learning could be when both participants were engaged in the work. This mirrored data collected from observed tutorials.

Participation was also a visible variable within observed tutorials, as tutors and writers interacted through genuine dialogue, pointing each other to ways of knowing and establishing mutual understanding. The following excerpt illustrates such observed exchanges:

> TUTOR. This is kind of like way back in the beginning. We've got the inserted phrase. . .
>
> WRITER. Sure. Non-extension phrases, right?
>
> TUTOR. Yeah, exactly.

In this instance, the tutor referred to a previous topic, began explaining a concept, and validated the writer. The multilingual writer offered confirmation, recalled information, and provided an explanation for the suggested edit.

Other observed interactions demonstrate the role of participation and the relational aspect of tutors and multilingual writers valuing each other as participants within the tutorial:

> TUTOR. Okay, so then products would be plural. So, have the apostrophe outside the s.
>
> WRITER. Okay. That's what I was wondering, I wasn't sure.
>
> TUTOR. Yeah, no, thank you for bringing me back to that.
>
> WRITER. Then this is wrong, right? "All salesmen are. . ."
>
> TUTOR. Oh, yeah, I didn't even catch that, thank you.
>
> WRITER. No, yeah, no problem I just saw it, so that's good we're both doing it right?
>
> (shared laughter)
>
> TUTOR. Tag teaming it. Okay, any other questions?
>
> WRITER. Not for that.

This evidence of tutors and writers as active participants aligns with how tutors described effective tutoring exchanges following the training intervention. Observed participation also mirrored multilingual writers' focus-group descriptions of tutoring roles and relationships. They were happy to have tutors to take the lead within tutorials and to provide information and options related to writing and language. However, multilingual writers were also adamant about their role as participants, particularly in owning the process and product of their work, offering input, and making final decisions about their writing and language use. No matter the tutorial context or content, though, tutors and multilingual writers actively engaged with each other, supporting rich data that described participation as central to learning interactions.

Common Ground. The research also revealed common ground as mediating learning within tutorials. Establishing common ground primarily occurred as participants made use of shared language or experiences. Following the intervention, when tutors described effective tutorials with multilingual writers, tutors noted the importance of being "on the same page" and "having a connection from the get-go." They shared instances where "something clicked" between them and the multilingual writer. A new tutor spoke of needing to find a common level of language proficiency in order to work effectively with multilingual writers. A bilingual tutor described code switching and code meshing in a tutorial and how her own language learning experiences helped her connect with a multilingual writer personally and academically: "I had gone through that, and I felt like that maybe came into the tutorial as well, where I didn't want her to go through that and didn't want her to feel like 'OK, my minority voice is not good enough.'" This tutor understood common ground as influencing her interactions and relationships with multilingual writers.

Multilingual writers also sought connection with tutors through shared language and language experiences. Within several tutorials, participants used more than one language to increase understanding of a concept or establish a personal connection:

> TUTOR. Hmmm. So, "Faced investigations not only by law enforcement, but by, something like that." (crosstalk) Does that seem to fit your idea more?

> WRITER. Gracias. Thank you.

TUTOR. No problem. De nada. "Faced." What did we say? "Faced criminal. . ."

In this example, a multilingual writer used more than one language, and a monolingual tutor replied in Spanish to establish the use of multiple languages as acceptable common ground within the tutorial. Additionally, since the participants had collaborated on the wording of a sentence in English, the tutor asked, "What did we say?" to make sure they were capturing their shared use of language.

Just as the common ground of shared language facilitated learning interactions and relationships within tutorials sessions, a lack of explicit understanding of sentence-level language frustrated opportunities for learning and relationships between participants. Although tutors received initial training in explicit sentence-level language as part of the intervention, in post-intervention survey and interview responses, they acknowledged a need for continued language learning. A new tutor lamented that he often felt the recommendations he gave multilingual writers were "pointless" because his understanding of English language conventions was innate, and he was unable to provide clear reasons for suggested revisions. Following the tutor training intervention, several multilingual writers also expressed tutors' lack of shared language experience impeded their interactions with tutors. They spoke of tutors not adequately addressing language concerns as "superficial" or "rude." They described tutors as *unwilling* rather than *unable* to help. These writers saw tutors' lack of knowledge about sentence-level language as relational, demonstrating the need for shared language as common ground and foundational within learning interactions.

Throughout observed sessions, participants also worked to establish common ground by identifying and drawing upon shared experience. Multilingual writers expressed value in working with tutors they already knew, and participants connected over a range of personal and academic experiences—classes, majors, procrastination, travel, current events, wedding rings:

WRITER. I like your ring. It's beautiful.

TUTOR. Oh, thank you, yeah.

WRITER. I got married last semester, I mean, last year.

TUTOR. Congratulations. Me, too.

WRITER. Oh my gosh. That's so exciting.

TUTOR. What are you working on today?

WRITER. I'm working on my analytical report. Yesterday I was here, and the girl was helping me out. . .English is not my first language, so it's hard for me to write in English.

TUTOR. Right, it's hard.

Establishing common ground and working from a shared space and a desire for shared understanding appeared to facilitate strategies and exchanges in observed sessions, including building rapport, negotiating, instructing, and scaffolding. Within the data, shared experiences offered relational connection between tutorial participants.

Validation. Results indicated that validation mediated participants' learning interactions within tutorials. Multilingual writers sought validation of their writing choices, and tutors wanted confirmation that their tutoring approaches were useful. In addition to individual, affective experience, validation was transferable and relational among participants.

In focus group discussions following the intervention, multilingual writers noted that writing tutors played an important role in confirming writing choices. Multilingual writers worked with tutors to understand the effectiveness of their text and sought validation from tutors before submitting work to instructors. In addition to describing the need for validation, multilingual writers sought validation throughout observed tutorials. Questions such as "Is that right?" and "Do you think that's okay?" appeared frequently, as did tutors' validation of revision and language choices via utterances of "Yeah, that works," "Yep," "Uh-huh," and "Exactly." These linguistic markers of seeking and providing validation were a steady undercurrent within learning exchanges, appearing 220 times across the ten observed sessions.

Tutors also sought validation from multilingual writers. Throughout observed tutorials, tutors requested confirmation that their tutoring approaches were of use. Tutors asked writers whether explanations were clear or if feedback aligned with the writer's needs or expectations. Tutors cited writers' use of revision strategies or application of concepts as validating the effectiveness of learning exchanges. Tutors also described feeling validated when multilingual writers returned to work with them again. As one new tutor explained, validation as a tutor occurs "when

ESL [multilingual] students come back that you've worked with and they trust you. And knowing that you did something right the first [time], that the scaffolding worked and like built their confidence in you and you helped them to do well on their assignment or paper." Throughout the data, validation emerged as an important relational component, underscoring the relational and participatory nature of learning and providing markers to guide interactions within tutorials.

Beyond providing confirmation of the effectiveness of writing and tutoring choices, validation addressed participants' affective needs. Both tutors and multilingual writers connected validation with confidence, participation, and establishment of common ground. These connections primarily occurred when participants validated emotions. In observed sessions, tutors validated multilingual writers' frustrations with writing and language learning:

WRITER. I don't know. This is really hard.

BILINGUAL TUTOR. For sure. I feel you.

While all instances of validating emotions were coupled with another emotional or motivational technique—optimism, empathy, encouraging ownership, etc.—acknowledging the expressed feeling seemed a vital bridge to extending motivation or encouraging continued participation within the tutorial. This ongoing relationship of validation between tutor and writer seemed particularly important since transmission of such affect means a sharing of energy (Brennan 6). Validating the experiences of another seemed to provide solidarity by indicating commitment to understanding and a desire to make meaning within a shared space. As Ahmed explains in *The Cultural Politics of Emotion*, "Solidarity does not assume that our struggles are the same struggles, or that our pain is the same pain, or that our hope is for the same future. Solidarity involves commitment, and work, as well as the recognition that even if we do not have the same feelings, or the same lives, or the same bodies, we do live on common ground" (189). Collaboration within tutorials appeared enhanced through validation as the transmission of affect offered possibilities to motivate and energize participants individually and collectively.

Confidence. In addition to participation, common ground, and validation, confidence—specifically as self-efficacy—emerged as an affective and relational variable influencing learning interactions. The influence confidence played within tutorials was amplified by the training intervention and made visible via mixed-methods analysis. As previously described, the tutor training intervention encouraged a shift from deficit to contextual thinking about multilingual writers and included explicit training on sentence-level language, allowingtutors and writers to more effectively scaffold within tutorials in multidirectional and participatory ways. The intervention provided cognitive and experiential learning support for tutors as they encountered and wrestled with sentence-level language, but it did not address the emotional or affective labor of learning and shifts in identity. A notable result of the training was a change in confidence as tutors identified less as experts and more as learners and expert-outsiders.

Following the training intervention, tutors recognized their need to learn more about the cultural, contextual, and linguistic aspects of working with multilingual writers, resulting in decreased confidence when tutoring multilingual writers. Tutors were more aware of the boundaries and systems multilingual writers navigated, leading to post-intervention questions such as "What are ways that I can better embrace other writing styles?" and "How can I help a Japanese student write in a way that makes sense to them AND in a way that will make sense to their professor?" These types of responses not only reflected a shift in tutors' roles and relationships with multilingual writers and writing, but the responses also marked a shift in identity and confidence.

This shift in tutors' confidence was reinforced by quantitative survey data. According to post-intervention survey responses (see Table 2), tutors experienced both a wider range and statistically significant difference in confidence scaffolding with multilingual and native-English speaking writers, $p < 0.01$. The effect size—$PS_{dep} = .56$—suggests that if randomly sampled, fifty-six percent of tutors would report feeling less confident scaffolding with multilingual writers than monolingual peers.

Table 2. Comparison of tutors' post-intervention confidence using scaffolding with writers

	Confidence scaffolding with writers whose first language is English	**Confidence scaffolding with multilingual writers**
N	16	16
Median	5	4
Range	1	3
p-value	0.01	
pSdep	0.56	
Z	-2.81	

As tutors increasingly identified as learners in relation to multilingual writers and writing, their confidence in facilitating learning interactions with multilingual writers shifted.

Multilingual writers also revealed how confidence mediated tutoring interactions. In focus groups and observations, multilingual writers exhibited or noted their lack of confidence speaking and writing in English. They were apologetic, used humor when describing their English being "bad" or "embarrassing," and identified themselves solely as learners. Across the data, confidence appeared as an affective, mediating variable—connected to identities, roles, and relationships within tutorials—and was likely transmitted between participants, potentially influencing individual and collaborative learning.

DISCUSSION

Certainly, tutoring is complex, contextual work that requires mental and emotional effort. Within the limited space and time allotted to tutorials, tutors and writers must establish the needed relationships and environment to be able to work together. Tutors and writers not only seek to better understand writing concepts and produce written text; they must work to define roles and processes to make learning exchanges and collaboration possible. In writing centers, as in other learning environments, "educating is not something one does *to* students through implementation of a set of techniques. Rather, it is something educators do *with* learners in the context of meaningful relationships and shared experiences" (Kolb et al. 218). Ideally, in learning exchanges between tutors and writers, roles and relationships are dynamic, shifting as participants individually and collaboratively encounter and traverse borders and boundaries.

While tutors and multilingual writers experience and participate in a range of relational and emotional work, participants in this study revealed participation, common ground, validation, and confidence as shaping learning opportunities and experiences within tutorials. Active and authentic participation allowed tutors and writers to understand the boundaries of each other's expertise and function as co-learners. Since each tutor, writer, and learning and writing context was unique, tutors and writers established common ground at these crossroads and found shared personal and academic space and language to move beyond individual boundaries and engage in collective work and collaborative learning. Validation functioned as a relational tool to acknowledge movement across borders involving new concepts or practices. Validation also allowed for empathizing and recognizing mutual understanding when borders and boundaries impeded learning and learners. The confidence tutors and writers brought with them into a session was potentially transmitted, amplified, or extinguished as individuals worked together to move beyond personal cognitive and affective boundaries. These mediating factors confirm the sociocultural nature of tutoring and learning as seen in both writing center theory and the interdisciplinary scholarship guiding this study. These relational and affective aspects of tutorials also present implications for tutor education, administrative work, and ongoing research into interactions between writing tutors and multilingual writers.

Participation within tutorials is essential to learning, as findings from this study reinforce. Learning is not given or received; it is co-constructed through participants' interactions. Participants in this study echoed existing scholarship that positions effective tutoring interactions as participatory, leading to learning for both tutor and writer (Hall 72; Lunsford and Ede 12; Nowacek and Hughes 178; Lee 61). According to Thompson, "Unless the relationship between the tutor and the student is highly interactive, learning is not likely to occur, even though active participation is not by itself sufficient for learning" (419). Participation is needed within tutorials, but the type and quality of participation matters. Ben Rafoth explains, "interaction is not only essential to learning generally but to learning language specifically. And the more this interaction also involves a positive relationship, the better" (40). The dynamic relationships and roles visible in this study demonstrate how participation increases opportunities for multidirectional learning within tutorials.

While learning is made possible through participation, tutors and writers must establish "enough common ground for ongoing mutual engagement" (Wenger et al. 35). Findings indicate that connection can be established through personal and academic connections, but shared language and language experience provide vital common ground. For tutors and multilingual writers to traverse boundaries and create new spaces for learning, understanding language systems and contexts matters. Language as shared space can be especially effective when it includes shared identity or understanding of the cultural and contextual aspects of language (Blazer 22; Nakamaru 107; Effinger Wilson). Language as common ground may also include understanding how to make use of multiple languages and literacies within different contexts, including valuing other languages and practices such as code-meshing (Green 73; Rafoth 20). Such perspectives and practices were apparent within several observed tutorials where participants jointly made use of multiple languages, comparing and building upon shared language and literacy knowledge and experience. Additionally, as participants noted, shared language often includes shared proficiency and explicit understanding of language. As previous scholarship suggests, writers need sufficient proficiency to communicate with tutors (Kim 71). However, tutors in this study also identified their need for sufficient sentence-level language proficiency to communicate with multilingual writers about language choices. These findings reinforce previous research that recognizes explicit sentence-level language knowledge as valuable common ground for tutors and writers (Weigle and Nelson 222; Eckstein 376).

In addition to establishing common ground to move learning forward, validation mediated tutors' and writers' ability to remain on a shared path throughout tutorials. Tutors sought validation that their tutoring choices were effective, and multilingual writers sought validation that they were understanding and applying writing concepts successfully. This multidirectional, formative feedback appearing throughout the data aligns with the idea of writing center tutorials as places where "talking in the middle" occurs (Harris 27). Since peer tutors are not teachers, and multilingual writers are not supervisors, validation allows participants opportunities to explore the boundaries of language, literacy, and learning in meaningful ways with reduced risk. In this way, validation is not simply a cognitive tool to facilitate task progress or completion. Validation motivates learners (Hyland and Hyland 215; Finkelstein et al. 70) and reinforces shared direction and energy in collaborative learning.

Research also indicates how confidence changes the dynamics of learning exchanges. Tutors and multilingual writers in previous studies have described feeling discomfort in tutoring sessions (Bromley et al.; Kim 68), which is expected since confronting boundaries precedes collaboration and transformative learning (Akkerman and Bakker 146). A multilingual writer's lack of participation within a session may leave the tutor's attempts to assist the writer unvalidated and cause the tutor to have decreased confidence in their ability to tutor effectively. A writer unable to establish common ground with a tutor may question the tutor's ability or desire to help, resulting in a lack of confidence in the learning exchange and tutoring relationship. Additionally, tutors' and writers' confidence prior to a session can influence learning interactions. Tutors lacking confidence with sentence-level language rules may avoid addressing multilingual writers' concerns in that area. Multilingual writers who lack confidence speaking English may participate less within a tutorial where English is the only language used.

Issues of confidence intertwine with issues of identity, roles, and relationships within learning exchanges (Denny 33, 119; Calhoun Bell and Reddington Elledge 17; Grimm, "Attending" 9). Shifts in confidence are inherent within learning interactions as boundary work. Multilingual writers and tutors as brokers or expert-outsiders consistently move between knowing and not knowing, belonging and not belonging (Akkerman and Bakker 142; Wenger 110; Nowacek and Hughes 172). Just as boundaries are not inherently negative and are necessary for learning, shifts in confidence can be useful within tutorials to motivate participation, encourage risk taking, signify a need for increased understanding, lead to seeking validation or common ground, and initiate reflection on other relational and affective variables influencing learning exchanges. A monolingual tutor's lack of confidence in working with multilingual writers may encourage the tutor to seek validation and common ground. It may position the tutor to participate as an authentic and active learner wanting to move beyond the personal barrier of their own background and understand the work and experiences of multilingual writers. On the other hand, a monolingual tutor's lack of confidence working with multilingual writers may be felt and sensed by the writer, amplifying the lack of shared space and identity and validating the writer's own lack confidence in the tutor's ability to cross the boundaries needed to make collaboration and effective learning possible. Confidence adds to the complexity of tutoring relationships and interactions.

Since tutoring, writing, and learning are not merely cognitive or procedural undertakings, tutors within writing center communities need support in relational and affective work. As this study suggests, training can help tutors reimagine and revise their relationship and work with multilingual writers. However, the work of rethinking and retooling to better traverse boundaries and facilitate learning must be understood as including affective effort. Just as writing centers ideally give writers space to reflect, discuss, explore, and practice learning and writing in a resource-rich environment, tutors need writing centers to function as similar spaces for them and their tutoring. They need writing centers to be places where they can practice using new knowledge, understand systems and boundaries, and explore new relationships with writers. In writing centers as learning spaces, tutors need to be able to participate with other learners, find common ground, receive validation, and address issues of confidence in their ongoing work as boundary crossers and expert-outsiders.

Establishing writing centers as learning spaces where affective and relational aspects of tutoring are explored alongside the cognitive and procedural should be central to ongoing tutor education. Although working with multilingual writers involves the familiar work of navigating and negotiating boundaries, underlying issues of power and identity add context and complexity to these collaborations. As this study suggests, tutors need additional mental and emotional support as they see themselves reframed as expert outsiders, become more aware of assumptions and systems, and recognize working with multilingual writers and writing as contextual. Rather than offering siloed training modules, the cognitive, affective, and relational work of tutoring should be understood as ongoing within writing centers as learning communities.

If writing center administrators expect tutors to engage in learning as expert-outsiders and participate in collaborative learning across boundaries, administrators need to support and model this work themselves. Administrators signify the value of relational and affective work when they make it visible to tutors. Although administrators are often siloed within disciplines as part of existing academic systems, they can engage in interdisciplinary scholarship and use it to train tutors. Administrators should model the shift from expert to outsider in their role as educators, approaching learning interaction—such as tutor education—in responsive and relational ways. Administrators as learners and boundary crossers should employ inquiry alongside expertise and provide transparency with affective work when reflecting on and revising their approaches to learning exchanges with tutors.

As with any research, this study has limitations. Given the vast scope of affective and relational work within learning interactions involving tutors and multilingual writers, the narrow focus of this study on four mediating factors was intentional. However, additional research and discussion is needed to adequately address issues of power and privilege associated with language, identity, and culture, including the reality that "achieving the desired peer collaborative relationship becomes a complex . . . task of undoing culturally taught behavior" (Blau et al. 28). The focus on influences and on the specific demographics for this action research study is not an attempt to reduce or oversimplify the complex nature of learning exchanges within tutorials. Despite its limited scope, this study offers additional insights into this ongoing, multifaceted work.

CONCLUSION

Understandably, this study invites additional research into interactions between tutors and multilingual writers and the affective and relational work involved in learning and moving between boundaries and systems. As Grimm suggests, "The tutoring situations that are not clear, not comfortable, not coherent in familiar ways are the ones that call for closer inspection" ("Attending" 18). Further research might examine how shifts in identity, roles, and relationships influence power dynamics within tutorials or how participants' perceptions of each other impact interactions. Research is needed on interactions between multilingual tutors and multilingual and monolingual writers. Subsequent studies may examine how roles and relationships shift when tutors and writers each have an explicit understanding of English at the sentence level or examine how shared knowledge might influence self-efficacy or session satisfaction. Additional studies may include how roles and relationships shift when tutors and writers each have an explicit understanding of English at the sentence level or examine how shared knowledge might influence self-efficacy or session satisfaction. Research is also needed on the experience of multilingual writers, their identities, and their roles, including how they might function as expert outsiders within sessions with monolingual tutors. Similarly, more insight is needed into the relational and affective work of writers and tutors in unpacking and understanding the challenges language learners experience within settings and systems that favor a single standard of academic English. On a very practical level, writing center scholars and practitioners must consider how the policies of individual writing centers—session length, use of multiple languages, attention to grammar, repeat visits, tutor education pedagogy, etc.—impact tutors' and multilingual writers' participation, ability to find common ground, use of validation, and confidence within sessions.

More than anything, this study provides another starting place for additional research related to the interactions between writing center tutors and multilingual writers, preferably interdisciplinary research that includes the perspective of multiple stakeholders and seeks to bridge theory and practice. Certainly, writing centers are crossroads and boundary spaces where "identity and the politics of negotiation and face are always present and require inventory and mapping" (Denny 28). This study adds to the mapping of learning interactions between writing tutors and multilingual writers, offering new perspectives into the roles and relationships possible and the affective work already present. Who we are, who we learn with, how we participate in learning, and how we map this work matters for structuring learning within tutorials and understanding our work as writing centers and learning communities.

WORKS CITED

Ahmed, Sara. *On Being Included: Racism and Diversity in Institutional Life*. Duke UP, 2012.

—. *The Cultural Politics of Emotion*. Routledge, 2004.

Akkerman, Sanne F., and Arthur Bakker. "Boundary Crossing and Boundary Objects." *Review of Educational Research*, vol. 81, no. 2, 2011, pp. 132–69.

Blau, Susan, et al. "Guilt-Free Tutoring: Rethinking How We Tutor Non-Native-English-Speaking Students." *The Writing Center Journal*, vol. 23, no. 1, 2002, pp. 23–44.

Blazer, Sarah. "Twenty-First Century Writing Center Staff Education: Teaching and Learning Towards Inclusive and Productive Everyday Practice." *The Writing Center Journal*, vol. 35, no. 1, 2015, pp.17–55.

Brennan, Teresa. *The Transmission of Affect.* Cornell UP, 2004.

Bromley, Pam, et al. "L2 Student Satisfaction in the Writing Center: A Cross-Institutional Study of L1 and L2 Students." *Praxis: A Writing Center Journal,* vol. 16, no. 1, 2018.

Calhoun Bell, Diana, and Sara Redington Elledge. "Dominance and Peer Tutoring Sessions with English Language Learners." *Learning Assistance Review,* vol. 13, no. 1, 2008, pp. 17–30.

Creswell, John W. *Educational Research: Planning, Conducting, and Evaluating Quantitative and Qualitative Research.* 5th ed., Pearson, 2015.

Denny, Harry C. *Facing the Center: Toward an Identity Politics of One-to-One Mentoring.* Utah State UP, 2010.

Eckstein, Grant. "Grammar Correction in the Writing Centre: Expectations and Experiences of Monolingual and Multilingual writers." *Canadian Modern Language Review,* vol. 72, no. 3, 2016, pp. 360–82.

Effinger Wilson, Nancy. "Stocking the Bodega: Towards a New Writing Center Paradigm." *Praxis: A Writing Center Journal,* vol. 10, no. 1, 2012.

Finkelstein, Stacey R., et al. "When Friends Exchange Negative Feedback." *Motivation and Emotion,* vol. 41, no. 1, 2017, pp. 69–83.

Green, Neisha-Anne S. "The Re-Education of Neisha-Anne S. Green: A Close Look at the Damaging Effects of 'A Standard Approach,' the Benefits of Code-Meshing, and the Role Allies Play in this Work." *Praxis: A Writing Center Journal,* vol. 14, no. 1, 2016.

Grimm, Nancy. "Attending to the Conceptual Change Potential of Writing Center Narratives." *The Writing Center Journal,* vol. 28, no. 1, 2008, pp. 3–21.

—. *Good Intentions: Writing Center Work for Postmodern Times.* Heinemann, 1999.

Gutiérrez, Kris D., et al. "Remediating Literacy: Culture, Difference, and Learning for Students from Nondominant Communities." *Review of Research in Education,* vol. 33, no. 1, 2009, pp. 212–45.

Hall, R. Mark. *Around the Texts of Writing Center Work: An Inquiry-Based Approach to Tutor Education.* UP of Colorado, 2017.

Harris, Muriel. "Talking in the Middle: Why Writers Need Writing Tutors." *College English,* vol. 57, no. 1, 1995, pp. 27–42.

Hyland, Ken, and Fiona Hyland. "Interpersonal Aspects of Response: Constructing and Interpreting Teacher Written Feedback." *Feedback in Second Language Writing: Contexts and Issues,* 2006, pp. 206–24.

Ivankova, Nataliya. *Mixed Methods Applications in Action Research: From Methods to Community Action*. SAGE Publications, Inc., 2014.

Kim, Eun-Young Julia. "'I Don't Understand What You're Saying!': Lessons from Three ESL Writing Tutorials." *Journal of Response to Writing*, vol. 1, no. 1, 2015, pp. 47–76.

Kolb, Alice Y., et al. "On Becoming an Experiential Educator: The Educator Role Profile." *Simulation and Gaming*, vol. 45, no. 2, 2014, pp. 204–34.

Lee, Cynthia. "Second Language Learners' Self-Perceived Roles and Participation in Face-to-Face English Writing Consultations." *System*, vol. 63, 2016, pp. 51–64.

Lunsford, Andrea A., and Lisa Ede. "Reflections on Contemporary Currents in Writing Center Work." *The Writing Center Journal*, vol. 31, no. 1, 2011, pp. 11–24.

Mackiewicz, Jo, and Isabelle Thompson. "Instruction, Cognitive Scaffolding, and Motivational Scaffolding in Writing Center Tutoring." *Composition Studies*, vol. 42, no. 1, 2014, pp. 54–78.

Nakamaru, Sarah. "Theory In/To Practice: A Tale of Two Multilingual Writers: A Case-Study Approach to Tutor Education." *The Writing Center Journal*, vol. 30, no. 2, 2010, pp. 100–23.

Nicklay, Jennifer. "Got Guilt? Consultant Guilt in the Writing Center Community." *The Writing Center Journal*, vol. 32, no. 1, 2012, pp. 14–27.

Nowacek, Rebecca S., and Bradley Hughes. "Threshold Concepts in the Writing Center: Scaffolding the Development of Tutor Expertise." *Naming What We Know: Threshold Concepts in Writing Studies*, edited by Linda Adler-Kassner and Elizabeth Wardle, Utah State UP, 2015, pp. 171–85.

Rafoth, Ben. *Multilingual Writers and Writing Centers*. UP of Colorado, 2015.

Schunk, Dale H., and Maria K. DiBenedetto. "Self-Efficacy: Education Aspects." *International Encyclopedia of the Social and Behavioral Sciences*, edited by James D. Wright, 2nd ed., vol. 21, Elsevier, 2015, pp. 515–21.

Severino, Carol. "Writing Centers as Linguistic Contact Zones and Borderlands." *The Writing Lab Newsletter*, vol. 19, no. 4, 1994, pp. 1–5.

Shouse, Eric. "Feeling, Emotion, Affect." *M/C Journal*, vol. 8, no. 6, 2005.

Thompson, Isabelle. "Scaffolding in the Writing Center: A Microanalysis of an Experienced Tutor's Verbal and Nonverbal Tutoring Strategies." *Written Communication*, vol. 26, no. 4, 2009, pp. 417–53.

Vygotsky, Lev Semenovich. *Mind in Society: The Development of Higher Psychological Processes*. Harvard UP, 1978.

Weigle, Sara Cushing, and Gayle L. Nelson. "Novice Tutors and their ESL Tutees: Three Case Studies of Tutor Roles and Perceptions of Tutorial Success." *Journal of Second Language Writing*, vol. 13, no. 3, 2004, pp. 203–25.

Wenger, Etienne. *Communities of Practice: Learning, Meaning, and Identity*. Cambridge UP, 1998.

—, et al. *Cultivating Communities of Practice: A Guide to Managing Knowledge*. Harvard Business Review Press, 2002.

8 "Can't We Just Stick to the Writing?": Empathy Narratives for Social Justice Tutor Training

Celeste Del Russo

Tutors assemble for the first session in a series of training around empathy and social justice work. The goal of the session, *Facilitating Difficult Tutoring Sessions*, is to prepare tutors to identify strategies they can use with students when engaging in topics they find emotionally taxing, politically charged, and generally . . . complicated. Halfway through the session, Alyssa raises her hand to speak.

"Can't we just stick to the writing? What if I don't want to debate feminism and the #metoo movement when I don't have the energy for that?"

A few tutors nod their heads, others squirm uncomfortably. After what seems like a long silence, another tutor, Leigh, raises her hand: "Sure, we can focus on organization and clarity and grammar, but I don't see how we can engage in social justice work if we just ignore sexist or racist ideas to persist."

This brief narrative illustrates two main areas of concern for this chapter. First, it demonstrates the challenges of implementing a social justice mission in the writing center, including the challenges of tutor investment. Second, it gestures to the emotional labor required by this important work. I *want* to answer the tutor's question, "Can't we just stick to the

147

writing?" with a resounding no: for so many of us who come to writing center work, it has always been about more than "just the writing." It is connecting with students, providing safe learning spaces, listening, valuing identities, and sharing compassion. However, understanding the range of our tutors' commitment and approaches to social justice are important if we are to truly implement these practices into our centers. This chapter explores empathy as an emotion at the core of writing center work and central to social justice tutor training. At its most basic definition, empathy is the ability to understand or relate to another person's experience. I describe our center's shift towards a social justice framework by way of integrating empathy into tutor training, and in doing so, this chapter expands the notion of empathy to demonstrate how this emotion can be honed in tutor training and practiced as a skill in application, especially for centers looking towards socially just futures.

Before I make a case for empathy training as a way *towards* deepening social justice work in the center, I want to consider the shift towards social justice in writing centers. To do that, I turn to the resounding presence of centers that directly take on social justice work. These leaders acknowledge historical and current inequities in higher education (KU Writing Center), embrace language difference and value the unique experiences of writers from across learning differences (Rowan University), define and discuss social justice issues in the context of student writing (Teaching and Learning), and foster humanity overall (Undergraduate Writing Center). Centers such as these have taken a necessary shift towards what Laura Greenfield notes as a new paradigm for writing centers (4–5). In our scholarship, we envision a new role for anti-racism and social justice work in the center, mainly by bringing race, power, and identity to the forefront of tutor education and providing practical application of anti-racist pedagogy in writing center tutor training (Aikens; García 45; Blazer 19). Specifically, Romeo García positions tutors as "theorists of race and racism" (38), imagining them as rhetoricians "working towards a transdisciplinary approach in putting race and power into dialogue" both in and beyond the center (50). Finally, our conference themes bring directors and tutors together to share research, writing experiences, tutoring strategies, and training that focuses on activism in the center, including the 2018 article, "Writing Centers and Activism," and the 2020 article, "Decolonizing Writing Center Practices," by The Mid-Atlantic Writing Centers Association, MAWCA. Given these moves towards social justice, it is clear that there is simply so much more to writing centers than "just the writing."

Our center had also made this turn beginning in 2016, bringing social justice to the core of our tutor training. Since then, our staff has co-developed and facilitated workshops on topics such as "The Meaning of Social Justice," "Valuing Language Diversity," and "Facilitating Difficult Dialogues," where we tackle topics related to privilege, racism, and ableism. These workshops have framed our writing center work as being motivated by our social justice vision. Since then, our staff has co-developed and facilitated workshops on topics such as "The Meaning of Social Justice," "Valuing Language Diversity," and "Facilitating Difficult Dialogues," where we tackle privilege, racism, and ableism, framing our writing center work in literacy and language as social justice issues. We worked collaboratively on social justice statements for our writing center. Still, tutors struggled with ways to negotiate what social justice looked like in their practice and were uncertain whether or not it was their job to engage in conversations with students in order to "make them woke" or push them to "acknowledge their privilege," especially when these conversations could be emotionally exhausting.

To try to understand why tutors felt limited in practicing social justice in the center, and to educate myself on how I might better prepare tutors, I returned to my own instincts about the qualities that make an excellent tutor. I continuously came back to the idea that being a strong tutor was always so much more than focusing on or being "just about the writing." Yes, strong tutors are strong writers, rhetorically adaptable, and have a tendency towards mentoring and guiding students, but demonstrating empathy has always been at the top of my list. I end every training session with my tutors by reminding them that having empathy and understanding for their student writers goes a long way in establishing trusting relationships. When tutors share challenging experiences with students and they just cannot seem to connect, I ask them to consider these questions: What life experiences inform a student writer's perspective or ideology? What literacy experiences shape their ideas about their writerly identities? How might you empathize—or not—with these experiences? I believe this line of questioning can lead to deeper connections between tutors and student writers, and I wonder, then, if perhaps tapping into tutors' notions of empathy might lead to deeper understandings of how they engage in social justice writing center work.

I understood that tutor education that recognized and validated empathy demanded reflection. If our goal was to develop a more empathetic writing center space around a social justice mission, we would need to consider empathy as a reflective practice. To this end, I developed a reflective journaling assignment for tutors around empathy and social justice. Drawing from the wealth of tutor education scholarship available to us as writing center scholars and administrators, we understand that engaging tutors in this type of meaningful reflection and journaling activity is essential in honing practice. This is certainly true from the point of view of both empathy scholars (Lape 5; Oweidat and McDermott) and social justice scholars (García 50), who call for centering these respective issues in tutor education, extending tutor education in empathy or diversity beyond special topics modules and into the daily lives of tutors through journaling and reflection activities.

Exploring the affective domain of tutoring writing is useful in explaining how empathy can be used to understand tutors' struggles with social justice work. Scholars in this collection, such as Anna Rita Napoleone, note centers must take into consideration the affective dimensions of the literacy work we ask tutors to do. In "Mixed Emotions and Blended Classed Positions: Circulating Affect in the Writing Center," she considers how emotions inform relationships, reflect tensions, and are felt through power structures. Emotions' ability to inform relationships and expose power dynamics is the outcome of social justice work. Paying attention to the affective domain and how it informs tutoring practices is also central to honing empathy in one's practice. The ability to relate to one another's feelings or experiences—to seek out and foster empathy—takes practice and negotiation, and in the process, poses challenges. In my experience in working with some of my most self-described "woke" tutors, they are continually challenged by the emotional work involved and have experienced what Luke Iantorno might describe as performing positivity and avoiding other negative responses that might lead to emotional exhaustion. Still, as the pieces in this edited collection suggest, exploring emotions in the writing center—as Lauren Brentnell, Elise Dixon, and Rachel Robinson indicate—can actually afford us with new ways to resist grand narratives that favor neutral emotions. Along with others in this collection, this chapter seeks to explore how using narratives to identify and hone emotions, such as empathy, can become beneficial to building sustainable and socially just practices in the writing center.

What Is Critical Empathy?

Empathy scholars have conducted grounded research, identifying the opportunities for connection and relationship-building often disguised in moments of affect (Haen 4) and for the integration of frameworks of empathy into tutor training (Lape 3). Noreen Lape notes, "an empathetic writing center may be the best place to cultivate the understanding, connection, and agency writers—and tutors—need to grow" (6). Honing empathy can result in the kind of connection and rapport building necessary to engage students in activities that will ultimately support their writing goals. Rapport and trust, two byproducts of empathy, are necessary if tutors and students are to grow together and address the types of support student writers need in visiting the center. An empathetic writing center is attentive to students' needs and reasons for struggling—or not struggling—with writing, acknowledges these challenges and successes as part of a wider web of literacy and writing experiences, and pairs students and tutors with the common goal of building trust and rapport. Building an empathic writing center can help in speaking back to damaging narratives about student writers who might be labeled in problematic ways. For example, a tutor might be distressed about a student who comes in repeatedly having not made changes between drafts. The tutor might easily dismiss their actions as laziness—where the student wants the tutor to write the paper for them—when in fact there could be a multitude of reasons that student struggles to write independently. While a prescriptive center might use a one-size-fits-all approach to tutoring, an empathic center trains tutors to ask questions, finds commonalities, and listen to different experiences that shape a student's ideas about writing. An empathic center then uses that knowledge to develop a course of action for growth. In this case, understanding the roots of a student's writing anxiety can help tutors develop scaffolding activities, make better use of time in the center, and set goals for writing independently. An empathic writing center creates space for this growth.

The concept of critical empathy expands on traditional notions of empathy by acknowledging empathy as a rhetorical construct, a tool that can be harnessed during tutoring sessions to develop a critical consciousness. Critical empathy acknowledges empathy as a shifting process of inquiry and understanding. Eric Leake underscores the rhetorical nature of critical empathy:

Teaching empathy as rhetoric has broad application as a suitable means of more closely examining the personal, social, and rhetorical functions of reason, emotions, and judgments. Empathy can be a means of invention, a heuristic, a way of considering audience and situation, an instrument of revision, and a tool for critical analysis. Teaching empathy as rhetoric attunes us to all of its possible uses and liabilities as a means of persuasion. (Leake para 12)

For centers embarking on social justice tutor education, honing critical empathy as a rhetorical construct can result in acknowledging commonalities and differences, potentially opening up space in tutoring sessions for students and tutors to question, debate, and negotiate in productive ways. Nancy Effinger Wilson and Keri Fitzgerald draw from empathy to coin the term "empathic intellectuals," noting that growing empathic intellectuals is directly connected to tutors' exposure to diverse populations, opinions, and backgrounds, wherein tutors recognize and reflect on their own bias and prejudice (13). Critical empathy moves beyond lay definitions of empathy as understanding or relating to another's point of view. Rather, critical empathy is a negotiation, and honing critical empathy is uncomfortable and challenging. It provides opportunities for tutors to consider a range of perspectives, to question assumptions—their own and others—and to evolve their understanding beyond one-dimensional thinking (Oweidat and McDermott). In this way, growth is measured beyond the capacity of teaching writing skills or strategies by exploring critical frameworks for understanding literacy and writing and honing critical thinking.

Within this framework, I view empathy as a core emotion for social justice training. I also see empathy as a rhetorical tool tutors can use when engaging in social justice work. In *Radical Writing Center Praxis: A Paradigm for Ethical Political Engagement*, Greenfield equates empathy with "resonance," writing, "resonance is the locus of connection, the moment of empathy felt deep in the body by the listener and shared with the storyteller" (144). Here, Greenfield's words help to advance my ideas about empathy and social justice work in two ways: invoking empathy as a narrative or story that can be shared and felt, thus demonstrating an acknowledgement of a desire to uncover various narratives or positionalities; and invoking empathy and its ability to craft a narrative in relationship with audience, purpose, and text, thus demonstrating how empathy is a negotiation and a conversation framed by interactions with other individuals who possess a range of differing experiences. Collectively, these studies complicate definitions of empathy to include critical frameworks necessary for countering institutionalized racism, sexism, bias, and homophobia. They also provide a strong framework for empathy training in connection to social justice. When combined with social justice work, critical empathy becomes a more dynamic characteristic that can be taught and practiced in relation to privilege, something that tutors learn and acknowledge through their training.

Sometimes these lessons are messy. One day in the center, a tutor, named Erica, was working with a student on a paper for a creative non-fiction class. The student used the word "ratchet" to describe an interaction she had with a work colleague. The tutor, trying to understand what the word "ratchet" meant in this context, asked the student to explain. The student said, "I guess I mean ratchet like 'ghetto' and 'Black.'" The tutor paused, taken aback, and not knowing how to react in that moment, responded that the student might want to revise her word choice as "ratchet" might not be the best choice, rhetorically, for her audience.

Nearby, a second tutor, named Rhea, waiting for her shift to start, overheard this interaction and felt immediately unsafe and unsettled. She came to me later in the day to share what she had heard and expressed that she would like the opportunity to meet with this student to talk to her about the problematic use of the terms "ghetto" and "ratchet." She used this opportunity to share her reaction as a Black woman overhearing this conversation. The next day, we invited the student into my office, where Rhea carefully outlined that she felt the need to address the racist language she overheard and that she wanted the student to know her words were harmful and perpetuated negative stereotypes of Black women. The student apologized, acknowledging that the words she used were hurtful and that she had heard others speaking in these terms, not realizing their impact. Rhea noted to me later, as an aside, that she was not really looking for an apology, and though she was doubtful that the student felt any remorse, she felt it was imperative that she make the student aware that she would not tolerate her language.

This example demonstrates the emotional energy required in striving for a socially-just writing center. First, in not responding to the racist undertones of the student's word choice, Erica inadvertently placed the burden to speak up on her colleague, a Black tutor. While Erica attempted to address the word choice as not the best rhetorical fit, she did not address the harmful impact of racially charged terms used in the paper.

Second, Rhea invested emotional energy in preparing her response and in anticipating the student's reaction. Building a socially-just writing center means being attentive not only to how we react to -isms in student writing but also being supportive and proactive in speaking out on behalf of our colleagues and staff. It means doing this often and repeatedly.

Attuning to critical empathy alters relationships within social justice tutor training. Tutors may struggle, as in the opening narrative, with the question of "do I practice activism in the center? And if so, *how*?" Further, Greenfield continues: "writing can't be an ethical end goal and neither can the ability to write well when we do not articulate the work such writing and writers do in the world" (87). Yet, that struggle becomes lessened when tutors understand that conversations around racism, sexism, and other institutional -isms are very much a choice made in the moment of each individual tutoring session. Equipping tutors with the tools they need to engage in these conversations—providing training around social justice and empathy—can empower tutors to make choices to answer this call, instead of leaving them feeling unprepared or somehow failing to not engage students critically. This next section shares a model for tutor training with critical empathy at the center.

TRAININGS FOR SOCIAL JUSTICE AND CRITICAL EMPATHY

> *I don't think this is something we need to label ourselves [a social justice mission] as we already have a department that works with Social Justice on campus. We should offer to be a support system and a partnership, but other than that, it becomes too complicated. Our students should have one centralized place to go if something should occur, but they should know that our writing center is a safe place where they can be comfortable and honest, and that we can help be a liaison for them to our social justice office.*

> —Tutor reflection

The sentiment that our job is not to "do" social justice work—shared in one of our earliest workshops, "The Meaning of Social Justice"—highlights the idea that social justice work is contained on our campuses, confined to the offices of a specific department with this particular mission. It is a sentiment held by some of our tutors. Our center would achieve our social justice mission through cross-campus, collaborative social justice training that centralized a framework of empathy. My goal in developing social justice modules was to draw from the aforementioned scholars in order to cultivate a culture of critical empathy in the writing center by expanding our center's definition of empathy as contextual—with the understanding that critical empathy cultivates the foundation for social justice work in the center and thus offers opportunities for tutors to better engage and identify with social justice work.

Through a combination of specialized workshops and reflective empathy narratives, our training for social justice and critical empathy sought to meet the following objectives:

- Introduce tutors to concepts such as privilege and institutional racism; socioeconomic factors as barriers to higher education; and how writing is impacted by identity.
- Engage tutors already experienced in social justice work and experts on campus in providing workshops and group activities to explore these concepts.
- Provide a space for tutors to explore concepts of multi-partiality and cultural humility, major components of empathy, in relation to their roles as writing center tutors.
- Identify tutors' working definitions of empathy and expand tutors' definitions of critical empathy through a rhetorical framework.
- Provide a space for exploring the agentive potential of empathy in alignment with social justice work.
- Listen and acknowledge all the ways that learning occurs and respect each individual's approach. This means making sure that we listen and actually hear our student writers and respect their experience.

Over the course of the first year we brought empathy into our social justice training, we led sessions including topics such as: "The Meaning of Social Justice," "Facilitating Difficult Dialogues," "Engaging Mindfulness in Tutoring Writing," "Neurodiversity: Tutoring Writers Across Ability," and "Language Diversity as Asset." These sessions were facilitated by myself, experienced tutors, and in collaboration with campus offices designated as experts in their respective areas. These included the Office of Social Justice and Conflict Resolution, Counseling and Psychological Services, and the Academic Success Center. In each session, our staff learned the basic guidelines for participating in discussion respectfully and with their own identities in mind; engaged in scenario building and response; and practiced techniques for empathetic listening, respecting, and working with students across difference.

Empathy Narratives. I was curious to understand how tutors were defining empathy, how they were reflecting on and responding to the social justice workshops and training that were the core of our mission, and how they were seeing connections between empathy and social justice. To this end, I invited interested tutors to participate in a thirteen weeklong journaling activity to reflect on their own understanding of empathy and social justice. Ten tutors volunteered and were asked to write empathy narratives drawing from the following, open-ended prompts: How do you define empathy in terms of your role as a tutor? What does it look like to practice empathy in a session? What does your activism or social justice work look like in the writing center?

These questions were purposely left open so tutors could draw from their weekly experiences of tutoring in connection with their journal responses. Tutors were asked to journal once a week, responding to any one or as many of the questions they felt drawn to. The impetus for the empathy narratives was to extend the discussion and make connections between the training received in the fall semester and the role of empathy in social justice work in the center—whether it be through their tutoring practices or how empathy informed their role as tutors beyond the center. The following section addresses some of the common themes that emerged in both the empathy narratives and the focus group in terms of how tutors defined empathy, related empathy to social justice, and understood activism as tutors.

SHARING EMPATHY NARRATIVES: EXPANDING TOOLS FOR SOCIAL JUSTICE WORK

Tutor narratives elicited a range of responses to their understanding of empathy and the practice of honing critical empathy. I share themes emerging in tutors' narratives as they reflect on their evolving understanding of empathy and social justice work resulting from their training. Evolving definitions emerged as tutors honed their practice of critical empathy by exploring connections between *critical empathy and identity*, *critical empathy and allyship*, and *critical empathy and agency*.

Critical Empathy and Identity. In their empathy narratives, tutors drew from concepts such as privilege, cultural capital, and socioeconomic status to reflect on how their own positionalities impacted their writing and ability to connect, or not connect, with the student writers they tutor. One tutor writes:

> I think my identity as a bisexual woman allows be to speak to issues of gender and LGBT+ fairly confidently. However, I am also white, neurotypical, and from an upper middle-class family. Soon after I began tutoring, I realized how I was assuming a base knowledge and perspective because of those attributes. I have been working these past couple of years to be aware of these projections and not assume anything of my clients (while not underestimating either). Thinking about how my identity can help me empathize but also acknowledge difference in the same session.

Here, practicing empathy means acknowledging commonalities and valuing difference. This goes beyond a surface definition of empathy, where the inclination is to search for common ground, dismissing the potential to see difference as a learning opportunity. This tutor's observation, connected to ideas around valuing difference in life experiences, demonstrates a more nuanced idea of empathy, infused with a social justice framework. Also noted is a deeper awareness of empathy as "perspective," stating that one quality of empathy is being able to see circumstances through another's point of view but also recognizing that perspective is informed by our own privilege.

Similarly, the following tutor addresses "mindset," a term we unpacked in our training for social justice and honing critical empathy. Exploring mindset is to name and unpack the identities and backgrounds that might impact learning and tutoring. To explore mindset, tutors were asked to reflect on questions such as: what are my social and personal identities? How might these identities impact my mindset when working with student writers? For tutors who identify as white and heteronormative, exploring mindset might work to decentralize their experiences and make space for alternative perspectives. In the following narrative, a tutor works through a topic addressed in our sessions around working-class mindsets and how this mindset impacts students' experiences of higher education.

> I am a white, cisgendered, able and neurotypical woman. I also come from a background where I worked outside a lot as a child with/for my dad building things, gardening, maintaining the

house/yard. I learned what hard work is, which I translated to working hard through school. I try and keep a working-class mindset when I am aware that I have a mindset that I'm applying so that I am not complacent with what I have or what I am doing. I want to make sure that I am valuing what I'm doing so that I can later value what I have done to get where I am.

This narrative demonstrates how tutors practiced critical empathy by acknowledging how learning occurs and respecting individuals' approaches. By identifying and unpacking her own working-class mindset—"hard work gets the job done"—the tutor above outlines goals associated with this mindset, such as working hard and non-complacency. However, focusing social justice tutor training around inequities in higher education for underrepresented student groups provides this tutor with the ability to also name and acknowledge her privilege, despite having a working-class mindset. Acknowledging their privilege allows this tutor to name how their identities might impact their tutoring. In a follow up discussion with this tutor, she is pressed by her colleagues to unpack the working-class narrative of "hard work pays off" to understand that this is not always the case for minoritized students in higher education. Had she not undergone the type of reflection on questions around her identity, privilege, and mindset, she might not have understood that so well. Tutors who acknowledge their own privilege and their own positionalities can address how their identities might affect the way they tutor and practice critical empathy and social justice in the center.

Critical Empathy and Allyship. While tutors described empathy as "the ability to put yourself in someone else's shoes, emotionally" or as "being able to understand and feel what another person is feeling," tutors' narratives noted expanded definitions that included the way lived experiences both fostered and complicated their own ability to connect with others. Complicating the concept of empathy was the idea of "allyship" and what it meant to be an ally to minoritized populations who visited the center, such as first-generation students, multilingual students, LGBTQ+ students, or POC. A challenge for our staff—both white, heteronormative staff and minoritized staff—was that they felt ill-equipped to address systemic issues related to racism, homophobia, and other discriminations as they appeared in the writing center or in student writing. One self-identified, cisgendered, white woman tutor wrote that her privilege by race and sexual orientation meant that she "needs to work to present myself as an ally so that those with different identities feel safe and can be open and welcome" but did not feel confident in how to accomplish this by means other than "being kind, providing affirmations, and paying attention to voice intonation or body language." A second tutor expanding on this unsurety wrote,

> I feel that as a middle-class, white female I used to feel like I did not have the expertise or life experience to discuss race, religion, class, etc. So, empathy to me is to listen and to see circumstances through another's perspective, especially if you have experienced similar circumstances as another person. It is to truly understand how another person views things and accept that, without projecting your own ideas about what they should do or feel onto them. I express connection in a way that makes the other person feel understood.

This tutor understood the value of exploring aspects of identities that have commonalities and recognized these similarities can help in bonding, understanding, and communicating, perhaps creating a space for allyship. However, as noted in our social justice training, creating space is only the first step towards allyship. LGBTQ+ and POC tutors on our staff expressed that while they often felt empowered to address common microaggressions and stereotypes as they occur during sessions, they also experienced emotional exhaustion. The message from our LGBTQ+ and POC tutors was that they cannot do this work alone. The emotional impact on minoritized groups who must consistently educate white people about systemic racism, homophobia, and other issues, was a topic we addressed with the message that minoritized groups and the call from our LGBTQ+ and POC staff being "we can't do this work alone."

Through a combination of social justice training around allyship and a reflection on critical empathy, tutors can begin to identify ways to do this work. Critical empathy is a tool for advancing perspective and sharing strategies for working with student writers in relation to varying beliefs, identities, and experiences. Practicing strategies for intergroup dialogue include setting intentions, voicing, reflecting, and suspending judgement. Some guiding questions for this module included: *How do I respond when I'm activated? Where are my discomforts? What are my strengths?* Tutors can begin to identify dialogue as a transformational tool for generating new knowledges and for supporting one another's approaches to social justice work. These strategies are important for practicing empathy in tutoring sessions, as in the following narrative, where these strategies are reflected upon:

> I try to be unbiased in my tutoring to help students craft their own argument and opinion. If it leans toward the offensive side I would begin by asking them questions about their viewpoint and purpose of writing, so I know if what they're trying to communicate lines up, so I know if I'm taking something out of proportion just cause I don't agree with it. If they truly are being offensive then I would try to present another viewpoint to shift how they understand and present their argument, and if needed, blatantly say that their words may come across offensive, or that it does for me as a reader, and explain why.

This narrative also demonstrates how one tutor might grapple with issues of bias and disagreement during a session. When the tutor does not make assumptions about a student's opinion, preferring to ask questions to find deeper connections and not assume the student is intentionally being offensive, they open a line of questioning that provides space for voicing opinions and positionalities. The tutor's ability to avoid assumptions also speaks to honing critical empathy to explore multi-partiality and cultural humility—both for tutors and student writers. In establishing a line of inquiry into the student's point of view, the tutor acknowledges that their opinion is only one of many, and rather than providing feedback that ignores the student's viewpoints, the tutor follows a line of inquiry to develop the student's ideas and come to an understanding. Additionally, in connecting to and situating writing within the rhetorical context of the argument, the tutor addresses bias and disagreement in terms of audience and purpose. The connection here between social justice and empathy is that the tutor is acknowledging their own bias and trying to understand where the student is coming from. Trying to understand and empathize with different viewpoints and opening lines of inquiry suggests that tutors and student writers explore topics together and find ways to treat each other as respectfully as possible, while not limiting students' right to speak their views. It also opens space for discussion to debate topics and explore perspectives from multiple angles.

Critical Empathy and Agency. A third theme emerging from the narratives is that of the agentive potential that honing critical empathy can have when aligned with social justice work. In the following narratives, tutors define empathy in relation to social justice in the writing center, finding that honing critical empathy has assisted them in identifying an agentive potential for both themselves and student writers. In these narratives, tutors identify institutional challenges students face when writing for academic audiences, naming challenges for students of color, academic racism around Standard American English, and limitations for students with disabilities. These tutors were open to the idea of bringing social justice to the forefront of tutoring sessions:

> In sessions, I think it's being open to discussing the social justice issues that come up during sessions. This might be writing related, such as addressing language diversity or the lack thereof in higher education. It's also willing to discuss social justice topics that come up in the content of their writing, as comp classes often have students tackle topics like oppression, representation, or other social issues. I think it's also about offering programs and services that support students of marginalized identities. We are a place that can offer support when traditional higher education fails students.

For some tutors, writing centers were a natural space for countering systemic racism, sexism, and inequity. Tutors identified moments when doing so was possible in a session and positioned the writing center as a space for this work to happen on campus. To amplify the center's role in social justice, several tutors articulated the potential for critical empathy to help students *and* tutors engage in a dialogue to address systemic -isms and issues together. For example, one tutor stated, "I believe that writing centers should work to break down barriers and educate people about their biases while we work to edit papers." The narratives here provide a space for tutors to reflect on and think about these roles for the writing center and negotiate what they believe their position to be when it comes to social justice. Throughout, tutors noted the agentive potential for the center to advocate for student writers and to help students advocate for themselves.

Agency was also represented by acknowledging the different ways students approach writing tasks and the tutors' goal of best amplifying students' "voices" or "visions" of their projects. Responding to students where they are in the writing, with their topic and with their frustrations, became an important component of critical empathy and social justice work. Tutors saw their goal as to remind student writers that what they have to say matters, or as a tutor describes, "to give them back their voice that may have been undercut in other areas of their lives." Having discussions about political and social issues and being a resource for marginalized students were two ways tutors felt they might encourage students to step into and use their identities for the betterment of society, as in this tutor narrative:

> Social justice in the writing center starts with listening rhetorically, that is openly and with the knowledge that there are gender, racial, and social differences between tutors and tutees that impact how we understand the world and communicate. Next, tutors can work collaboratively to help tutees craft their message and find their authentic voice so that their voice can be heard outside of the session, outside of the paper.

Overall, writing empathy narratives and honing critical empathy helped tutors infuse a new level of engagement around their roles as tutors towards an agentive potential. Tutors demonstrated their ability to practice empathy in ways that were meaningful to them, their tutoring styles, their identities, and their opinions about writing centers' roles in social justice.

As a whole, the above empathy narratives suggest a more nuanced understanding of empathy that ranges in definition from an emotional capacity to understanding another's point of view, to critical empathy, to disruption. Returning to the objectives for the center's social justice and critical empathy tutor training, we can begin to see how these narratives show tutors reaching towards an empathetic and socially-just responsive writing center space. By incorporating notions of privilege, institutional racism, cultural humility, and identity into their tutoring reflections, and by invoking critical empathy as a rhetorical strategy for engaging in activism and social justice work, tutors note an awareness of the agentive potential for this work in the center. This is a significant shift in the ethos of our center towards a more empathetic space.

What Does It Mean to "Stick to the Writing?"

What does it really mean, then, when tutors ask, "Can't we just stick to the writing?"

On the surface, "sticking to the writing" indicates an avoidance of confrontation or emotion during tutoring sessions. Sticking to the writing suggests focusing on organization, structure, a strong thesis, grammar, and syntax over disruption.

However, as demonstrated in the empathy narratives, "sticking to the writing" can have a more expansive definition. One end goal of our training and our empathy narratives was that we worked towards expanding tools for engaging in social justice work, Conversations around critical empathy helped us do that. In our writing center, there has been an important shift in the narrative around what it means to stick to the writing. Now, sticking to the writing means examining bias and acknowledging identity and past experiences with writing. Without key training around social justice issues, tutors would not have the language or ability to navigate how language and literacy are politicized, socialized, and embedded in one's lived experiences and realities. Sticking to the writing now also means understanding individuals' backgrounds with literacy and learning and how that impacts their experience of writing in college. Addressing the rhetorical aspects of one's argument is "stick[ing] to the writing" by invoking audience awareness as a way for student writers to see how their arguments might be perceived by others. Several tutors noted how they would "turn attention to the audience" or "check for reading comprehension or interpretation" to begin seeing how these strategies could be perceived as moments of agency to intervene and open dialogue, address bias, and practice activism in the session.

"Sticking to the writing" could also mean drawing from lessons learned in sessions on cultural humility and multi-partiality, where tutors acknowledged that changing everyone's mind or opinion was not the end goal of a session. In these cases, practicing critical empathy and exploring perspectives in sessions looked more like negotiation or dialogue. The narratives suggest that training for social justice by way of critical empathy has been successful in helping our tutors bridge the gap between the desire for social justice and participating in social justice in a way that aligns with their individual identities, tutoring styles, and experiences. The deep dive into social justice work takes patience and prioritizes empathy—empathy for our student writers but also for our tutors. Critical empathy work in the center has the potential to generate narratives that celebrate and respect tutors' individual approaches and emotions surrounding social justice work. As a staff, they feel empowered by the variety of ways to be social justice-forward, understanding their roles as dynamic, ranging, and dependent on one's identity, tutoring style, and beliefs.

Whether tutors identify as agents for student voices, guides in helping students make writing choices, allies in confronting racism and calling out deficit discourse, or mentors in checking privilege, I suggest a nuanced framing of critical empathy and social justice work in writing centers that accounts for the positionalities our tutors inhabit across several factors such as privilege, identity, style, and emotional intelligence. In their narratives and responses to tutor training, tutors demonstrate some shared terminology for social justice work and understand critical empathy and activism work as fluid and rhetorical. They understand the ways their own identities impact their tutoring and are able to articulate this through empathy narratives. Tutors participate in activism in the center in relation to their own personal conceptions of their tutor roles. Tutors also acknowledge that they respect the range of approaches to activism exhibited by their colleagues. If we, as directors, are to continue to provide open dialogues for social justice missions in our centers, we need to know where our tutors are in terms of their definitions of critical empathy and their opinions on the role of activism. We need to provide spaces for tutors to address their concerns and opinions on social justice work and reflect on ways they "do" activism in the center. Training that allows for a discussion around the varied approaches to social justice work and the center's institutional role can assist tutors in making their way towards engaging in activism. Further explorations of training that place critical empathy at the center of social justice training can provide insight into centers as they shift towards more socially-just centers.

Works Cited

Aikens, Kristina. "Prioritizing Antiracism in Writing Tutor Education." *How We Teach Writing Tutors: A WLN Digital Edited Collection*, edited by Karen Johnson and Ted Roggenbuck, 2019.

Blazer, Sarah. "Twenty-First Century Writing Center Staff Education: Teaching and Learning Towards Inclusive and Productive Everyday Practice." *The Writing Center Journal*, vol. 35, no. 1, 2015, pp. 17–55.

Effinger Wilson, Nancy, and Keri Fitzgerald. "Empathic Tutoring in the Third Space." *The Writing Lab Newsletter*, vol. 36, no. 9–10, 2012, pp. 11–13.

García, Romeo. "Unmaking Gringo-Centers." *The Writing Center Journal*, vol. 36, no. 1, 2017, pp. 29–60.

Greenfield, Laura. *Radical Writing Center Praxis: A Paradigm for Ethical Political Engagement.* Utah State UP, 2019.

Haen, Mike. "The Affective Dimension of Writing Center Talk: Insights from Conversation Analysis." *WLN: A Journal of Writing Center Scholarship*, vol. 42, no. 9–10, 2018, pp. 2–9.

KU Writing Center. "KU Writing Center Mission and Diversity Statements." *The University of Kansas*, writing.ku.edu/mission-diversity-statements.

Lape, Noreen. "Training Tutors in Emotional Intelligence: Toward a Pedagogy of Empathy." *The Writing Lab Newsletter*, vol. 33, no. 2, 2008, pp. 1–6.

Leake, Eric. "Writing Pedagogies of Empathy: As Rhetoric and Disposition." *Composition Forum*, vol. 34, 2016.

MAWCA. "Call for Proposals: Writing Centers and Activism: Uncovering Embedded Narratives." *The Mid-Atlantic Writing Center Association*, mawca.org/2018callforproposals/.

—. "Call for Proposals: Decolonizing Writing Center Practice: A New Vision for a New Decade." *The Mid-Atlantic Writing Center Association*, mawca.org/2020-cfp/.

Oweidat, Lena, and Lydia McDermott. "Neither Brave nor Safe: Interventions in Empathy for Tutor Training." *The Peer Review*, vol. 1, no. 2, 2017.

Rowan University Writing Center. "About the Writing Center." *Rowan University*, www.rowanwritingcenter.com/about-us.html.

Teaching and Learning Center. "Inclusion and Anti-Racism." *University of Washington-Tacoma*, www.tacoma.uw.edu/tlc/our-mission.

Undergraduate Writing Center. "Mission and History." *University of Vermont*, www.uvm.edu/undergradwriting/mission-history.

9 Crybabies in the Writing Center: Storying Affect and Emotion

Lauren Brentnell, Elise Dixon, and Rachel Robinson

Because academics are trained to be intellectuals, we often struggle when talking about feelings. Crying is an embodied response to our experiences, and physical bodies are generally ignored in the academy in favor of the mind. Indeed, "as a trigger for meaning making that is rooted so completely in the body, embodied response is barely legitimated in academia" but is often "a driving force behind much scholarly activity" (Knoblauch 54). For instance, while our academic interests are often embodied—in our excitement around them or in our embodied positionalities that motivate our endeavors—we frequently see those interests as solely intellectual. Writing centers, as academic and often social justice-oriented spaces, hold the trappings of similar complicated relationships to the body, and therefore, also hold tears. *Client* tears—theorized in writing center scholarship—are often triggered by, or are a driving force for, writing (Lape; Gillespie and Lerner; Ryan and Zimmerelli). In this collection, Genie Giaimo outlines the many ways that writing center consultants and administrators are at the edges of our emotional labor and wellness. For many academics, present at those edges of emotional labor and wellness are tears. Yet, in writing center lore and practice, crying is an activity we only whisper about, if we talk about it at all.

In this chapter, we argue for cultivating writing center spaces where emotional vulnerability is supported and crying is made viable. We advocate for those in writing centers to become crybabies. Though the term "crybabies" is often used negatively, we use it specifically to focus on the physical and embodied act of crying. Instead of simply advocating for the visibility of tears—*crying*, the verb—we focus on the crybaby—*crier*, the noun. The act of crying is important, but by focusing on the crybaby, we're centering *people* as well as the act. Judith Nelson argues that any theory of crying as an overwhelming response must account for both its emotionality and physicality (11). Similarly, Jeffrey Kottler calls for scholars to recognize the multiplicity of factors that lead to crying, including emotions but also socialization, situation, positionality, and interpersonal affect (83). We view crybabies in the writing center through a complex lens that accounts for the emotions that cause people to cry, the bodily response of crying itself, and the reaction that crying causes in others. For our purposes, crybabies are people in writing centers who physically shed tears. Understanding that "tears demand a reaction" (Lutz 19), we wish to reclaim this term from its negative connotations of whiners and complainers and rebrand it to focus on the physical act of crying.

Certain types of vulnerability, like crying, may be useful for rethinking emotional practices in the writing center. For example, crying—especially when enacted by a consultant—may serve as a learning moment in which beneficial relationships are established. Crying can offer opportunities to explore our subjective and affective[1] experiences in the center as a resistance to grand narratives and lore about consultant emotional neutrality. Through telling our stories, we hope to create spaces where writing center scholars and consultants can see the value of emotions as ever-present parts of writing center work.

We want to make space for crybabies in the writing center while thinking through the complexities that crying may present. In the following section, Rachel discusses writing center lore and grand narratives surrounding displays of emotion and crying, including how we respond to and interact with criers. She also shares her own story of being a crybaby in the writing center, asking us to consider what it would be like to construct a space that values "breaking down." Next, Elise considers the complexity of white women's tears and how they complicate our calls for open crying in the writing center. While doing so, she questions the power dynamics of crying and whether tears are genuine, violent, or both. Finally, Lauren concludes by asking what we can do with crying in the writing center and whether tears can become a means for us to act

---

1. Affect serves as a collective, socio-political umbrella term to describe emotional states; emotions are temporary, personal affects.

towards social justice, create community, or make our writing processes visible. We close with a call to consider crying as part of—and not separate from—writing center work and provide further recommendations for what administrators and consultants can do to encourage and respond to crybabies in the writing center.

(Why) Do People Cry in the Writing Center?

Part of the grand narrative of writing centers is that they operate differently than other academic spaces—they exist to be spaces outside traditional classroom models where writers have control. In writing center lore, centers are supposedly more comfortable for all students, more welcoming for all types of writers, more willing to challenge academic notions of "standard English," and more open to listening—all while existing on the margins of academia (Grutsch McKinney).

Because they shift away from traditional classroom hierarchies, writing centers are often marked as spaces where students can be their whole selves, including their emotional selves (Blitz and Hurlbert). However, many scholars have *also* challenged writing centers' views of themselves as writing utopias (Denny; Green; Grutsch McKinney)—including whether they are spaces where writers feel comfortable being emotional. While there is some truth in our narratives, "the effect of the writing center grand narrative can be a sort of collective tunnel vision" (Grutsch McKinney 5). Grutsch McKinney argues that this tunnel vision can cause writing centers to miss seeing opportunities for evolving (5–6). I, Rachel, argue that part of this evolution away from seeing centers as utopic could involve embracing embodied discomfort, like crying, in writing centers.

Why does crying make us uncomfortable? Perhaps because as intellectuals, bodies sometimes make academics uncomfortable, and crying in public is always an embodied, interpersonal act. For some of us, crying is deliberate; we have a clear emotional reaction to an event or feeling. For others, crying might seem counterintuitive to the situation; for example, we might cry out of frustration or anger rather than sadness. Whatever the reason, "the act of shedding tears has as much depth, symbolism, and meaning as a poem or a dream . . . Crying, too, touches all the themes that bind us together in the totality of human experience. Crying, quite simply, has soul" (Nelson xi). Crying, then, is a physical and soulful act—to share the emotional experience of crying means sharing a piece of one's soul and body. Sharing space with someone who cries is an act of holding space for the crier's most vulnerable parts and, therefore, is a powerful act of relationship-building. When we cry in a public space, like the writing center, we make that soul social and re-ceptive to others' interpretations. As receivers of someone's tears—and sometimes even as the criers—we might not ever know all the emotions associated with them. As Tom Lutz argues, "Tears are sometimes con-sidered pleasurable or profound, and sometimes dangerous, mysterious, or deceptive" (21). Because tears can be so mysterious, "our reactions to other people's tears are to some extent improvised" (Lutz 21). We fum-ble with our words around criers; we do not necessarily know how to help them. We sometimes cannot fix why they're crying or soothe their associated emotions. Sara Ahmed says, "emotion is the feeling of bodily change" (5). When one *feels* fear or anger, it is a reaction to a sensation in our body—higher blood pressure, a racing heart, and sweaty skin. Our embodied tears, then, "are the most substantial and yet the most fleeting, the most obvious and yet the most enigmatic proof of our emo-tional lives" (Lutz 29). Our bodies hold our reactions, and sometimes we cannot control them.

In writing centers, how we respond to these expressions of emotions changes our orientations to the space; we become aware of the layers of emotions held in that space by all who inhabit it. When our reactions leave of our bodies, they change the environment. The parties involved suddenly have a choice, not just with what to do with a feeling but with what to do with the bodily expressions of those feelings. "Once what is inside has got out," Ahmed says, "then my feelings also become yours, and you may respond to them" (8). For example, if we cry during a ses-sion, the table where we cried forever becomes *that table*, the consultant we cried with becomes *that consultant*. We are suddenly sharing some-thing intimate with the people, places, and things we might not have wanted to, and now those things have our personal, emotional associa-tions. A writing center pen seen outside of the writing center could even carry the orientation because our emotions have gotten stuck to it like a memory. This stickiness is a "form of relationality, or a 'with-ness,' in which the elements that are 'with' get bound together" (Ahmed 91). Crying in the writing center sticks the writing center to us. It creates an elaborate web of relations that is both seen and unseen, causing us to sometimes "catch" an emotion or feeling simply because of the space we are in. The writing center, as a place full of heightened emotions, is always sticky, and as consultants, we feel that.

Consultants *assume* there will be tears from writers in the writing center because we understand the writing center as a safe enough space for everyone—a space "becoming brav*er*" (Hallman Martini and Webster). Centers can be spaces where writers share personal stories, personal writing, and personal vulnerabilities. Emotions often run high as the pressures of deadlines feel enormous. For just as often as they are filled with rested, content, steadfast, eager, happy people, writing centers are also filled with anxious, tired, overwhelmed, sad, angry people, and yet . . . they are not full of crybaby consultants. Crying is the bodily symptom of many of these heightened emotions, yet we are much less willing to embrace crying in writing centers than, say, laughing or even angry outbursts. "We recognize in crying a surplus of feeling over thinking," says Lutz, "and an overwhelming of our powers of articulation by the gestural language of tears" (21). Crying "messes up" our faces, disrupts our composure, makes us apologize, causes us to feel shame, and causes us to *feel*. Ahmed says that shame is an emotion that is felt on and in our bodies "insofar as shame is about appearance, about how the subject appears before and to others" (104–5). When one feels shame from crying, they feel that their changed appearance is exposed as "apart" from others not crying (105). Ahmed calls the exposure of this apartness "wounding" (105). Sharing one's writing in a writing center already is a vulnerable process. Therefore, if crying in writing centers *also* makes people feel shamed, wounded, and apart from others, it is no wonder crying is not embraced by more consultants and clients.

Writers come into writing centers with their thoughts all a-jumble and their ideas in flux, and they need help breaking them down into tangible threads they can follow. Breaking down ideas is a first step in the writing process for many. Breakdowns are also a first step in the emotive process for many. As Lutz says, "By encouraging us to shift our attention from our thoughts to our bodies, crying can wash away the psychic pain we feel simply by diverting our attention from it" (23). What, then, is crying in the writing center, if not an exercise in breaking down? What would it look like if writing centers saw crying the same way we saw outlining ideas, drafting papers, working shifts, going to meetings, and reading emails? What would it look like if crying was just seen as part of the writing and writing center process? What would it look like if writing centers valued the breakdown as much as the break down?

As I write this, I am approaching the seventeen-month anniversary of my mother's death, and I remember how many times I have broken down in the writing center. In fact, I was in the writing center when I found out about my mother's second stroke. Everywhere I look in the writing center, I see traces of her, even though she never visited the space. The table closest to the conference room is where I was when I saw the notification on the family group chat that she had that second stroke. The table facing the window is where I sat and cried while everyone avoided me after I came back from her funeral. The coordinator office is where I hid from prying eyes and stage whispers wondering if I was okay. The middle office in the back is where I shared countless stories about my mother and her life with my co-assistant director last year. I cry openly all the time in the writing center. I use the tissues.

Writers feel comfortable enough, safe enough, and welcome enough to share their high stakes, high pressure, sometimes highly experimental writing with us, and consultants listen, ask questions, and are engaged, despite whatever is going on outside the writing in front of them or the session they are in. Similarly, literature exists about clients in need of comfort, or even a shoulder to cry on from consultants (Ryan and Zimmerelli; Gillespie and Lerner). Consultants are encouraged to remain compassionately stoic both when working with writing and when working with writers' tears, but this is a disservice we, as administrators and the writing center community, continue to perpetuate, even as perhaps the bulk of us have cried in this space ourselves.

CAN (WHITE) TEARS BE GENUINE *AND* VIOLENT?

In late January 2017, just weeks after Donald Trump's inauguration, I, Elise, drove from Lansing, Michigan, to the Detroit airport with friends to protest President Trump's executive order to ban the entry of people from seven Muslim-majority countries and suspended entry of refugees. The drive was nearly two hours long and the weather was frigid, but on the way home, I felt energized by my actions in the wake of what had been a horrifying beginning to Trump's exhausting term as president. My friends and I scrolled through photos we had taken of ourselves with our signs, and I eventually chose a few to post: one photo of us holding our signs among fellow protesters with serious faces and another similar pose of us smiling. While we had attended the protest for serious reasons, there was joy to be found in solidarity with others who believed just as strongly for the cause.

The next day, I sat in the writing center with a different set of friends: three graduate students in the writing group I facilitated. I was a paid consultant, but the writing group had quickly become a friendship circle, one in which we could vent to each other about our anxieties over our graduate programs and our new president. Toward the end of our session, our conversation turned more personal, hovering over what we had done during the weekend. Somehow, the topic of my presence at the airport came up. To my surprise, Rohit, a PhD candidate from India studying education technology, raised his voice to me, asking why I felt comfortable posting a smiling photo of myself protesting when there were people at the airport in chains. What gave me the right to so blatantly take advantage of a moment of true heartache for many for my own social media benefit?

I balked. I felt a catch in my throat and could feel blotches of red begin to dimple my chest and neck. My body wanted to start crying. My mind knew the instant relief of tears was a bad idea, and my identity as a white woman of immense privilege was clear to me. I had read articles, tweets, and blog posts about the weaponization of white women's tears; I knew that often when white women cried after being called out or in by a person of color, those tears killed any productivity in the conversation, put the focus on the white person's pain, and shut down the person of color's entire point (Hamad; Motwani Accapadi; Ajayi Jones; @blackgirlinmain). For a brief moment, no one spoke. The four of us—two white women, an Indian man, and a Latinx woman—found ourselves in a racially-charged conversation in the writing center, where I was supposedly the "professional" in the room. None of the complexities were lost on me; I fought hard to regain my composure, send the tears back behind my eyes, and engage with Rohit as thoughtfully as I could.

In the writing center conference room, I choked back tears of hopelessness, of white guilt and shame, of not knowing how to be a good activist, of feeling called out by a person of color, and of feeling like a bad white person. The tears came from a genuine place of hurt and confusion, but I also knew that sharing my hurt and confusion through tears was not going to help. I knew my tears could be met with impatience, and that such impatience was deserved.

It still hurt.

I cried in my car on the way home.

On the one hand, I want to call for the safety of all people's vulnerabilities in the writing center, even—and perhaps especially—tearful vulnerability. On the other hand, I know that tears *do* silence people, especially minoritized people who are doing the emotional labor of calling out or calling in someone doing harm. I certainly do not want to be in the camp of white women calling for everyone to cry if and when they want to, without acknowledging the power dynamics around whose tears are valued and whose tears are not. This leaves me at an impasse. Is it even ethical to call for tears in the writing center as a white woman?

This question is even further complicated by a history of writing centers having been run by—mostly white—women (Banschbach Valles et al.). Writing centers are coded as homey or cozy spaces, but when those spaces are primarily constructed by white women, those home spaces can still be coded as white and, therefore, as mostly comforting to other white students. Grutsch McKinney argues that "homes are culturally marked. If a writing center is a home, whose home is it? Mine? Yours? For whom is it comfortable?" (25). Indeed, when the homemaker is a white woman, that home's aesthetics are only comfortable to some. According to Faison and Treviño, "Aesthetics are invested with ideas about not only who will populate a space, but also what they will find both pleasing and comfortable. Within this imaginary the dominant culture and its upper middle-class, white ideologies are often hidden in, enacted on, and inscribed within writing center pedagogies. . ." Writing centers have been critiqued in the past for being spaces inscribed by femininity. Race further complicates the space as only *for some*, even as writing center directors often claim their centers are *for everyone*. Because they have been cultivated by white women, objects, signs, and bodies in the writing center adhere to the concept of whiteness, and therefore elicit the embodied response *to* whiteness—whatever that embodied response may be.

Part of the reason I feel comfortable crying in the writing center from time to time is because it always *has* felt like a home to me. But homes are not neutral, and I realize as I grow as a scholar and citizen that my comfort in this space is not either.

During my undergraduate years, my college boyfriend—we will call him Matt—physically and emotionally abused me. One of the things he would often do after abusing me was cry. After an explosion, I would open my squeezed-shut eyes and uncover my face, huddled in the corner of the bathroom floor, to see Matt across the room in the same position, sobbing. In the beginning of the abuse, I would crawl across the room and cradle him in my arms as he would tearfully, genuinely apologize again and again. I would find myself comforting *him*, even though *I* was the one he had hurt. As the abuse progressed, I lost patience for Matt's tears, seeing them as weapons he used to minimize my own pain and, ultimately, my worth. Yet, he cried with abandon, hiccupping as his body shook. Crocodile tears streamed down his reddened face. I did not know that these kinds of tears could be faked. While he might never admit to his culpability in the abuse, I do think he felt ashamed of himself. Looking back, I think his tears were both weapons and genuine expressions of anguish.

Knowing that I have found myself on the other end of violent tears, tears used to silence my pain, I wonder what it means to call for writing centers to be spaces where crybabies are welcome. My tears of white guilt, cried in the solitude of my car after my writing group, were genuine. Had I cried in the writing center in that particular moment, I believe they would have also been violent.

Can white tears *have* integrity? When or do they have a place in any space, including the center? I have no real answers for these questions. Harry Denny writes, "recipes for 'how to' are not so interesting to me as the questioning of 'what makes possible' dynamics that might go unrecognized" (88). Like Denny, I am less interested in how to answer these questions as I am in considering what these questions around white tears can make possible in the center. I am asking these questions to begin a conversation.

What Do We Do with Tears in the Writing Center?

I, Lauren, do not think of myself as a crybaby. I rarely cry, so the moments when I do stand out to me. I have cried twice in the writing center. Once, I had just learned of the death of a friend. The second time, I had a particularly fraught meeting about my dissertation project, which dealt with institutional responses to sexual violence, and in particular, with how program administrators could enact trauma-informed, care-based approaches. Because I was doing this research at Michigan State University—in the midst of the Larry Nassar scandal—there was a particular kind of scrutiny around my work, and I was confronted by one administrator who left me feeling like my project was going to be impossible to do. I barely made it out of the meeting before the tears started coming. As I walked up to my office, I ran into some friends. They listened.

After they calmed me down some, I left, still sniffling, to walk over to the writing center to find a space of solitude and vulnerability—but also a space where I could talk to others and move forward. I needed the center in that moment to talk through my emotions, and specifically to work my emotions into my dissertation itself. I needed people to help me answer questions: how could I use the meeting I just left as motivation? How could I talk about it in my methods? How could I ethically represent the administrators-as-participants in my study, given what they were doing to uphold the institutional values I was critiquing?

Through my experiences, I have thought a lot about what it means to make space for crying in the writing center. Rachel's story makes me question how we can create spaces where crying and vulnerability is an option for everyone. Elise makes me wonder if it is even possible for white women leaders, like the three of us are, to try to create this kind of vulnerable space given our own positions of power. Their stories and my own experiences make me think. What do we do with the tears and emotions that show up at our door?

Our goal has been to open up space for emotions—and specifically for crying in the writing center—while also acknowledging the complexities and power dynamics of those expressions. We want to acknowledge that crying is not an equal act, even as we still call for space for it to happen. What I am left with is the question of how to make crying into a productive act. Crying in and of itself can be incredibly beneficial and powerful; however, there are further benefits if we reflect on crying as a way to create community or to talk about social justice.

As writing center consultants and administrators, we are trained to comfort criers just enough to shut them up. As Rachel notes, we are taught to handle crying with some compassion and are often trained to suggest offices and resources around campus, such as counseling centers (Ryan and Zimmerelli; Gillespie and Lerner; Blitz and Hurlbert). However, this response outsources crying to other spaces in the university and asks students to put it on hold within the center. Sure, you can cry here, we say. Writing is personal. Sometimes it makes us cry. But you only have a limited amount of time in this space, so let us redirect your attention back to your writing and take your emotions elsewhere, outside of the writing center.

Crying is uncomfortable, often for everyone involved—it is uncomfortable to feel unable to stem or control your emotions publicly, and it is uncomfortable to watch another person feel such emotions. In a writing center context, crying is seen as unproductive. It is a block to meaningful discussions on the writing itself, so the goal of a session is to acknowledge the crying, then to put it aside. We hand the writer a tissue and return to the paper, give them *writing* help, not *emotional* help. Instead, what would happen if we viewed crying as part of the process, a way to learn and move forward? Specifically, what if the crying was put into the writing rather than set to the side of it? I offer some theories of thinking about crying in the writing center as productive, ones we use to make recommendations in the conclusion.

Crying as Social Justice Literacy. Howard Stevenson, in his conversations about promoting racial literacy in educational contexts, discusses the need for people of all raced positionalities to tell stories and expose emotions about their experiences with race. Specifically, he notes that everyone—including white people—has a story about race, and if we are invited to tell those stories to each other, we will end up with a lot of emotions in the room. Instead of shying away from these emotions, Stevenson uses them to promote conversations about race, community, and culture, and to help people from different racial backgrounds come to understand their experiences. In a writing center context, we might think about the stories behind tears, ask people to reflect on what those tears reveal about positionalities, and use them to create conversations about difficult topics, rather than allowing them to create distance between people.

Crying as Community or Relationship-Building. Studies on therapists crying in therapy reveal that nearly three-quarters of therapists report crying during sessions with clients (Blume-Marcovici et al.; 't Lam et al.). However, these therapists often have conflicting views about crying during sessions. Some remark that it feels unprofessional or even unethical; while others claim that being open in their emotions with clients helped them form an essential therapeutic relationship. When we considered the act of crying in the writing center, particularly the act of crying-as-consultant, we had similar conflicting feelings. Some of us hold back because it feels unprofessional—as though it is decentering the attention from the writer—but sometimes, crying can allow us to make essential connections with writers.

Crying as Writing Process. Finally, crying can be part of the writing process, rather than separate from it. When I cried over the problems I was having with my dissertation, I did not separate the tears from my research methodology. Because I was working with a trauma-informed, care-based methodology that asked me to pay attention to the impact the research was having on my body, the experiences I had crying became part of my research and writing process—and eventually, part of my dissertation. I was not handed a box of tissues, told to go to a therapist, and then get back to writing. Instead, I was told to think about whether I could use what I had gone through in my project. Could I write about the experiences as a data collection problem, for example? I did—and my dissertation was stronger for it. Had I placed the crying away from my research, it would not have done the same kind of embodied, care-based work I wanted it to do. As a result, I want to consider how crying may have a space within—some—writing projects and think about how it can be invited into the writing center rather than asked to wait outside.

IT'S OUR CENTER AND . . . WE'LL CRY IF WE WANT TO?

Making space for crying to do social justice work takes practice and critical reflection, so we want to invite more consideration for what crying can be in the writing center. We are not uncritically calling for consultant waterworks; rather, we hope to begin a critical conversation on crying as an embodied practice of vulnerability that can create space for relationship-building, processing, and difficult conversations. In addition, we offer these suggestions for how to incorporate and respond to crying within the writing center as a starting place for making space for crybabies.

Crying as Social Justice Literacy. Crying can be a vehicle for social justice. As Lauren described in the previous section, Stevenson importantly emphasizes *everyone* sharing stories and emotions, rather than just the person crying. This can disempower potentially violent tears, such as the white women's tears Elise warns us about. People may cry, but the tears are not the center of attention. In particular, when we share stories of how, when, and why we cry, we can create connections across differences and facilitate action-oriented goals. One way to practice crying as social justice literacy in the writing center is to provide space during training to discuss individual consultations as opportunities to enact social justice simply through affirming our own and our clients' emotions. We suggest offering a reading—like Michael Blitz and Mark Hurlbert's "If You Have Ghosts"—to consultants to discuss the emotional connections we have made with clients, especially those who differ from us in varying ways. This conversation can act as a "way in" to training crybabies who use their emotional literacies from a social justice orientation.

Crying as Community and Relationship-Building. Amy Blume-Marcovici et al. recommend that therapists who cry take special consideration to keep the explanations of their crying client-centered, such as describing what about the client's story caused them to cry or asking the client to discuss how they felt about the crying in relation to the session (417). We make a similar recommendation for consultants who cry: find ways to ask writers to think about their emotions or interactions with crying to help create that empathetic relationship. During Elise and Rohit's conversation about the protest, their relationship could have deteriorated had Elise actually cried publicly, rather than alone in her car. Instead, Elise was able to consider the situation and avoid crying. On the other hand, Lauren understood in her dissertation struggles that she needed to find comfort in a space that felt safe in that moment: the writing center. Both Elise and Lauren relied on their intuition, even during moments of emotional upheaval. Encouraging consultants to trust their intuition in the moment—even when the moment is emotionally-charged—and to read the room for signs of safety for all involved is one way to advocate for crying as community and relationship-building.

Crying as Writing Process. When our clients cry in the writing center, acknowledging that crying is not a barrier to writing but part of the writing process can make crying more acceptable. Drawing on Kottler's framework of crying as a *language*, we argue that we—as writing center consultants, administrators, and writers ourselves—must find ways to use this language of crying, alongside the other languages we use, to write. Kottler recognizes the complexities of this language by arguing that we come to understand crying as we start to identify certain aspects of where it comes from. We identify the emotions that may trigger tears, the positionalities of those who are allowed to cry and those who are not, the ways we are socialized to react to crying, and the physical impacts crying has on us. By asking our crying consultants to think through these aspects of their tears, administrators respond more empathetically to crying than we would by simply ignoring it, and we might help consultants recognize the network of reasons that led them to cry in the writing center. This recognition may help them incorporate crying into their writing process and even into their writing. As Steven Corbett and Katherine Villarreal argue in this collection, when we facilitate a dialogue that incorporates both writers' stories and consultants' emotions, we can recognize how emotion is already part of our everyday writing center practice.

We believe that crying is and can be a key part of the writing process, of life in the writing center, and of critical engagement with social justice in the academy. While we acknowledge that crying is fraught with emotional and vulnerable baggage that most academics do not wish to address, we argue that crying is an embodied, scholarly practice necessary for developing more empathetic, social justice-based pedagogy, both in and out of the center.

WORKS CITED

Ahmed, Sara. *The Cultural Politics of Emotion*. Routledge, 2004.

Ajayi Jones, Luvvie. "About the Weary Weaponizing of White Women's Tears." *Awesomely Luvvie*, 17 Apr. 2018, awesomelyluvvie.com/2018/04/weaponizing-white-women-tears.html.

Banschbach Valles, Sarah, et al. "Writing Center Administrators and Diversity: A Survey." *The Peer Review*, vol. 1, no. 1, 2017.

@blackgirlinmain (Shay Stewart Bouley). "A few weeks ago, I had lunch with a childhood friend. White girl from the Southside of Chicago, she's now a professor here in NE. Our friendship ended at 18. Why? White woman tears. I told her she made me feel like a charity case and it hurt her feelings." *Twitter*, 16 Apr. 2018, twitter.com/blackgirlinmain/status/986030856643981315.

Blitz, Michael, and C. Mark Hurlbert. "If You Have Ghosts." *Stories from the Center: Connecting Narrative and Theory in the Writing Center*, edited by Lynn Craigue Briggs and Meg Woolbright, National Council of Teachers of English, 2000, pp. 84–93.

Blume-Marcovici, Amy, et al. "Examining our Tears: Therapists' Accounts of Crying in Therapy." *American Journal of Psychotherapy*, vol. 69, no. 4, 2015, pp. 399–421.

Denny, Harry C. *Facing the Center: Toward an Identity Politics of One-to-One Mentoring*. Utah State UP, 2010.

Faison, Wonderful and Anna Treviño. "Race, Retention, Language and Literacy: The Hidden Curriculum of the Writing Center." *The Peer Review*, vol. 1, no. 1, 2017.

Gillespie, Paula, and Neal Lerner. *The Longman Guide to Peer Tutoring.* 2nd ed., Pearson, 2007.

Green, Neisha-Anne S. "The Re-Education of Neisha-Anne S. Green: A Close Look at the Damaging Effects of 'A Standard Approach,' the Benefits of Code-Meshing, and the Role Allies Play in this Work." *Praxis: A Writing Center Journal,* vol. 14, no. 1, 2016.

Grutsch McKinney, Jackie. *Peripheral Visions for Writing Centers.* Utah State UP, 2013.

Hallman Martini, Rebecca, and Travis Webster. "Writing Centers as Brave/r Spaces: A Special Issue Introduction." *The Peer Review,* vol. 1, no. 2, 2017.

Hamad, Ruby. "How White Women Use Strategic Tears to Silence Women of Colour." *The Guardian,* 11 May 2018, www.theguardian.com/commentisfree/2018/may/08/how-white-women-use-strategic-tears-to-avoid-accountability.

Knoblauch, A. Abby. "Bodies of Knowledge: Definitions, Delineations, and Implications of Embodied Writing in the Academy." *Composition Studies,* vol. 40, no. 2, 2012, pp. 50–65.

Kottler, Jeffrey. *The Language of Tears.* Jossey-Bass, 1996.

Lape, Noreen. "Training Tutors in Emotional Intelligence: Toward a Pedagogy of Empathy." *The Writing Lab Newsletter,* vol. 33, no. 2, 2008, pp. 1–6.

Lutz, Tom. *Crying: The Natural and Cultural History of Tears.* W.W. Norton and Company, 1999.

Motwani Accapadi, Matma. "When White Women Cry: How White Women's Tears Oppress Women of Color." *The College Student Affairs Journal,* vol. 26, no. 2, 2007, pp. 208–15.

Nelson, Judith Kay. *Seeing Through Tears: Crying and Attachment.* Routledge, 2005.

Ryan, Leigh, and Lisa Zimmerelli. *The Bedford Guide for Writing Tutors.* 6th ed., Bedford/St. Martin's, 2016.

Stevenson, Howard C. *Promoting Racial Literacy in Schools: Differences that Make a Difference.* Teachers College Press, 2014.

't Lam, Catelijne, et al. "Tears in Therapy: A Pilot Study About Experiences and Perceptions of Therapist and Client Crying." *European Journal of Psychotherapy and Counseling,* vol. 20, no. 2, 2018, pp. 199–219.

10 Groans and Sighs: What are Nonlexical Vocalizations Doing in Face-to-Face Tutorials?

Mike Haen

As described in this collection's introduction, writing center researchers have recently embraced evidence-based approaches to understanding emotion and affect (c.f. Babcock and Thonus; Lawson). In studies of writing center interaction, much of the affective focus has been on the role of *affiliation*, or sympathetic expressions, in response to writers' troubles-telling and complaining (Godbee; Mackiewicz and Thompson, "Motivational"). Tutors' affiliative responses can help build rapport in the tutorial, thereby contributing to a conducive and productive environment for learning. For example, Mackiewicz and Thompson highlight how tutors "express understanding of" difficult situations that writers describe ("Motivational" 47). In the excerpt below, the tutor (T) in Mackiewicz and Thompson's study acknowledges the anticipated trouble that the writer (S) describes in line 9.

9. S.   [Interrupts] I have a feeling that I'm going to be writing it all over tonight.
10. T.   Yeah, you probably will be, you know. And with these revisions it always
11.   ends up being (1-2 seconds) You know, it's always a lot of work in order to
12.   try to get a better (1-2 seconds) to try to write a better paper. (61)

Mackiewicz and Thompson explain that this tutor "sympathizes with the student" through "acknowledging the difficulty required for such an extensive revision" (61–62). The repetition of "always" also seems to be doing the work of normalizing the student's trouble as something many writers experience. Similarly, in this collection, Bell's findings from her mixed methods study show the importance of tutors validating and acknowledging multilingual students' expressed emotions to motivate them and encourage their participation.

Beyond interactional analyses that highlight how tutors express support—for example, by normalizing a perceived difficulty or validating troubles—recent research has examined the role of emotion in tutoring by synthesizing data from audio=recorded tutorial sessions, surveys and interviews (Follett). This chapter complements and extends that recent work by focusing more narrowly on the production of two nonlexical vocalizations that are commonly associated with negative emotion in social interaction: sighs and groans. While interviews provide useful insights on emotion and can access "participants' authentic experiences" to a degree (Potter and Hepburn 4; ten Have), they are also reconstructions of experience from memory that interviewers shape with interviewees. This is not meant to dismiss interview or survey methods altogether, but to highlight their limits for achieving a deeper understanding of how emotion and associated interactional features—like sighs—"function within the session" (Rowell 29). By drawing on and applying concepts and principles from conversation analysis, CA, in this chapter, I attempt to advance that deeper understanding, while acknowledging Grutsch McKinney et al.'s point in chapter one of this collection about different methodologies presenting different affordances and limitations.

Before proceeding, a quick note on terminology: I use *affect* and *emotion* interchangeably in this chapter. I am aware that scholars in this collection, in cultural studies, and in related disciplines make important theoretical distinctions between these terms— like Schmitz and Ahmed. However, I am indifferent to those theorized, fine-grained distinctions for now, as it is unclear from their interactional conduct that the tutors and writers in this chapter care about those distinctions. My goal is to explicate participants' moment-to-moment understandings of each other's conduct in tutorials—a goal that aligns with CA's scholarly roots (see Heritage on the sociological origins of CA). This is not to say that analyses of emotion in tutorial interactions with a cultural studies lens are not useful, but rather, that drawing on those particular theoretical distinctions is outside the scope of this chapter's inquiry.

In this chapter, I analyze interactional sequences from three tutorials with a focus on two nonlexical vocalizations that are commonly associated with negative emotion: sighs and groans. The term "nonlexical" refers to units of speech that are not conventional words, such as *aargh*, *ugh*, and laughter. First, I explore the social actions, or interactional work, that tutors perform with these nonlexical vocalizations—sighs; response cries or what I call "groans". Second, I consider how these features shape subsequent trajectories and sequences of interaction for tutorial participants.

In social interaction, interlocutors can display affect with various interactional resources, including vocalizations as well as embodied actions. Most research on affect and vocalizations in social interaction has drawn from foundational work by sociologist Erving Goffman, who explained that *response cries*, like "ah!" or "ugh!," externalize a "presumed inward state" (794). They are also described as "flooding up" sounds or "exclamatory interjections" that are not conventional words (Goffman 800). Research informed by CA has shown how certain kinds of vocalizations are central to producing displays of emotion like surprise, disappointment—like "oh"—and irritation, depending on situational usage and placement in a sequence of interactions (Couper-Kuhlen, "Sequential"; Reber; Wilkinson and Kitzinger). Changes in delivery of the vocalization, like loudness, along with embodied behavior, like facial expression, can be mobilized by interactional participants to express some affective stance. For example, in response to a parent rejecting their child's request of "Can I please get that dress," the child's pained response of "uhhh!" departs from "local prosodic 'norms' in prior talk" such as volume and pitch (Couper-Kuhlen, "Affectivity" 461). In this case, the child is expressing a negative affective stance. However, this conduct might not necessarily be relevant or hearable to participants in the moment as a *serious* emotional expression. Recent research on response cries in board game interactions, for example, illustrates that participants may treat these sounds "as displays of (suffering) affect" but then downgrade the seriousness of the suffering and display a willingness to continue with the gameplay (Hofstetter 59).

Like response cries or groans, *sighs* are often implicated in displaying emotions like sadness as well as resignation (Hoey; Teigen). In the scholarship on dyadic talk about writing, sighs are also implicated in moments of mutual frustration, general awkwardness, or interactional trouble (Black; Janangelo; Gilewicz and Thonus). Writing in *WLN*, Marnie Larkin recalls a writer who "emitted a long sigh" at the start of a session (9). As frustrations grew, Larkin explains that "soon my sighs, too, were filling the room" (9). Likewise, in her book, *Between Talk and Teaching: Reconsidering the Writing Conference*, Laurel Johnson Black describes a frustrated instructor who sighs before complaining about student papers in a conference, which Black claims placed the student in an awkward position (128–129). In writing center scholarship, sighs also materialize in moments of *giving up* (Gilewicz and Thonus 41–42) and exasperation (DiPardo 192). In their article "Close Vertical Transcription in Writing Center Training and Research," Magdalena Gilewicz and Terese Thonus describe a case in which a student sighs after the tutor directs the student to "compose orally" (42). Specifically, the tutor says "give me an example. . .how would you phrase it?" The authors explain that the student's subsequent sigh indicates that they are experiencing some trouble with the tutor's directive to compose aloud. Though these representations are common in scholarship and popular discourse more broadly, interlocutors sigh to do other things besides conveying negative affect or expressing some trouble with the preceding interaction (Hoey).

This chapter's analysis of interaction in three tutorials augments the conventional stories in writing centers and writing studies about what these nonlexical vocalizations or "sighs" mean for participants and how they might shape the trajectory of interaction. Drawing on recent research in language and social interaction, I demonstrate first that tutors sigh to show they are preparing to do some new or different action in the unfolding interaction. In doing so, the participants do not seem to clearly attribute negative affect to these sighs. Second, in addition to sighing at transition points between actions, tutors featured in this chapter produce sighs and another kind of nonlexical vocalization—a *response cry* (Goffman) or "groan"—when their attempts to compose aloud stall or fail. In these cases, after tutors' vocalizations and adjoining talk or complaints, participants promptly resume the in-progress activity of *composing aloud* or formulating spoken-written language in their subsequent turns. I conclude by discussing how future research in this vein might be useful for helping tutors build reflective, evidence-based dispositions about their practice, especially about the typical interactional trajectories that lead up to these vocalizations and about trajectories—or sequences—that follow them.

Data Collection and Methods

The data comes from a larger project funded by Midwest Writing Centers Association, MWCA, and International Writing Centers Association, IWCA, grants. From 2015–2018, I video-recorded ten tutorials, ranging from thirty to sixty minutes, at a large public university and a private university in the Midwestern United States. Five tutors and five writers participated. The tutors included two doctoral students, one post-doctoral student, and two undergraduate students. Writers included two graduate students and three undergraduate students. Each session typically began with the tutor and writer setting an agenda or identifying issues to discuss. They then proceeded to read the draft aloud. In some cases, they stopped intermittently to discuss potential revisions, and then continued reading. Other times, the writer read the draft without stopping, and they then discussed it. In this chapter, I analyze five examples from three tutorials, as these examples demonstrate the main functions of sighs and groans observed across the ten tutorials. Example one is from a tutorial in which participants discuss a think piece on Donald Trump's business acumen for an independent study course in political science. Examples two and three show participants working on a medical school personal statement. Examples four and five show participants drafting headlines and leads for a media writing course.

Like prior studies of writing center interactions (Denny; Godbee; Thonus), my method is guided by principles from CA. Researchers employing CA begin by observing patterns in audio- or video-recorded interactions through initial transcriptions, and then examine those patterns more rigorously through fine-grained transcription and recursive interaction viewing (Sidnell). Throughout the process of transcription and re-viewing, researchers build collections of interactional phenomena, like sighs. My approach draws on two concepts in CA: *participants' orientations* and *action*. By grounding claims about the phenomena in *"participants' orientations"* to the preceding interaction (Sidnell 79), CA is attuned to how participants respond to one another's turns because those responses show how participants understand one another and interpret the actions they are performing—for example, advice-giving. In other words, CA "treats participants' own understandings as having primacy relative to analysts' understandings" and the methodological orientation "shows through most plainly in the CA 'proof procedure'" (Stivers and Heritage 665). The *next-turn proof procedure* involves an analyst looking at the *next-turn*, or the "recipient's response" to prior turns and actions (Sidnell 79). This procedure elucidates how speakers interpret one another's turns and actions as interaction unfolds, and it informs this chapter's analysis about the role of vocalizations in tutorial interactions.

Another central area of interest in CA, and a main interest here, is on how participants take turns to accomplish *actions*. *Action* refers to the main job that the turn—or sequence of turns—is performing (Levinson). When a writer performs the action of *asking* via a question, it is designed to elicit a tutor's *answer* as a responding action (Sidnell). A main action in writing center talk, such as tutors' advice-giving, is often built through multiple turns forming sequences of talk. For example, Christopher Leyland, who examines writing tutorials involving L2 writers, finds a "consistent pattern of actions" in cases in which writers resisted tutors' advice (271). He characterizes an advising sequence, and *actions* within it, as follows:

> Action A: tutor's initial advice; for example, "maybe . . . you could have a kind of little introduction paragraph . . ."
>
> Action B: student resists; for example, "but I think this sentence works for my introduction since it . . ."
>
> Action C: tutor adapts their advice; for example, "okay but . . . maybe here . . . seems like a natural break"
>
> Action D: student accepts, and consensus is achieved; for example, "yeah so I can open a new paragraph" (276).

Several of my examples resemble Leyland's data, in that participants are often trying to achieve a joint consensus—as seen in Action D—about what to do with the draft or about how to write and revise certain parts. Throughout the chapter, I adhere as much as possible to the aforementioned CA concepts. I also highlight "the prosodic packaging" or volume of a turn and "the type of interactional activity in which it is deployed" (Reber 9). Each example is transcribed with simplified Jeffersonian conventions, which are standard for CA (see Appendix). I **bold the vocalizations** of interest and use an arrow "->" to mark "next-turns" or responses to the prior turn. I also highlight and describe relevant features like gaze, hand gestures, and other kinds of embodied behavior that coincide with participants' talk.

ANALYSIS

I now explore how vocalizations or "sighs" matter for participants and how they might shape the trajectory of interaction or the sequencing of actions in tutorials. I demonstrate, first, that tutors sigh to show they are preparing to do some new or different action in their talk, without the participants clearly attributing negative affect to these sighs (Hoey;

Sacks). Elliot Hoey, who applies CA, defines *sighing* as "an audible or visible expiration of relatively great intensity, out of sync with normal breathing" (177). He adds that "sighing criterially consists of an out-breath"—marked as **hx** in the transcripts—which may be preceded by an in-breath—marked as **h**—and a brief silence (177). I adapt his criteria for this chapter. Second, in addition to sighing at transition points between actions, tutors produce sighs and another kind of nonlexical vocalization—a *response cry* (Goffman) or "groan"—when their attempts to compose text aloud stall or fail. In response to the tutor's negative stance, a writer can momentarily "take the lead" in the tutorial interaction and the in-progress activity (see Examples Four and Five).

The interaction shown in Example One comes from the tutorial where the graduate student tutor and undergraduate student writer discuss the writer's "think piece"—described this way by the participants—for an independent study course. In this example, the tutor, T1, produces a sigh at a transition point between the writer, W1, completing the activity of reading aloud—as seen in line 01—and the tutor giving a *first* assessment of the draft—as seen in line 07. Indeed, after his sigh, T1 describes his positive assessment as the "first" thing he "wants to say" about the draft—as seen in lines 06–07. Just before the sigh, the tutor leans back in his chair[3] and turns his left hand over so his palm faces upward. He keeps it in that position until his outbreath ends.

(1)

1.	W1.		((reading aloud)) and that's where I got.
2.			(1.0) ((T1 moves left hand and palm faces
3.			upwards))
4.	T1.		**h hx** um
5.			(2.0)
6.	T1.	->	I'm gonna. well I'm- alright. so: what I wanna say
7.			is first is like <u>really</u> <u>awesome</u> <u>writing</u>
8.	W1.		thank you, thank you

After his sigh and a pause in line 05, T1 does repeated "self-repair" of his talk by stopping or interrupting his turn to "deal with something which is being treated as a problem in what [he] has said, or started to say, or may be about to say" (Kitzinger 230). That is, he abandons his in-progress turn of "I'm gonna" and starts again with "well I'm," before producing the positive assessment of the "writing" in line 07. W1, in his turn at line 08, thanks T1 for the praise. Altogether, the sigh and pausing in lines 03–05, along with the tutor's embodied conduct and "self-repair" of his talk, displays that he is trying to carefully decide what he should say first about the draft. Though sighs are conventionally associated with negative affect, the positive assessment and gratitude would seem to conflict with such an understanding of this particular sigh. Rather than carry a negative affective valence, the sigh prefaces a transition to the next topic of talk or next course of action (Hoey)—*making a first evaluation* of the draft after reading aloud is completed.

Similarly, the tutor shown in Example Two produces a sigh when *transitioning* back to a prior course of action—writing notes with pen and paper. The graduate student tutor, T2, and undergraduate student writer, W2, are discussing the writer's personal statement for medical school. In the personal statement, the writer discusses how seeing an advertisement for a Ronald McDonald House event, "McHappy Day," in her home country of Brazil influenced her to pursue her dream of becoming a pediatric oncologist. Just before the transcribed talk, the tutor starts simultaneously writing and reading notes about a potential revision for the writer's draft but stops to elicit information from the writer about McHappy Day and its geographical location, as seen in lines 01–03. Moving her gaze from her notes to W2, T2 elicits this information and tries to confirm her understanding, in part, because the writer moved frequently throughout her childhood and adolescence. T2's sigh is characterized by an in-breath that is slightly longer than the out-breath in line 08, and the sigh prefaces T2's resumption of notetaking.

(2)

1. T2.		((looking down while writing notes))
2.		so you no longer thou- so mexico city didn't have
3.		the mchappy day <u>right</u>? ((T2 starts gazing at W2))
4.		(1.0)
5. W2.		I don't think so. ((T2 continues gazing at W2))
6. T2.		okay
7. W2.		not the [same way as
8. T2.		[**h hx** so ((T2 looks down and writes notes))
9. W2.		as in brazil, at least
10. T2.	->	((writing revision and reading it aloud on notepad))

While the writer's answers in lines 05, 07, and 09 extend past the tutor's sigh in line 08, she stops talking soon after the tutor resumes notetaking in line 10, which suggests the writer understands that more talk from her is unnecessary for the tutor's current notetaking. T2's "so" in line 08, which immediately follows the sigh, is a relevant part of her return to notetaking. A well-developed body of social interaction research has demonstrated that "so" is commonly used as a marker for causal or inferential connections in interaction and for transitioning to new topics and actions, especially suspended or pending courses of action (Bolden; Howe; Raymond). T2's sigh and the adjacent "so" appear to mark some transition to a different course of action—for example, writing notes—which was momentarily suspended by the tutor to ask a question and elicit information from the writer.

In contrast to the first two examples, the tutor's sigh in Example Three more clearly suggests some momentarily "resigned or defeated" stance (Hoey 187).

(3)

1.	T2.		<u>this</u> we need to tie in a little bit
2.	W2.		okay
3.	T2.		um
4.			(1.0)
5.	T2.		furthermore, ((both looking at draft))
6.			(2.0)
7.	T2.		**hx**
8.	W2.		(xxx) ((looking at draft))
9.	T2.	->	darn it
10.			(3.0)
11.	W2.		hmm
12.			(2.0)
13.	T2.		h maybe even <u>furthermore</u> ((speaking revision aloud in
14.			combination with writer's original text))
15.	W.		okay=
16.	T2.		maybe?
17.	W2.		=so like switch,
18.	T2.		yeah
19.	W2.		those two [ideas?
20.	T2.		[<u>yeah</u>
21.	W2.		let's see okay ((prepares to write with pencil))

The talk that follows the sigh suggests, in a more transparent way than the talk in examples one and two, that the tutor is displaying or express-ing negative affect at this moment in the interaction (line 09). . The tutor sighs in line 07, producing a quiet out-breath after starting to formulate *spoken-written language, SWL,* for a passage in the personal statement from line 05. SWL refers to "the spoken language that both tutors and student writers produce for potential use in the student writer's written product" (Mackiewicz and Thompson, "Spoken" 47). This "composing aloud"—as it is also sometimes referred to—is in service of making a clearer connection or "tie in" between two disconnected ideas that the tutor has identified.

T2 quietly says "darn it" after the sigh. Taken together, this suggests some negative affective stance. During a pause in line 10, the writer continues looking at the draft and displays she is aligned with the on-going activity of trying to formulate language for the draft, seen with "hmmm." After another pause, T2 tries again to propose a revision, and W2 checks her understanding of it in lines 17 and 19. The tutor con-firms the writer's understanding, and the writer prepares to implement the change in line 21. In sum, and as shown in recent research (Hoey), the first two examples demonstrate how sighs can carry no discernible affect and mark a transition to another action that moves tutorial busi-ness forward—whether to prepare to praise the draft after reading aloud or to resume taking notes. These examples contrast with convention-al portrayals of sighing in writing center scholarship (Black; Janangelo; Gilewicz and Thonus). Example Three shows how sighs index or indi-cate a negative affective stance. In this case, the writer and tutor move on with the activity of formulating SWL after this momentary expression of trouble.

In Examples Four and Five, the tutor, T3, "groans"—or produces what Goffman calls a "response cry"—in her attempt to formulate lan-guage for a news story assignment. These vocalizations are paired with embodied behavior—for example, hunching over—that indicates a neg-ative affective stance. These affective displays emerge after the writer rejects the possible written language and accounts for why he cannot use it—for instance, he cannot use the word "and." In response to T3, the writer laughs, thus orienting to the tutor's display as non-serious. He then promptly continues with attempts to compose aloud or find the ap-propriate words for the news headlines he is working on.

Just prior to the beginning turns shown in Example Four, the tutor suggests a new version of some SWL that the writer, W3, had rejected because it included the word "and," which for this part of the assignment, the writer evidently cannot use. W3 asks T3 to repeat the newest version of SWL in line 01, and W3 begins the first part at line 05. T3 builds from W3's talk about the first part and, in lines 07–09, repeats what she said in her turns before line 01. In response, W3 then rejects the SWL again in lines 10–11). T3 then groans in line 12 and says "WHAT?" while bringing her hand to her head and hunching over. T3's conduct comes off as displaying negative affect or suffering of some kind.

(4)

1. W3.		alright, so can you say that again?
2. T3.		sure
3. W3.		so,
4. T3.		[uh
5. W3.		[suit filed on april first by ellie madison says,
6.		(1.0)
7. T3.		<u>she</u> suffered permanent bodily and mental injuries,
8.		incurred medical expenses and lost income, slipping
9.		on a green <u>bean</u> hehe I don't know
10. W3.		well that's the thing, you can't say <u>and</u>. that's the
11.		thing.
12. T3.		**AHH** ((brings hand to forehead and hunches over))
13. W3.	->	sa(heh)ys
14. T3.		**WHAT?**
15. W3.	->	ellie madison says
16.		(2.0)
17. W3.	->	she ((writing))
18. T3.		<u>why</u> would they put it there if you can't use it,
19. W3.		I don't know.
20.		(1.0)
21. W3.	->	says she <u>suffered</u> permanent
22.		(2.0)
23. T3.		bodily

Following T3's groan in line 12, W3 repeats "says"—appearing earlier at line 09—with some interspersed laughter. Here, the writer's turn briefly acknowledges the tutor's vocalization but continues pursuing suitable SWL for his purposes. After exclaiming "what?!" in a loud volume, the tutor complains in line 18. Complaining involves a speaker "expressing a grievance about some state of affairs for which responsibility can be attributed to some particular complainee" (Pillet-Shore 2). In this example, T3 produces an indirect complaint that targets a non-present "they," which apparently refers to the authors of the assigned workbook that the students are working from. While writing, W3 responds to T3's complaint with "I don't know," which seems to treat T3's complaint as a question that calls for an answer, as opposed to a complaint that calls for some affiliation or display of sympathy. After a second of silence, W3 continues the composing aloud he tried to do earlier in lines 13, 15, and 17, and T3 joins him in that effort in line 23. Perhaps not surprisingly, there seems to be a consistent orientation to the activity of achieving suitable SWL, as demonstrated in the writer's responses to the tutor's groan and complaint. The writer, at least temporarily, takes the lead here in composing possible text.

The fifth and final example exhibits a similar trajectory leading up to and following the tutor's groan and embodied conduct. T3 produces a response cry after a first failed attempt and a sigh after a second failed attempt to formulate possible written language. Specifically, after T3 completes her advice about writing two sentences, W3 rejects the advice based on another restriction associated with the assignment in line 03: "can only be one sentence." In line 06, T3 produces a groan in a loud volume along with embodied behavior that can be interpreted as conveying negative affect. She brings her hand to her face, like the previous example, and slightly hunches over while dropping the pencil she is holding. W2 then laughs, treating the matter as not entirely serious. T3 assesses the situation as "so stressful" in subsequent turns in line 08. In returning W3's earlier laughter, T3 also appears to treat the matter in a less serious way than her words "this is so stressful" would indicate on their own.

(5)

1. T3.		whose jobs have been <u>threatened,</u> period um
2.		(2.0)
3. W3.		oh no it can only be one sentence.
4. T3.		oh
5. W3.		like it can't be two sen[tences
6. T3.		[**UGH** ((brings hand to face and drops pencil))
7. W3.	->	hehe
8. T3.		heh **this is so stressful uhhm**
9.		(1.0)
10. W3.	->	hehe
11. T3.		that's a long sentence, okay
12. W3.		but I mean as long as it's not like thirty words
13.		then it's okay
14. T3.		well you say company union so maybe say presidents
15.		from <u>respective,</u>
16.		(2.0)
17. W3.		<u>but</u> then I don't say their names
18. T3.		**hx** I don't know
19. W3.	->	like I think sayin their names the way
20.		we had last time [soo (xxx)
21. T3.		[you wanna do <u>that</u>. okay
22.		(2.0)
23. W3.		((writing)) president

After the tutor reassesses the problem in line 11, the writer qualifies
the tutor's assessment about the sentence's length in lines 12–13. T3
tries to formulate some SWL again in lines 14–15, and W3 again resists
it. T3's subsequent sigh and "I don't know" from line 18 seem to take a
resigned or defeated stance toward the task and her thwarted efforts in
formulating a revision. The tutor's conduct in this moment leaves space
for the writer to propose a revision in lines 19–20, which the writer does,
and the tutor quickly agrees with in line 21. W3 then begins writing
that revision in line 23. With Examples Four and Five, the writer treats
the tutor's groans, complaints, and embodied conduct as laughable and
non-serious, and he advances the activity of *composing aloud* through
his turns-at-talk.

Conclusions and Implications for Tutor Education

In this chapter, I analyzed the interactional and affective work tutors
perform with their vocalizations—sighs and response cries—and considered how those vocalizations and participants' adjacent conduct—com-

plaining—shape trajectories of tutorial interaction. Rather than adopt a prescriptive stance about the kinds of emotion that are acceptable in tutorials, I have attempted to illustrate two observations about what might matter to these participants. First, in contrast to past scholarship that often portrays sighing as indicative of mutual frustration, general awkwardness, or interactional trouble in dyadic talk about writing (Black; Janangelo; Gilewicz and Thonus), participants in these tutorials produce sighs to do slightly different interactional work, and their co-participants appear to interpret them as such. Sighs can convey no affective valence, as in Examples One and Two, when they signal transition to another topic or action. Hoey's recent conversation analytic study comprehensively analyzes this dimension of sighing in ordinary interaction as well as some pedagogical talk—for example, a math homework tutoring session. With Example One, the tutor produces a sigh in his turn after the writer finishes reading his draft aloud. The sigh is part of how the tutor prepares to make *a first evaluation* of the draft after reading aloud: "what I wanna say is first is like really awesome writing." In the second example, the tutor's sigh and adjacent discourse marker "so" signal some transition to a different course of action—writing notes—which was momentarily suspended. To understand sighing in tutorials as mainly indicative of negative emotion would mean that we also miss the other interactional work it can and does perform.

The second takeaway of this chapter is that *composing aloud*, or formulating spoken-written language (Mackiewicz and Thompson, "Spoken-Written Language"), might be one important context for our field to explore to build evidence-based understanding of negative affect and how it matters for tutorial participants in their interactions. Indeed, Gilewicz and Thonus allude to the challenge of composing aloud in their "Close Vertical Transcription" article. In Examples Three, Four, and Five shown in this chapter, tutors' nonlexical vocalizations—sighs and groans—occur when tutors visibly struggle to compose aloud. In the third example, the tutor struggles to formulate a possible sentence that the writer could add to the draft, and her negative affect is indexed with a sigh and phrase: "darn it." She seems to be displaying some momentary trouble in finding suitable language for the writer's draft. In the fourth and fifth examples, the writer resists the tutor's suggested spoken-written language because of restrictions associated with the writing task— the prohibition against using "and." The tutor's groans and complaints follow, and the writer briefly acknowledges them, treating them as non-serious with laughter. The writer's next turns advanced the activity of formulating suitable written language.

The analytic approach taken in this chapter offered some insight into how affect and affective displays were relevant to participants as they engaged in different activities in writing center tutorials. Future work might explore the relationship between certain affective displays and activities or actions, with an eye towards helping tutors reflect on their practice.

For example, the tutor's pained expression in Examples Four and Five is related to the immediate prior talk, in which the writer resisted the advised written language or revision repeatedly. New tutors might consider how they and their writing center colleagues respond in similar interactional trajectories and examine how writers participate in these kinds of moments. As scholars like Gilewicz and Thonus and R. Mark Hall have explained, asking tutors to view and transcribe their own video-recorded sessions can lead to more nuanced understandings. Hall, who explains the applications of activity theory for analyzing transcripts, highlights one such transcription assignment in which he asks his tutoring staff to consider "what tutors and tutees are *doing* together—what *activities* they're engaging in, and how those activities either forward or inhibit learning" (72). In the case of affect in tutorial interaction, new tutors might complete a similar transcription assignment in which they observe nonlexical vocalizations in their talk—and writers' talk—with the goal of describing how these features seem to matter to both participants. Through closely observing and transcribing these interactions, tutors can collaboratively document and discuss the kinds of tutorial activities, like composing aloud, in which both tutors and writers produce vocalizations associated with affect. They can consider how these features are relevant and prove consequential in interaction *for the participants*. Paying attention to writers' negative affective stances might also reveal missed opportunities for more effective *rhetorical listening*, which Steven Corbett and Katherine Villarreal describe in this collection. Future research should more systematically analyze common activities in which tutorial participants' affect becomes relevant, so that we can build a more robust understanding of the role of emotion in tutorial interaction.

WORKS CITED

Babcock, Rebecca Day, and Terese Thonus. *Researching the Writing Center: Towards an Evidence-Based Practice*. Peter Lang, 2012.

Black, Laurel Johnson. *Between Talk and Teaching: Reconsidering the Writing Conference*. Utah State UP, 1998.

Bolden, Galina. "Implementing Incipient Actions: The Discourse Marker 'So' in English Conversation." *Journal of Pragmatics*, vol. 41, no. 5, 2009, pp. 974–98.

Couper-Kuhlen, Elizabeth. "On Affectivity and Preference in Responses to Rejection." *Text and Talk*, vol. 32, no. 4, 2012, pp. 453–75.

—. "A Sequential Approach to Affect: The Case of 'Disappointment.'" *Talk in Interaction: Comparative Dimensions*, edited by Markku Haakana, et al., Finnish Literature Society, 2016, pp. 94–123.

Denny, Melody. "The Oral Writing-Revision Space: Identifying a New and Common Discourse Feature of Writing Center Consultations." *The Writing Center Journal*, vol. 37, no. 1, 2018, pp. 35–66.

DiPardo, Anne. "Whispers of Coming and Going: Lessons from Fannie." *The Writing Center Journal*, vol. 12, no. 2, 1992, pp. 125–144.

Follett, Jennifer R. *"How Do You Feel About This Paper?" A Mixed-Methods Study of How Writing Center Tutors Address Emotion*. 2016. Indiana University of Pennsylvania, PhD dissertation.

Gilewicz, Magdalena, and Terese Thonus. "Close Vertical Transcription in Writing Center Training and Research." *The Writing Center Journal*, vol. 24, no. 1, 2003, pp. 25–49.

Godbee, Beth. "Toward Explaining the Transformative Power of Talk About, Around, and For Writing." *Research in the Teaching of English*, vol. 47, no. 2, 2012, pp. 171–97.

Goffman, Erving. "Response Cries." *Language*, vol. 54, no. 4, 1978, pp. 787–815.

Hall, R. Mark. *Around the Texts of Writing Center Work: An Inquiry-Based Approach to Tutor Education*. Utah State UP, 2017.

Heritage, John. *Garfinkel and Ethnomethodology*. Polity Press, 1984.

Hofstetter, Emily. "Nonlexical 'Moans': Response Cries in Board Game Interactions." *Research on Language and Social Interaction*, vol. 53, no. 1, 2020, pp. 42–65.

Howe, Mary. *Topic Change in Conversation*. 1991. University of Kansas, PhD dissertation.

Hoey, Elliott. "Sighing in Interaction: Somatic, Semiotic, and Social." *Research on Language and Social Interaction*, vol. 47, no. 2, 2014, pp. 175–200.

Janangelo, Joseph. "The Polarities of Context in the Writing Center Conference." *The Writing Center Journal*, vol. 8, no. 2, 1988, pp. 59–82.

Kitzinger, Celia. "Repair." *The Handbook of Conversation Analysis*, edited by Jack Sidnell and Tanya Stivers, 2013, pp. 229–56.

Larkin, Marnie. "Tutor's Column." *The Writing Lab Newsletter*, vol. 17, no. 3, 1992, pp. 9.

Lawson, Daniel. "Metaphors and Ambivalence: Affective Dimensions in Writing Center Studies." *WLN: A Journal of Writing Center Scholarship*, vol. 40, no. 3–4, 2015, pp. 20–27.

Levinson, Stephen C. "Action Formation and Ascription." *The Handbook of Conversation Analysis*, edited by Jack Sidnell and Tanya Stivers, 2013, pp. 103–30.

Leyland, Christopher. "Resistance as a Resource for Achieving Consensus: Adjusting Advice Following Competency-Based Resistance in L2 Writing Tutorials at a British University." *Classroom Discourse*, vol. 9, no. 3, 2018, pp. 267–87.

Mackiewicz, Jo, and Isabelle Thompson. "Motivational Scaffolding, Politeness, and Writing Center Tutoring." *The Writing Center Journal*, vol. 33, no. 1, 2013, pp. 38–73.

—. "Spoken Written-Language in Writing Center Talk." *Linguistics and Education*, vol. 47, 2018, pp. 47–58.

Pillet-Shore, Danielle. "Complaints." *The International Encyclopedia of Language and Social Interaction*, edited by Karen Tracy, Wiley and Sons, 2015, pp. 1–7.

Potter, Jonathan, and Alexa Hepburn. "Qualitative Interviews in Psychology: Problems and Possibilities." *Qualitative Research in Psychology*, vol. 2, no. 4, 2005, pp. 281–307.

Raymond, Geoffrey. "Prompting Action: The Stand-Alone 'So' in Ordinary Conversation." *Research on Language and Social Interaction*, vol. 37, no. 2, 2004, pp. 185–218.

Reber, Elisabeth. *Affectivity in Interaction: Sound Objects in English*. John Benjamins, 2012.

Rowell, Christina. *Let's Talk Emotions: Re-envisioning the Writing Center through Consultant Emotional Labor*. 2015. East Carolina University, Master's thesis.

Sacks, Harvey. *Lectures on Conversation*. vol. 2, Blackwell, 1992.

Schmitz, Sigrid, and Sara Ahmed. "Affect/Emotion: Orientation Matters. A Conversation Between Sigrid Schmitz and Sara Ahmed." *Freiburger Zeitschrift für GeschlechterStudien*, vol. 20, no. 2, 2014, pp. 97–108.

Sidnell, Jack. "Basic Conversation Analytic Methods." *The Handbook of Conversation Analysis*, edited by Jack Sidnell and Tanya Stivers, 2013, pp. 77–100.

—, et al. *The Handbook of Conversation Analysis*. Blackwell Publishing, 2013.

Stivers, Tanya, and John Heritage. "Conversation Analysis and Sociology." edited by Jack Sidnell and Tanya Stivers, pp. 659–73.

ten Have, Paul. *Understanding Qualitative Research and Ethnomethodology*. SAGE Publications, Ltd., 2004.

Teigen, Karl Halvor. "Is a Sigh 'Just a Sigh'? Sighs as Emotional Signals and Responses to a Difficult Task." *Scandinavian Journal of Psychology*, vol. 49, no. 1, 2008, pp. 49–57.

Thonus, Terese. "Discourse Analysis, Critical Discourse Analysis, and Conversation Analysis." *Theories and Methods of Writing Center Studies: A Practical Guide*, edited by Jo Mackiewicz and Rebecca Day Babcock, Routledge, 2020, pp. 173–85.

Wilkinson, Sue, and Celia Kitzinger. "Surprise as an Interactional Achievement: Reaction Tokens in Conversation." *Social Psychology Quarterly*, vol. 69, no. 2, 2006, pp. 150–82.

APPENDIX. SIMPLIFIED CA TRANSCRIPTION KEY

Markings	Meaning in Transcript
hx	outbreath
h	in-breath
(1.0)	pause measured in seconds
WORD	(all caps) loud speech
word	stress or emphasis
(xxx)	uncertain hearing/unintelligible talk
[words]	(aligned brackets) start and end
[words]	of overlapping speech
= (equal signs)	continuous speech with no break
heh	laughter
-	word cutoff
. (period)	falling intonation
, (comma)	continuing intonation
? (question mark)	rising intonation

11 POSITIVE AFFECTIVE DISPLAY AND EMOTIONAL LABOR IN THE WRITING CENTER: A QUALITATIVE STUDY

Luke A. Iantorno

I n her highly influential *The Managed Heart*, Arlie Hochschild defines emotional labor as the on-the-job management of felt emotions and emotional expression, often performed in response to organizational requirements for professional employee behavior. In the broad swathe of research about the expenditure of emotional labor in service-oriented professions, employees are more likely to outwardly display positive emotions in response to work-related stressors because of professional and organizational expectations (Rafaeli and Sutton 23; Waldron 121–22; Fineman and Sturdy 631). In my own professional experiences in writing centers and on-the-job observations of fellow tutors, we routinely expend positive emotions during our interactions with student writers and with each other. Previous literature about the expenditure of emotional labor in educational and service-oriented professions informs readers that routinely utilizing positive emotions in daily interactions with others could result in emotional exhaustion, negative affective displays, and eventual burnout (Bellas 97; Wharton 206). Based on past research about the effects of emotional labor in higher education, I wondered which forms of emotional labor my fellow writing center professionals participate in and how they respond to the daily stressors of writing center work—for example, following consecutive or stressful consultations.

In the years I have spent as a writing consultant at three separate institutions of higher education, everyone I worked with had something to say about on-the-job stressors in the privacy of the breakroom or during weekly staff meetings. My colleagues and I would discuss clients or whatever stressor was affecting us emotionally that day. We needed to vocalize our stress while others listened, empathized, and offered their support. Unfortunately, that was usually where the conversation about emotions in our writing center ended. Discussions about how to cope with on-the-job stress—or how our expenditure of emotional labor could impact work performance—were frequently absent. While customer service professionals and teachers have primarily been the subjects of emotional labor research, such as the work of Debra Meyer and Mary Guy et al., studies have typically overlooked the role emotional labor plays in the daily work of writing center employees.

The lack of research into the expenditure of emotional labor in writing centers could be due to our resources seemingly existing on the fringes of higher education and are thus considered less important than heavily subsidized university offices and programs. To echo the sentiments of Bonnie Sunstein, writing centers typically exist and operate in small liminal spaces—both physically and conceptually—within the wider university environment (18, 22). Perhaps writing center staff labor is not viewed as significant as that of faculty. Maybe we hold onto the belief that we will simply discover ways to cope with work-related stress and move on with our lives. Whatever the reason, we should consider the ways writing center staff expend emotional labor because directors and tutors provide essential services to students. These services include active and empathic listening, collaboration, constructive feedback, and writing instruction—typically offered with positive affect displays, what Cynthia Haynes-Burton might call "the 'pathos,' or emotions, of writers" (51). Broadly, positive affect displays may be verbal or non-verbal cues— tone of voice and facial expression—that employees present to customers and co-workers while on the job (Metts and Planalp 295). Such displays of positive emotions further reflect the cultivation of emotional intelligence by which tutors can identify their "own and others' feelings and emotions, to discriminate among them and to use this information to guide [their] thinking and actions" (Salovey and Mayer 189). While professional requirements, institutional values, and perceived expectations may shape the work directors and tutors do in writing centers, service with a smile often foregrounds that work.

In service-oriented professions, researchers discovered that employees who routinely expend positive affect displays in their interactions with customers were more likely to participate in surface acting or deep acting to maintain a professional and friendly demeanor (Tracy; Gosserand and Diefendorff; Sliter et al.; Holman et al.). When employees participate in surface acting or deep acting in the workplace, they suppress felt emotions and subsequently replace those emotions with ones not truly experienced (Hochschild). Hochschild writes that when we participate in surface acting, "we deceive others about what we really feel, but we do not deceive ourselves" (33). In other words, surface actors pretend to appear happy while their felt emotions do not change. If someone participates in deep acting, they conceal negative emotions and attempt to sincerely feel the positive emotions they show others; deep actors become capable of "deceiving oneself as much as deceiving others" (Hochschild 33).

The daily display of positive emotions from staff—as they serve student writers—could eventually lead to an increase of emotional labor, especially if a tutor suppresses one emotion for another in order to maintain a friendly demeanor during a session. In Leigh Ryan and Lisa Zimmerelli's "Coping with Different Tutoring Situations," they recommend that tutors be "kind and sympathetic" (99), and "patient, polite, and supportive" (101) when confronted with "troublesome—or perhaps even difficult—situations while tutoring" (99). In providing positive responses to student writers, Bethany Mannon confirms that "Consultants do not always recognize the emotional labor of tutoring (and might perform it unconsciously), but many clients appreciate this service" (62). On-the-job participation in positive affect displays, especially to maintain professional appearances and a friendly work environment, certainly reflect the broader issue of writing center staff performing emotions deemed appropriate and necessary for student service work. In Anna Rita Napoleone's chapter in this collection, she reveals that emotions performed in writing centers are circulated and regulated rather than individualized. To that end, she argues that emotions are inextricably linked to multiple identity markers and performances. While my chapter does not focus on how personal identities influence the performance of appropriate emotions in writing centers, it does examine the different emotions writing center staff perform in their daily interactions with clients and each other.

To better understand the role emotions and emotional labor plays in writing centers, I designed and distributed an online RedCap survey during the 2019 spring semester to directors and tutors employed at Texas Tech University's undergraduate and graduate writing centers. In this chapter, I draw from the responses of voluntary participants who self-evaluated their on-the-job performance of emotions, particularly positive affect displays. The survey also asked respondents a series of open-ended questions, which gave them the opportunity to elaborate on how they managed the emotional effects of job-related stressors, as well as how the center could help staff better discuss the emotional labor components of writing center work. Elements from the survey could help writing center directors learn more about the emotional needs of their employees and help both directors and tutors better consider work-related stressors. The results of this project may also serve as a baseline for future research about emotional labor in writing centers.

Literature Review

Research about emotional labor in higher education has often focused on how academe overlooks and undervalues the role emotions play in the face-to-face and service-oriented work performed in classrooms and at other sites of academic discourse. Current literature about emotional labor in writing centers similarly examines the personal experiences of directors and tutors and how the expenditure of emotional labor impacts on-the-job experiences. Elizabeth Boquet, Lisa Birnbaum, Michelle DeLappe, Donna Rabuck, Thomas Spitzer-Hanks, Kathleen Hunzer, Christina Rowell, and Margaret Tipper have all noted the benevolent qualities of writing center work that is "often carried out at a considerable remove from the academy's systems of economic rewards and political privileges" (Trachsel 33). Within the liminal spaces of writing centers, directors and tutors offer students and one another "refuge, nurturance, emotional support, [and] personal guidance" (Grimm 524). Writing centers have thus become polestars where the intellectual labor of active and empathic "listening, reflection, and collaboration are nurtured" (Miley 20). If the abovementioned labor requirements have fashioned current ideas of what writing centers represent, then self-reflection and self-evaluation can help researchers better understand the types of emotional labor tutors and directors expend.

In writing center scholarship, tutors and directors have published a fair amount of personal self-reflections and self-assessments about how emotions have influenced their work. A common narrative from these reflections is that the expenditure of emotional labor manifests from professional interactions with others, such as acknowledging and responding to the different emotions that writers bring to a tutorial (Barnett 12), empathizing with clientele (Massie; Hudson 10), and actively and empathically listening to clients (Weintraub 11; Schotka 54). Gayla Mills recommends that writing center staff must first understand that "[w]e can't respond perfectly to every emotional situation, but we can mentally prepare" (1–2). To better prepare for the inevitable emotions that consultants and clients expend during tutorials, Mills contends that directors and tutors should collectively learn about evaluating and responding to negative emotions, role-play different scenarios as part of professional development, and actively listen and thoughtfully respond to clients to help them remain on task (4–5). Like Mills, Lauren Bisson recommends that consultants should simply be aware and read the situation, and, if a client responds positively to a consultant's inquiry for either privacy or emotional support, then the client can eventually return to the session (15). While the above assessments strictly focus on emotions in the writing center, subsequent researchers evaluate how emotional labor influences the work of writing center staff.

In current literature about emotional labor in writing centers, two common themes emerge. First, writing center staff are responsible for acknowledging the ways emotional labor influences their professional identities; and second, emotional labor can positively affect the daily work of writing center employees. Alison Perry writes that directors and tutors must "validate the emotional ardor of writing center work" and "adjust conditions in the work lives of [writing center] staff to promote self-care and an overall climate of support" (par. 5) Julia Meuse would likely concur with Perry because, as Meuse affirms, "all writing is personal and the act of sharing it with others can be an anxiety-inducing, emotional experience" for both consultants and students. "Tutors," she writes, "must assume multiple roles simultaneously, striking a difficult balance between expert adviser, empathetic listener, and the imagined intended audience" (Meuse para. 2). In their empirical study of writing center directors, Nicole Caswell, Jackie Grutsch McKinney, and Rebecca Jackson likewise confirm the prevalence of unseen emotional labor. Based on their interviews with administrative staff, the authors discovered that the expenditure of emotional labor by directors simultaneously "both what made the work difficult and what made it rewarding" (195). Although Caswell et al. focus solely on the lived professional experiences of writing center directors, their conclusions demonstrate how the expenditure of emotional labor in writing centers is not always adverse. Rather, emotional labor—especially when expended on work someone has passion for—can facilitate both "satisfaction and visibility" as well as "recognition and affirmation" of the employee's efforts and successes (Caswell et al. 196). The positive components of emotional labor that contribute to the work performed by directors and tutors also supports, as Muhammad Saleem contends, "the relationships that we build with each other [in the writing center], what goes into building and sustaining them, and what it means to reciprocate" emotions (par. 18). Past research certainly reveals how felt emotions inform interactions between clientele and tutors and how emotional labor can shape professional identity. While empirical studies about the emotional labor of writing center directors and tutors do exist, additional research in this area could lead to increased understanding of the emotional labor obligations staff undertake daily.

METHODOLOGY

To learn about how writing center administrators and consultants expend emotional labor, I developed an online survey with fifty-seven questions using the data collection tool, RedCap. The purpose of the survey was to collect data about: the types of emotional labor writing center staff participate in; how writing center directors and tutors cope with emotional stressors; and how emotional labor influences the relationships between staff members and their clients. The survey asked participants open-ended questions and short answer responses about emotional labor and its effects on their work for the writing center. I specifically wanted to know if the expenditure of emotional labor influenced the quality of work, overall job satisfaction, perceptions of co-workers and clientele, and development of emotional intelligence. It was my intention that a self-evaluation format, especially the short answer questions, would encourage introspection from participants.

In the design process of the online survey, I selected respondent self-evaluation as the method of data collection. Self-evaluation from participants would also allow me to better infer relationships between survey responses. Prior to the current study, my own self-reflection and evaluation of the emotional labor I expend in the writing center altered my perspective of how I interact with colleagues and clients. Beyond maintaining a friendly demeanor and treating others with kindness and empathy, I did not consider the role emotional labor played in my own professional identity. The more I researched positive affect displays, the more I started to assess my own emotional labor and slowly understood how positive affect shaped my interactions with others as a professional writing consultant. As I evaluated my persona in the writing center, I realized that I often participated in surface acting to maintain a friendly demeanor in front of others. In a similar vein, self-evaluation could also allow participants to, likewise, reflect on their own experiences with emotional labor without intervention or unintended influence from the PI.

The target population for this study was writing center consultants and directors employed at Texas Tech's University Writing Center (UWC) and Graduate Writing Center (GWC). UWC consultants tutor undergraduate and graduate students, as well as university faculty and staff. Consultants at the GWC exclusively work with graduate students and postdoctoral fellows. Both writing centers employ tutors from diverse disciplines. While undergraduate tutors work alongside professional tutors at the UWC, only graduate and professional tutors work at the GWC. The survey did not ask respondents to indicate if they were part-time or full-time employees, undergraduate or graduate student consultants, professional consultants, or writing center administrators; this maintained anonymity. For the purposes of maintaining respondent confidentiality, the survey did not collect information about age, gender, or ethnicity either. While two survey questions provided respondents the opportunity to elaborate on whether their gender or ethnic identities informed their use of positive affect displays in the writing center, responses were non-identifying.

Upon receiving approval from Texas Tech University's Human Research Protection Program, IRB2019–295, I distributed a link to the survey via email, along with a description of the study—purpose, informed consent, data use, and privacy and security—to all currently employed UWC and GWC staff; n=28. Upon conclusion of the survey period on June 1, 2019, at midnight, the total number of participants who submitted responses was thirteen. While the small sample size may have limited the amount of data that could have been collected and analyzed, the thirteen respondents who completed a survey met the criteria for this research project. Although the opinions and experiences from the thirteen respondents may not be representative of all UWC and GWC employees, the respondents are a part of the same narrow target population recruited for the study. Lastly, while respondents greater than thirteen would have certainly provided the study with additional data, that data may not have offered new or unique information to the study.

I analyzed the survey questions by identifying common themes and inferring connections between responses. I considered individual survey responses as part of a broader conversation and established relationships across respondent answers as well as the similarities and differences between responses. All respondent comments were randomly allocated numbers between one and thirteen to separate one statement from another.

RESULTS

In order to measure perceptions of emotional labor requirements of writing center work, multiple choice questions asked participants to consider their own beliefs and experiences. Respondents identified positive emotional expressiveness (n=12), surface acting (n=4), deep acting (n=3), empathy (n=13), sincerity (n=12), and mindfulness (n=13), as types of emotional labor they performed in the writing center. Supplemental non-identifying questions included whether gender identity and ethnicity influenced respondents' participation in emotional labor. Seven participants concurred that their gender identity informed how they approach emotional labor in the writing center, while only two participants believed that their ethnicity shaped their practices of emotional labor.

Emotional Control. In response to survey questions about on-the-job emotional suppression, respondents admitted to participating in surface acting or deep acting at some point in their employment at the writing center. Responses include adjusting negative emotions to make positive emotions appear genuine (n=12), striving to feel faked emotions (n=11), and setting an intention to be in a good mood while interacting with clients and colleagues (n=12). Participants also reported neither pretending to display positive emotions (n=9), or faking positivity in the writing center, n=10. Similarly, respondents admitted that it was easy for them to be in a positive mood around colleagues and clients (n=9), as well as display positive emotions—for example, friendliness, optimism, kindness—consistently in the writing center (n=10).

While the above results indicate a preference for positive affect displays, additional responses show that emotional regulation helps achieve that positivity. Responses include controlling emotions in front of colleagues and clients (n=13), and wearing a "mask" to express appropriate emotions and attitudes while in the writing center (n=6). Moreover, participants admitted to exhibiting positive emotions even after receiving negative or critical feedback from a client (n=11), hiding disappointment after an unsuccessful writing tutorial (n=9), and concealing negative emotions when a colleague or client made them mad or upset (n=8). These responses imply that Texas Tech's writing center staff do participate in a certain level of emotional control; that control may be a result of perceived organizational requirements to maintain a professional and friendly demeanor in front of colleagues and clients.

Expressed and Felt Emotions. In response to questions about expressed and experienced emotions, eight respondents reported experiencing emotional exhaustion at some point during their employment with the writing center. While eleven people responded that they have felt negative emotions in the writing center, nine reported hiding those negative emotions from others. Respondents also reported experiencing high levels of stress, n=7, burnout, n=5, sadness, n=8, dissatisfaction (n=7), and anger or frustration (n=7). Twelve participants reported setting an intention to be in a good mood while interacting with clients and colleagues. While seven respondents admitted to conjuring up positive emotions, eleven participants agreed that emotions displayed in front of clients and colleagues were consistent with their actual emotions. In the current iteration of the online survey, no questions were asked to determine whether negative affect was the result of work-related stressors or dissonance between positive displays of emotion and felt negative emotions.

Professional Requirements. The final section of the survey focused on perceived, job-related requirements for writing center employees. Responses motion toward a vested interest in genuine, felt emotions to maintain a positive work environment, such as maintaining a friendly demeanor (n=11), offering advice in a nice way (n=12), empathizing with others (n=13), and, if something goes wrong at work, trying to make colleagues and clients feel better (n=13). Twelve respondents also revealed that both they and their co-workers talk about negative emotions with each other and that it was easy to sense and respond to the emotions of clients and colleagues.

The survey also asked elective short answer questions about coping with the side effects of emotional labor and requested recommendations for a training program or intervention that could help build emotional intelligence and empathy in the writing center. One respondent noted that "the opportunity to discuss tutorials and ask any questions" can assist with "the care and development" of consultants (Respondent 8). As well, another participant said that being able to "express my concerns professionally with clients in a productive way" can help consultants "be transparent about [their] struggles with [their] colleagues and supervisors" (Respondent 12). Likewise, respondents concurred that additional opportunities for communication between co-workers could help alleviate incidences of emotional labor, such as "debriefing sessions to talk about a client session" (Respondent 2) and checking in "on the well-being of everyone on a daily basis" (Respondent 3). During training and staff meetings, one participant mentioned that employees should openly "talk about compassion fatigue and emotional labor to ensure [that] everyone is aware of it and knows what steps to take when experiencing it" (Respondent 7). In that way, supplemental conversations about emotional labor "would build on existing models of open conversation and trust" through things like a weekly, in-service meeting or a professional development session, "but might also include more structured discussions early in training about coping with emotional labor and more formal means of mediating those feelings" (Respondent 11).

When participants described how they managed stress, negative emotions, signs of emotional conflict, and emotional exhaustion, active communication was a common theme. Participants mentioned conversing with other consultants and supervisors because of their ability to empathically listen (Respondents 5 and 7). Respondent 11 likewise writes: "[I] often talk through my reactions or stress level with supervisors. I appreciate that they are willing to hear those emotions even if they cannot always solve the problems." Additional respondents confirmed that communication with supervisors and co-workers can help one another discuss "the hard questions we might feel difficult to ask in a public setting" (Respondent 2) and "navigate the experiences of challenging sessions" (Respondent 9).

DISCUSSION

Based on the results, surveyed writing center staff acknowledged displaying positive affect towards co-workers and clientele. Participants also admitted a preference for conveying genuine positive emotions, cultivating emotional intelligence, being mindful of others' emotions, and showing empathy when interacting with others in the writing center. Respondents' preference for sincere positivity and actively empathizing with others perhaps illustrates a desire to maintain a positive and supportive work environment. Short answer responses likewise revealed preferences for building emotional intelligence and empathy and collaboratively discussing and resolving on-the-job stressors.

By sensing and responding to the emotions of others, survey participants likely consider responsiveness to felt emotions a paramount responsibility in the writing center. Noreen Lape affirms that when tutors "[learn] to identify feelings, both her own and the writer's" (3), they can develop "the ability to interpret correctly each writer's emotions" (4). Open and honest communication, managing emotional labor costs, and providing clients with empathy and assistance can first provide directors and consultants the opportunity to articulate their emotions and then discuss any work-related stressors affecting emotional well-being. Lape further contends that "identifying emotions is a habit of mind and being that tutors can cultivate with practice over time, resulting in deeper intuitions and sharper emotional instincts" (4). Actively reflecting and talking about emotions can—as per the recommendations of Lana Oweidat and Lydia McDermott—maintain a work environment built on nurturance and help employees cultivate their emotional intelligence. Emotional intelligence certainly exists at the forefront of writing center work because tutors consistently perceive, appraise, and respond to the emotions of student writers during consultations. Identifying and responding to the emotions of others in writing centers already has the potential of building tutors' emotional intelligence, as doing so could allow them to actively understand what different emotions—theirs and clients'—communicate during a session and how those emotions can affect—either positively or negatively—a tutorial. The cultivation of "empathetic listening and responding" further allows writing center staff "to 1) find a balance between acknowledging students' emotions and supporting their writing and 2) develop listening and responding strategies that support nondirective efforts that honor student agency" (McBride et al.). As well, professional development readings and activities that underscore emotional responsiveness could allow directors and tutors to share their knowledge about empathy, reflect on their own empathetic communication skills, and learn how to better empathize with the diverse experiences of clientele.

Practical and Policy Implications. The current research study offers practical and policy implications not only for Texas Tech University's UWC and GWC but for other writing centers, as well. One of these implications includes improving our overall understanding of how we as writing center professionals expend emotional labor. One way to increase our knowledge about emotional labor and how it can affect our work is to establish novel training components for new and returning tutors.

In their recommendations for how writing centers could implement an assistance program to reduce the potential negative impacts of emotional labor, respondents wrote that additional opportunities for open communication between employees could help promote personal well-being. Supplementing standard training curricula with the addition of readings that discuss the cultivation of active and empathetic listening, as well as emotional intelligence, is an important policy implication. Even writing centers that already encourage open communication among employees could also utilize supplemental in-house training across the academic year to educate staff to better recognize and appropriately respond to the emotions of clients. In addition to readings about open communication in the writing center, supplemental training could include scenario-based learning exercises that complement the best practices outlined in Ryan and Zimmerelli's *Bedford Guide*. The objective would be to increase employees' awareness about the potential effects performing emotional labor may have in their work with clients, as well as their own emotional well-being, how to value and develop emotional intelligence and empathy, and how to best respond to different emotions during tutorials.

For example, as part of our continuing professional development at Texas Tech's GWC, administrative staff and consultants read and discussed articles—such as Lape and McBride et al.—about emotional labor and emotional performance in writing centers. These conversations not only made us more aware of how emotional labor can affect our work with clients but also provided an opportunity for us to develop our emotional intelligence and empathetic listening. The addition of such readings to tutor training could help shape the policy of writing center administrators who would like their consultants to not just consider the emotional labor requirements of supporting students but also cultivate their own empathy. While the above recommendation motions towards an ideal for writing centers and their staff, directors and tutors may feel more inclined to perform positive emotions or participate in surface and deep acting in the presence of others because of either preconceived professional requirements, social norms, or personal preferences. The performance of positive emotions and regulation of negative ones in the academic space of writing centers certainly reflects Anna Rita Napoleone's concerns in this collection about peer tutors who feel like they must always *be on* in order to fit the institutional requirements of the job.

As discussed previously in the results section of this chapter, respondents indicated a preference for being empathetic and displaying genuine emotions while interacting with colleagues and clients. Therefore, an immediate practical implication of this result is that writing center staff should see mindfulness towards others' emotions as well as communicating honest emotions with others as fundamental components of their work. This could help maintain a friendly and positive work environment for both onsite and online writing centers. Directors and tutors should be mindful of their own and others' felt emotions but should not be reluctant to share and discuss those emotions when appropriate, echoing the sentiments of Lauren Brentnell, Elise Dixon, and Rachel Robinson in their chapter about supporting emotions and cultivating an awareness of the multilayered role emotions hold in these spaces. As before, additional opportunities for open communication in the writing center could allow staff to collaboratively build their emotional intelligence, be actively empathetic towards others, and create a common professional identity.

LIMITATIONS AND RECOMMENDATIONS FOR FUTURE RESEARCH

The current study about emotional labor and positive affect display in the writing center has several limitations. While the study was qualitative in nature, the researcher was unable to conduct follow-up interviews as initially planned. Therefore, analysis of survey responses was interpretive without supplemental participant input. One-to-one interviews or a focus group with writing center staff could have created a robust narrative analysis of participant experiences. A follow-up study could offer participants a new list of descriptive questions to scaffold the current survey. A future study could also examine how gender and ethnic identity inform the types of emotional labor directors and consultants expend and how other factors—like length of time worked in the writing center or one's professional role in the writing center—influence emotional labor.

Another limitation of the current study is sample size. Given that the number of survey respondents was thirteen—and was limited to only writing center staff at Texas Tech University—the results do not represent the experiences of all writing center tutors and directors at other institutions of higher education. While participants' responses did provide this study with richly detailed data, the small sample size represents only a portion of the target population. Future research with a similar survey design and instrument should increase the sample size to include writing centers at other institutions of higher education and determine if the findings of this study can be replicated with similar participants. As well, data collected from such a comprehensive study could help researchers better identify and understand common professional experiences of writing center staff.

CONCLUSION

The objective of this research project and chapter was to learn how writing center staff identified the emotional labor requirements of their work, the various types of emotional labor they participated in, and how they dealt with their expenditure of emotional labor. An underlying assumption was that tutors and directors did expend emotional labor, particularly positive affect display. Based on the findings, respondents identified positive emotional expressiveness, mindfulness, and empathy as the primary types of emotional labor expended in their daily work for the writing center. Participants further showed a noticeable preference for genuine displays of positive emotions—instead of faked positivity—while interacting with colleagues and clients. The primary practical and policy implication in establishing or expanding in-house support systems may help tutors negotiate the expenditure of emotional labor that could occur while working in a writing center. With such support systems in place, writing centers can continue to function as safe spaces where tutors and their supervisors can talk openly about on-the-job issues. As well, self-evaluating the ways we participate in emotional labor and communicating that labor with others can help maintain writing centers as places where we can talk about issues that we might otherwise feel difficult discussing. The disclosure of our felt emotions or work-related stressors to colleagues might not be the easiest conversation, but actively listening and responding in a thoughtful way is a fundamental part of the work we do every day.

WORKS CITED

Barnett, Robert. "The Invisible Couch in the Tutoring of Writing." *The Writing Lab Newsletter*, vol. 20, no. 4, 1995, pp. 10–12.

Bellas, Marcia. "Emotional Labor in Academia: The Case of Professors." *The American Academy of Political and Social Science*, vol. 561, no. 1, 1999, pp. 96–110.

Birnbaum, Lisa. "Toward a Gender-Balanced Staff in the Writing Center." *The Writing Lab Newsletter*, vol. 19, no. 8, 1995, pp. 6–7, wln-journal.org/archives/v19/19–8.pdf.

Bisson, Lauren. "Tutor's Column: 'Tears of a Tutee.'" *The Writing Lab Newsletter*, vol. 32, no. 4, 2007, pp. 14–15.Boquet, Elizabeth. *Noise from the Writing Center*. Utah State UP, 2002.

Caswell, Nicole, et al. *The Working Lives of New Writing Center Directors*. Utah State UP, 2016.

DeLappe, Michelle. "Midwifery in the Writing Center." *The Writing Lab Newsletter*, vol. 22, no. 9, 1998.

Fineman, Stephen, and Andrew Sturdy. "The Emotions of Control: A Qualitative Exploration of Environmental Regulation." *Human Relations*, vol. 52, no. 5, 1999, pp. 631–63.

Gosserand, Robin, and James Diefendorff. "Emotional Display Rules and Emotional Labor: The Moderating Role of Commitment." *Journal of Applied Psychology*, vol. 90, no. 6, 2005, pp. 1256–64.

Grimm, Nancy. "Rearticulating the Work of the Writing Center." *College Composition and Communication*, vol. 47, no. 4, 1996, pp. 523–48.

Guy, Mary E., et al. *Emotional Labor: Putting the Service in Public Service*. Routledge, 2008.

Haynes-Burton, Cynthia. "Constructing Our Ethos: Making Writing Centers 'Convenient.'" *Composition Studies*, vol. 20, no. 2, 1992, pp. 51–59.

Hochschild, Arlie. *The Managed Heart: Commercialization of Human Feeling*. U of California P, 1979.

Holman, David, et al. "Emotional Labor, Well-Being, and Performance." *The Oxford Handbook of Organizational Well-Being*, edited by Susan Cartwright and Cary Cooper, Oxford UP, 2008, pp. 331–55.

Hudson, Tracy. "Head 'Em Off at the Pass: Strategies for Handling Emotionalism in the Writing Center." *The Writing Lab Newsletter*, vol. 25, no. 5, 2001, pp. 10–12.

Hunzer, Kathleen. "Misperceptions of Gender in the Writing Center: Stereotyping and the Facilitative Tutor." *The Writing Lab Newsletter*, vol. 22, no. 2, 1997, pp. 6–10.

Lape, Noreen. "Training Tutors in Emotional Intelligence: Toward a Pedagogy of Empathy." *The Writing Lab Newsletter*, vol. 33, no. 2, 2008, pp. 1–6.

Mannon, Bethany Ober. "What Do Graduate Students Want from the Writing Center? Tutoring Practices to Support Thesis and Dissertation Writers." *Praxis: A Writing Center Journal*, vol. 13, no. 2, 2016, pp. 59–64.

Massie, Courtney. "On Gratitude, Empathy, and the Work We Do." *Axis: The Blog*, 21 Nov. 2016, www.praxisuwc.com/praxis-blog/2016/11/21/on-gratitude-empathy-and-the-work-we-do.

McBride, Maureen, et al. "Responding to the Whole Person: Using Empathic Listening and Responding in the Writing Center." *The Peer Review*, vol. 2, no. 2, 2018.

Metts, Sandra, and Sally Planalp. "Emotion Experience and Expression: Current Trends and Future Directions in Interpersonal Relationship Research." *The SAGE Handbook of Interpersonal Communication*, edited by Mark Knapp and John Daly. 4th ed., SAGE Publications, Inc., 2011, pp. 283–316.

Meuse, Julia. "Tutoring Sessions as Safe Spaces: Affecting Writing and the Personal Statement." *Another Word*, 9 Feb. 2016, www.dept.writing.wisc.edu/blog/tutoring-sessions-as-safe-spaces-affective-writing-and-the-personal-personal-statement/.

Meyer, Debra. "Entering the Emotional Practices of Teaching." *Advances in Teacher Emotion Research: The Impact on Teachers' Lives*, edited by Paul Schutz and Michalinos Zembylas, Springer, 2009, pp. 73–91.

Miley, Michelle. "Feminist Mothering: A Theory/Practice for Writing Center Administration." *Writing Lab Newsletter*, vol. 41, no. 1–2, 2016, pp. 17–24.

Mills, Gayla. "Preparing for Emotional Sessions." *The Writing Lab Newsletter*, vol. 35, no. 5–6, 2011, pp. 1–5.

Oweidat, Lana, and Lydia McDermott. "Neither Brave nor Safe: Interventions in Empathy for Tutor Training." *The Peer Review*, vol. 1, no. 2, 2017.

Perry, Alison. "Training for Triggers: Helping Writing Center Consultants Navigate Emotional Sessions." *Composition Forum*, vol. 34, 2016.

Rabuck, Donna. "Giving Birth to Voice: The Professional Writing Tutor as Midwife." *Writing Center Perspectives*, edited by Byron Stay, et al., NWCA Press, 1995, pp. 112–19.

Rafaeli, Anat, and Robert Sutton. "Expression of Emotion as Part of the Work Role." *The Academy of Management Review*, vol. 12, no. 1, 1987, pp. 23–37.

Rowell, Christina. *Let's Talk Emotions: Re-envisioning the Writing Center through Consultant Emotional Labor*. 2015. East Carolina U, Master's thesis.

Ryan, Leigh, and Lisa Zimmerelli. *The Bedford Guide for Writing Tutors*. 5th ed., Bedford, 2010.

Saleem, Muhammad Khurram. "The Languages in Which We Converse: Emotional Labor in the Writing Center and Our Everyday Lives." *The Peer Review*, vol. 2, no. 1, 2018.

Salovey, Peter, and John Mayer. "Emotional Intelligence." *Imagination, Cognition, and Personality*, vol. 9, no. 3, 1990, pp. 185–211.

Schotka, Roberta. *Academic Peer Tutor Training Manual*. Wellesley College Pforzheimer Learning and Teaching Center, 2014.

Sliter, Michael, et al. "How Rude! Emotional Labor as a Mediator Between Customer Incivility and Employee Outcomes." *Journal of Occupational Health Psychology*, vol. 15, no. 4, 2010, pp. 468–81.

Spitzer-Hanks, Thomas. "On 'feminized space' in the Writing Center." *Axis: The Blog*, 13 Apr. 2016, www.praxisuwc.com/praxis-blog/2016/4/13/on-feminized-space-in-the-writing-center.

Sunstein, Bonnie. "Moveable Feasts, Liminal Spaces: Writing Centers and the State of In-Betweenness." *The Writing Center Journal*, vol. 18, no. 2, 1998, pp. 7–26.

Tipper, Margaret. "Real Men Don't Do Writing Centers." *The Writing Center Journal*, vol. 19, no. 2, 1999, pp. 33–40.

Trachsel, Mary. "Nurturant Ethics and Academic Ideals: Convergence in the Writing Center." *The Writing Center Journal*, vol. 16, no. 1, 1995, pp. 24–45.

Tracy, Sarah. "Becoming a Character for Commerce: Emotion Labor, Self-Subordination, and Discursive Construction of Identity in a Total Institution." *Management Communication Quarterly*, vol. 14, no. 1, 2000, pp. 90–128.

Waldron, Vincent. *Communicating Emotion at Work*. Wiley, 2011.

Weintraub, Melissa. "The Use of Social Work Skills in a Writing Center." *Writing Lab Newsletter*, vol. 29, no. 5, 2005, pp. 10–11.

Wharton, Amy. "The Affective Consequences of Service Work: Managing Emotions on the Job." *Work and Occupations*, vol. 20, no. 2, 1993, pp. 205–32.

PART III: RELATIONAL ENCOUNTERS

12 Listening About Listening: Narratives of Affect, Diversity, and Feminist Listening in Writing Center Research Reporting

Steven J. Corbett and Katherine Villarreal

On May 1, 2019, about fifty faculty and students gathered for the inaugural Student Writing Projects Symposium at Texas A & M University, Kingsville. Faculty teaching writing-intensive courses across the curriculum gathered with their students to present on and listen to the engaging writing projects they had collaborated on together. The capstone of the symposium was the final roundtable session led by all of the staff from the University Writing Center, entitled "Top 5 Tips for Helping Students Navigate Writing Assignments." As the title suggests, tutors from our Center were there to offer any suggestion they could—from their substantial collective years of experience—on how to assist students in meeting the expectations of their writing assignments. At one point in the discussion, a tutor brought up the idea of the importance of motivational and emotional concerns in tutoring and how often they have worked with students who seemed emotionally stunted or even traumatized by their writing assignments and instructors. This set off what ended up being the most exciting moment of the five-hour event. Diverse tutors and instructors commenced debating the value of attending to the emotional needs of student writers—offering praise and other motivational scaffolding, in addition to critical feedback, whenever possible—versus being blunt with students about their writing issues and not sugar-coating direct instruction—and cognitive scaffolding—with unnecessary, even potentially counterproductive, affective concern. Emotions on both sides of the debate ran high as we listened to each other's stories of the choices involved in the coaching of writing. Tellingly, a large number of participants, in their post-symposium evaluation forms, mentioned the final roundtable as the best part of the entire event.

One thing all writing center and peer tutoring philosophies have in common is the belief in the primacy of the affective and emotional aspect of peer-to-peer pedagogies (c.f. Harris, *Teaching*; Harris, "Talking;" Lape; Lawson; Mackiewicz and Thompson; Corbett, *Beyond*; Corbett, "Learning;" Yoon and Stutelberg). Increasingly, reporting and analyzing the affective and emotional aspects of peer tutoring have become more nuanced in writing center research. For example, in the extant work of Jo Mackiewicz and Isabelle Thompson, the concept of motivational scaffolding involves elements of affective connections between tutors and student writers. Likewise, in "Training Tutors in Emotional Intelligence: Toward a Pedagogy of Empathy," Noreen Lape urges "when it comes to tutoring, emotional intelligence is no less important than knowledge of discourse conventions and the writing process" (1). The willingness and ability to listen carefully to and re-tell these studies and stories of affect will continue to be extremely important for writing center research reporting.

As studies have become more RAD—replicable, aggregate, and data-driven—we are actually gaining deeper insight into narratives of emotion and what it means to listen carefully *with* our research participants. Lynn Briggs and Meg Woolbright's collection, *Stories from the Center: Connecting Narrative and Theory in the Writing Center*, focuses on what can be learned from writing center practitioners' stories. The editors offer a distinction between "story" and "study" (xi). They see a study as primarily about other people's voices, as "controlled or objective" with little "contact with one's own life," while narrative and story can "give voice to that which would otherwise go unheard" (xi). Even twenty years after Briggs and Woolbright published their collection, can we still draw such a sharp distinction between "study" and "story?" Conversely, Thomas Newkirk, drawing on Linda Brodkey and Clifford James—and echoing the work of Clifford Geertz and Jerome Bruner—in "The Narrative Roots of the Case Study," argues that during research, whether qualitative or quantitative, we make new stories from the patterns of old narratives. For Newkirk, rather than allow the "methodological machine" the ostensible agency of reporting and interpreting the data, "[a] more honest strategy—for both quantitative and qualitative researchers—is to admit, from the beginning, that we are all storytellers" (134). The place of narrative in constructing both more positivistic and more interpretive ways of knowing has become essential to writing center research reporting. Drawing on our own and other's studies—and stories—we will argue, in this chapter, that the importance of continuing to listen to narratives of affect in the work that we do to more carefully inform the scholarship is as timely and warranted now as it has ever been. It is crucial, in fact, if we wish to continue realizing the important roles of identity and diversity in the work writing center practitioners and researchers choose to engage in. To this work, we propose a theory of practice that centers on feminist listening.

In exploring our claim about the importance of affective narratives in writing center research, we will begin this chapter theorizing the connections between pedagogical affect and feminist listening. Like Lauren Rosenberg and Emma Howes in "Listening to Research as a Feminist Ethos of Representation," we believe feminist listening seeks to understand "how listening can be channeled toward more ethical research practices. We are concerned with our own positions as feminist researchers and with the ways we interact with participants and students; thus, we aim to enact practices that tend to differences among others, while holding ourselves accountable for how our positions orient us as researchers" (77). We offer Rosenberg and Howes's three principles to guide feminist researchers—lingering on relationships, listening, and co-creating knowledge—as a heuristic for analyzing and reporting writing center case studies. *Lingering on relationships* involves slowing down and pausing—writing and reflecting *with* rather than *about* the fellow actors in our pedagogical interactions and research studies, whenever possible. *Listening* acts as the all-important bridge between lingering on relationships and co-creating knowledge. Feminist listening entails lingering on the state of mind and emotion of the people we work with, paying attention to how we design research projects, and becoming aware of what value we assign to how—and with whom—data is collected and reported. *Co-creating knowledge* involves listening for and seeking out ways of knowing and experiencing beyond our own and, whenever possible, with the people we interact with and our research participants—a process Rosenberg and Howes call "mutual contemplation" (81).

Next, we apply these feminist research connections to two of co-author Steven Corbett's writing center case studies as reported in the book, *Beyond Dichotomy: Synergizing Writing Center and Classroom Pedagogies*, and the essay, "Learning Disability and Response-Ability: Reciprocal Caring in Developmental Peer Response Writing Groups and Beyond." These case studies involve diverse participants—tutors, instructors, student writers, and researchers—in course-based tutoring, working together to build—sometimes successful, and other times unsuccessful—narratives of listening, relationship-building, and co-creating knowledge. Course-based tutoring participants find themselves trying to negotiate just what they are supposed to do now that the typical ecology of the tutorial has changed—tutors might find themselves in classrooms in a leadership role; tutors might find themselves in more in-the-know positions, where they are closer to course readings and the expectations of the course. Instructors, then, find themselves in situations where they have a very advanced student ready to help share in instructional efforts. In short, all participants try to build trust in one another's authority and roles. Tutors, finding themselves often more in-the-know, have to decide if they want to take on more authoritative or directive roles or try to be as non-intrusive or nondirective in the ebb and flow of classroom instructional conversation and momentum. Finally, tutors must face the age-old issue of balancing between attention to students' texts or students' products and awareness of the human-intensive quality of the work they are performing with fellow students and students' writing processes.

We will conclude this chapter with our thoughts on the implications and importance of the value of uniting pedagogical affect with feminist listening—*listening about listening*, à la Elizabeth Wardle and Douglas Downs's *Writing about Writing*—in terms of identity and diversity, for future writing center practitioners and researchers.

RESEARCH AT THE INTERSECTIONS OF FEMINIST LISTENING AND PEDAGOGICAL AFFECT

Feminist ideals—including the importance of authentic listening, relationship-building, valuing diverse identities and perspectives, and attending to emotions—have permeated writing center spaces and research reporting. If we care about equality, writing center practitioners should consider the idea of a feminist theory of practice. Feminism is the idea of political, social, and economic equality for people of all sexes, races, and abilities. Applying equality and diversity to the writing center should not be a difficult task, but writing center scholarship has shown that it has proved challenging. While feminist ideals permeate writing center scholarship, they involve a complicated matrix of identity, subject positions, agency, and point of view.

In one of the first articles on the subject of feminism in the writing center, the 1992 "The Politics of Tutoring: Feminism in the Writing Center," Woolbright reflects on the complexity of a feminist theory of practice. Woolbright describes how, for her, becoming more attuned to the ideals of equality and diversity resulted in the realization that when considering "the level of feminist pedagogy, the issue is one of power" (19). Woolbright notes that perceived, asymmetrical subject positions during tutorial sessions can present obstacles that can hinder success (19). Writing center scholarship has long featured tutors who express and push for students to take more action, assume more ownership of their writing, and become more driven towards their goals of writing proficiently. A big part of this motivational scaffolding recommends that tutors understand the importance of "feelings and be[ing] willing to address them in order to best serve writers and the goals of the Writing Center" (Seeley 4). Thus, decades-old writing center feminist ideals are still highly relevant for the ways they inform and inspire a current and future feminist theory of practice.

As tutors and researchers, we bring to the scholarly table our approach to not just writing but also to the conversations behind writing. For example, the focus of being grammatically correct—later-order concern— is not always the most important issue. Attention to someone's feelings might be even more important than higher-order concerns (Seeley; Lape; Lawson; Valentine; Haen; Phillips; Yoon and Stutelberg). When we shift the conversation of emotion in writing centers, we shift it by focusing on the person behind these emotions. We find ourselves running into labels that represent or are represented in our writing. The list of labels stems from the generic: tutor, student, and graduate. They branch off to: disabled, gay, Hispanic, Black, White, and so on. The list grows longer to the point that they are not just labels but actual internalized identities students and tutors bring into the writing center.

A feminist theory of practice encourages balancing between labels and our identity, where students question who exactly they are and need to be when writing a paper. Michelle Miley, in "Feministic Mothering: A Theory/Practice for Writing Center Administration," remarks, "The nature of my work as a writing center director means that I must also balance multiple relationships and identities" (21). Miley describes how her own identity becomes a process of negotiation while administering her writing center. Writing center scholarship has always been concerned with how creating discussions—instead of mandating solutions—and crafting new conversations on equality and inclusion can make centers more inclusive places (Dixon). Tutors need to be aware of what writing center scholarship has revealed about the value of people-first language and the value of delving into more conversations centered on students' feelings. Yet, Miley laments how feelings in the writing center are often debunked and erased in order to focus on more critical listening and peer tutoring strategies. She asserts that "having the work of a writing center described as 'just talking about feelings' diminishes and devalues what I believe is central to a necessary pedagogy writing centers offer in today's university systems" (17). Her research narrative unfolds more opportunities for emotion and listening to become stronger in the writing center spaces she inhabits by valuing feminist ideals.

Listening—and all it can do to enhance the affective dimension of our practice—has been a recurring topic in the narrative of writing center research (Harris, *Teaching*; Babcock and Thonus; Valentine), and it has concurrently encouraged a feminist ideology. Early on, in 1986, Muriel Harris emphasized the importance of listening in relation to all aspects of a tutoring session (*Teaching*). Harris states that when "we listen, we ask questions, we observe, we demonstrate strategies, and we respond with necessary information or answers to questions" (*Teaching* 55). Listening conveys importance and attentiveness to the student's writing and enhances the need for more awareness of the affective dimensions in the writing center (Harris, "Talking"). Being attuned to feminist principles in writing centers lead us to question: What kind of listening goes on in writing centers? Is the listening that occurs too concerned with how the writer feels? Is the listening that occurs too concerned with what the writer wrote? Mike Haen in "The Affective Dimension of Writing Center Talk: Insights from Conversation Analysis," expresses the need for more authentic listening and challenges how tutors praise and encourage students who visit writing centers, admonishing tutors to put "feel good emotions" last and critical instructional focus and specificity first (4). In his analysis of tutorial transcripts, Haen seeks to disrupt writing center narratives of affiliation that can supersede students' needs for critical feedback. Can this kind of authentic listening occur when tutoring without paying attention to affective concerns? Can it only be strengthened by staying open to students' emotional states? We believe attention to affective and critical concerns are by no means mutually exclusive. Increasingly, writing center research is demonstrating how emotion, listening, and critical feedback can go hand in hand. Tutors can use motivational scaffolding in coordination with direct instruction and cognitive scaffolding to encourage students to interact with them and their own essays (cf. Mackiewicz and Thompson; Lerner and Oddis, in this collection). Increasingly, writing center research is demonstrating how emotion, listening, and critical feedback can go hand in hand when tutors use motivational scaffolding in coordination with direct instruction and cognitive scaffolding to encourage students to interact with them and their own essays (cf. Mackiewicz and Thompson; Lerner and Oddis, in this collection). This approach can lead to the research-informed practice of feminist listening.

There is a direct connection between the idea of feminist listening and Krista Ratcliffe's concept of rhetorical listening. In the "Afterword" of the collection *Composing Feminist Interventions: Activism, Engagement, Praxis* the often-cited Ratcliffe describes why she believes "rhetorical listening, as well as other means for inviting listening into conversations . . . may serve as a feminist tactic" (509). She points to the chapters in the collection as examples of narratives of feminist research and teaching that merge personal and public spheres. Ratcliffe believes that becoming a student of feminist narrative—stories and studies involving the negotiation of identity, subject positions, agency, and points of view—can allow students, teachers, and researchers to listen more carefully. This can, in turn, lead them to become able to recognize "how power dynamics haunt their daily lives and then to discern when and how to perform activism, engagement, and other needed praxes" ("Afterword" 510). The willingness to *listen about listening* in the stories of the diverse students and colleagues we encounter can thus contribute to an ongoing narrative of feminist transformative teaching, learning, and research reporting.

CASE STUDIES OF FEMINIST LISTENING IN ACTION

Connecting feminist listening to rhetorical listening, we use Rosenberg and Howes's three principles as a heuristic to guide feminist researchers analyzing writing center research reporting: lingering on relationships with participants and communities; listening; and co-creating knowledge. We will use this feminist listening heuristic as a lens with which to continue our attempts at mutually contemplating the following case studies in order to illustrate examples—and the values of—successful and less-successful realizations of these feminist research principles.

Case Study One: A Cautionary Tale of Non-Listening. Steven Corbett's *Beyond Dichotomy: Synergizing Writing Center and Classroom Pedagogies* offers illuminating narratives of success, as well as a cautionary tale of course-based tutors making—or failing to make—affective and emotional connections with students and instructors in developmental composition courses. Corbett reports that one of the course-based tutors he studied closely, Julian, did not develop either salutary rapport with diverse students nor have much of an understanding of what was going on in the course. Julian's sense of himself as "reserved advisor" and the gross lack of communication between he and the instructor of the course, Anne, combined to co-construct a cautionary tale of affective and emotional disconnect (108). Anne intimated that she felt students and Julian did not get to know each other well enough on an individual basis to enable Julian to move past his nondirective "reserved advisor" approach—that he had learned during his peer tutor training—toward a method that might take into account the more individualistic needs and dispositions of each student. Julian stated that the "biggest roadblock . . . involved lack of regular communication between him and Anne" (92). Yet, not getting to know the students very well may not have been the major factor in Julian's problematic sessions. Careful transcript analysis helps illustrate Julian's most salient negative tutorial pattern—the fact that he talks too much while allowing relatively much less student talk-time—or, concurrently, tutor listening-time. Couple this with the fact that he often talks a lot before he has read the entire student's paper, and we are often left wondering why he is talking so much, often in the abstract, about the student's ideas and writing.

In his fourth session, Julian works with a highly reticent student who is having obvious trouble negotiating the assignment. We quote this excerpt at some length because it illustrates the extreme that Julian can go to in his verbosity, in his domination of the session:

> JULIAN: Yeah okay just get specific with it. Do you think we need to follow President Bush's plan because it affects everybody? How does it affect everybody? Like what's at stake? Like security? Like what else? What are the issues at play?

STUDENT: I don't know.

JULIAN: That's cool. Just make a note for yourself or something. I just think about it because that's the kind of stuff I read. That idea makes sense, right? Just kick it around. One thing to do is if you're totally like i"s not coming to you forget about it for a while because it looks like you've got a good structure of your body paragraphs, right? And this last sentence suggested like talking a little about there are many clear facts like what are you talking about? See where you can end up in your conclusion like ultimately we'll only need to listen to Bush ready to do this because these things are like like why do we need to? What is President Bush saying that we need to do these things for right? So he says that we need to do this because ABC right? Do we need to do for AB and C if he's right if he's correct right? Where Bush says what we need is for AB and C and you look at that and he is right we do need to do it for these reasons one of those can be your stakes because that's what you're talking about right? You just need to introduce them in a general way. I know I'm rambling but I'm trying to say that the topics are the central ideas of your body paragraphs. You can sort of like generalize about them; just sort of go back and connect them to claim. (yeah) FIVE SECOND PAUSE. That's got to actually do a lot. When I get stuck on opening paragraphs like I'll just because I don't know I don't know how the writing process goes for you but you my intro paragraph takes me and my claim takes me about as much time as writing half of my body paragraphs, so sometimes I'll write by pulling my quotes and I'll write the central paragraphs and then in writing them I'll be like oh I do have something to say in like my conclusion. I'll, I'll go back and generalize to make a claim. (all right) I'm talking a lot, like let me ask you a question. You guys have talked about rhetorical analysis right? So what do you think about the rhetorical analysis you have so far on Bush in this first and second paragraph?

STUDENT: I don't know what rhetorical means.

In this striking example, Julian . . . knows he is rambling, which causes him to actually slow down and ask a question that leads him to figure out the student does not understand the idea of

rhetorical analysis. This lingering moment of thoughtful pause
seems promising. Yet, rather than ask some questions that might
get the student thinking, allow time for a response, and maybe
even write some notes, notice how Julian will ask a question,
then answer it himself. . . . (61–62)

There are many similar examples across Julian's transcript. Julian often
will continue without waiting for the student to respond to questions
he's asked. Instead, we see "extended stretches where he tries hard to
offer useful suggestions" before the student has a chance to speak (62).

Comparing Julian's session to another reported in Sacha-Rose Phillips' *WLN* tutor's column, Phillips cogently relays a similar perspective
on the need for listening as a tool for our sessions and presents another
issue of the balance between identity and listening. In "Shared Identities,
Diverse Needs," Phillips reports on her struggles with her assumptions
during sessions that caused her not to listen carefully. She writes, "Tutors need to continuously center not only the identities of writers but
also their expressed needs" (29). Phillips relays how she failed to listen to
what the student wanted and instead focused on what she thought she
heard. While identity is important, Phillips admitted it was her own ESL
background that got in the way of her cognitive scaffolding. She focused
too much on her own identity, when it should have been the student's
identity she helped establish during the session. Woolbright states that
"when the topic shifts to the work on the student's paper, the pedagogy shifts to an uneasy subversion. . ." (23). Since Phillips dedicated too
much time on the paper instead of the student, she found herself unsure
as to where to take the session. This same question of how much to focus
on the text versus the "whole writer" surfaces in this collection with
Neal Lerner and Kyle Oddis's study of emotional knowledge in relation
to online tutoring. The same can be said for Julian and Anne in the narrative of a disconnected instructional relationship. Julian fully admitted
that he was too focused on fulfilling a role he thought Anne wanted him
to perform. Julian ended up focusing almost completely on the writer's
text, repeatedly paying little attention to their emotional states. For other
examples of applying Ratcliffe's rhetorical listening to analyzing failed
communication, see Valentine 110–111.

Yet, we must also ask questions involving the significance of lingering on relationships, listening, and co-creating knowledge from the researcher himself, Corbett. Julian, unfortunately, did not have the same
opportunity as the successful, course-based tutor, detailed below, to re-

deem himself in any way via consistent and productive interactions in the classroom. In Corbett's interview with Anne and Julian, both stated that if Julian had attended class on a regular basis, they felt that their experience would have been much more positive. Corbett reports that while designing this research study, in order to have a variety of collaborative approaches, he moved this team away from Anne's original desire to have Julian in-class on a much more regular basis. Anne was a graduate student who had worked in the writing center herself as an undergraduate. Perhaps Anne, holding so much writing center experience and knowledge of moving between center and classroom, felt it would be better—for her students and herself—if Julian could have been in much closer instructional proximity. Maybe, as Anne intimated, Julian was too conflicted and experienced too much metacognitive dissonance in negotiating his role. Julian seemed to spend too much time trying to get students to where he felt Anne wanted them to be, when what Anne was hoping for was some disruption of her teacherly authority. In relation to these developmental writers' identities, Anne said: "They're the quickest to bow to authority. They're the quickest to say 'well am I doing it right?' And the least likely in some ways to sort of say 'I don't think that's a useful way of approaching this question' or 'what can we do with this assignment to make it something real for me and not just some imagined scenario or something'" (Corbett, *Beyond* 92). Moreover, Julian's habit of talking a lot, passion for intellectual conversation, and fuzzy knowledge of the course texts and expectations caused him to speak in general and vague ways. Yet, a feminist-listening approach to research asks us to also question the role of the researcher in this narrative and to listen for possible "discordant notes" (Ratcliffe, "Rhetorical" 203) from everyone involved in a research project. Perhaps Corbett should have listened more carefully to, and tried harder to accommodate, Anne's desire to have Julian in the classroom on a more frequent and regular basis. Lingering on these types of problematic pedagogical moments—*listening about listening*—as Erica Cirillo-McCarthy and Elizabeth Leahy discuss in their chapter in this collection, might help future researchers design more successful, less conflict-ridden studies based on relationship-building and co-creating knowledge.

Case Study Two: When Participants Talk and Researchers (Choose to) Listen. Attention to emotion pinpoints just how deep our students' narratives can go and suggests how fruitful listening for people's stories can prove for writing center research. One set of narratives, reported in

Corbett's article "Learning Disability and Response-Ability," addresses the discussion around student and tutor identity, again in relation to the often-closer instructional contact afforded by course-based tutoring. Corbett reflects on the importance of authentic listening in course-based tutoring for the sake of strong and reliable instructional relationships with a student, named Max, and a tutor, named Sara. Both students identify as learning-disabled, LD, but present two different perspectives that offer examples of feminist pedagogical ideals. Max, self-identified as autism-spectrum, intimated how he struggled throughout his grade school years and approached college, especially his first-year writing course, with heavy trepidation. Sara approached Max with patience and an upbeat attitude—intent on identifying with and building a relationship with him—as she is a tutor also with a self-identified LD: dyslexia. Sara did not let her "LD identity" define her and rewrote her own identity as a course-based tutor instead. Her emotions fueled her to defy her own—and even her parent's—expectations and be a helpful tutor for Max and the other students in the course.

As a result, Max blossomed and regained his footing with his own "LD identity" by pushing himself. Max wanted to be equal to his peers but also did not want to be singled out or treated any differently. Max found that he was not singled out at all. In fact, he was listened to like the rest of the students in the course. The key importance of feminist listening comes into play in a classroom scenario reported by Corbett. The whole class is engaged in a peer review and response session. The tutor, Sara, who is circulating from group to group, sees and hears Max's struggles with the assignment and encourages him to persevere. Corbett writes:

> I noticed one student in particular, Max, having a visibly tough time understanding what he was supposed to be doing, while his two peer group partners seemed to be experiencing no trouble at all. The peer tutor, Sara, who was circulating around the room, saw that Max was having trouble. "I noticed Max looking nervous over in his seat so I went over to see what I could help him with. His partners, Kim and Adrianne, already had their computers set up and were starting the assignment. Max wasn't as far along. He hadn't even logged into the computer," she later said. Sara spent much of the remaining class session helping him get on track with the multiple organizational and communicative tasks students needed to negotiate during this peer review

and response session: working with online files, following the response guidelines and instructions, and reading and offering feedback to his group members. (Corbett, "Learning" 463)

To be identified and singled out by their disability is the last thing any student wants. Instead, Sara slowed down and listened to what Max struggled with, reshaping that into an emotional response that urged Max to keep trying. Max himself used his frustration and hesitation to continue to build a narrative of persistence and success for himself. Harking back to Lerner and Oddis's idea of the "whole writer," Sara focused on Max, the person, first, and his critical performances during peer review, second. Feminist theory points to the need for equality and equal opportunity for all students via a willingness to listen carefully for relationship-building opportunities. When tutors listen for—and respond to—what is most important in a particular situation, with a particular individual, sometimes a breakthrough moment can occur where the value of prioritizing the whole writer—including their emotional state—can make a powerful, positive impact. Max is an example of that. Instead of being seen as another LD student, he was listened to as a student, and this helped facilitate the rebranding of his own identity on his own terms.

Our review of Corbett's case studies above points to the narratives that can take place in collaborative writing center spaces, where stories are told that are rich in emotion and feminist listening—even cautionary tales like Julian's. Lape remarks that "emotional turmoil not only undermines the efforts of a struggling writer but also derails the interventions of an otherwise well-intentioned and conscientious tutor" (2; cf. Jurecic). Facilitating students' stories so that they become an important part of everyday writing center dialogues can help tutors come to terms with their own emotions during sessions and can remind researchers of the value of the affective in every aspect of writing center theory and practice. In contrast to Julian's story, when Corbett began designing the research that led to Sara and Max's story, he tried to listen more carefully to the desires of his participants. The instructor of the course, Mya, had requested that Sara—a former student of hers that she had developed a closer relationship with—be the course-based tutor. Mya also wanted Sara to be in the class every day. When it came time to interview all participants, Sara and Max both had a lot to say about the close relationship they had created during their experiences working together. This included a discussion about their personal experiences growing up neurodiverse. When Corbett asked if they were interested in talking more about their experiences at a local presentation and at a regional conference, they both gladly accepted. Both proceeded to share moving, emotional presentations with scores of intent listeners. Listening built relationships that enabled the co-creation of knowledge, knowledge that invites readers to *listen about listening*.

LISTENING (ABOUT LISTENING) LIKE A FEMINIST RESEARCHER: WHO ARE YOU IN THE WRITING CENTER (RESEARCH NARRATIVE) AND WHO AM I?

Having come full circle, now, we return to the question: How important are narratives of emotion to writing center practice? By implication, how important are emotions to the stories we report on in our research? What is at stake in rendering our stories is nothing less than chronicling and instantiating in our scholarship the diverse identities and life experiences of who we—and the people we encounter—are. In the second case study example above, both students held an LD-student identity but approached their narratives in two completely different ways (Corbett, "Learning"). Sara decided to become a tutor despite her LD, or neurodiversity, and Max worked past his and focused on not being defined by it. The significance of both of these narratives is that tutors have unique identities, identities in an ongoing state of flux. Every student and tutor is an open canvas and once they take part in a session or peer-review, they begin to fill in the plot in their narrative like a complicated screenplay. Yet, as Phillips cautions, "we tutors need to continuously center not only the identities of writers but also their expressed needs," so that balance is not forgotten (29). When tutors are guided by feminist listening principles—including lingering on relationships, relationship-building, and seeking to co-create knowledge—it shapes researching and reporting that practice.

An awareness of identity and ethos formation is key for feminist listening to thrive, and it is absolutely crucial for building a feminist-researcher theory of practice. Knowledge of the researcher, tutor, or participant is key. Answering feminist identity-questions can continue to open avenues for scholarship to aspire to, co-creating even more opportunities for diverse tutors and directors to extend their narratives and identities in the writing center. For co-author Katherine, "Kat"—being a 24-year-old Millennial, a first-generation college student, and a Hispanic woman—the need for more diversity and representation has always been a juggling act within her own writing center practice and research narrative. Kat is a non-Spanish speaking feminist and a tutor. What ties her to the writing center? What can she add to the narrative of her story and the writing center? She adds her insight to the dialogue here in South Texas, which varies from some of the scholars mentioned in this chapter. Corbett notes that listening and paying attention to a student or tutor's identity "offer[s] teachers a deeper view into what it means to listen, care, and persist in our best efforts towards inclusive teaching and learning" ("Learning" 470)—and by extension, research.

Corbett is a long-time contributor to the writing center scholarship narrative. He reveals part of his own research story when he reflects on the value of his interactions with Max and Sara, "two LD students . . . teaching me the true value of what it means to struggle, to persevere, and to make the most of what 'others' of all backgrounds and abilities have to offer" (Corbett, "Learning" 471). Corbett, being a 50-year-old, white, male, non-LD in South Texas—where it is predominately Hispanic—is another aspect of diversity and inclusion that makes every person's identity important. Despite these identities we see attached to our names, what tutors and researchers can focus on, first, is how we can listen to students before we rush to construct our own narratives about them. As co-authors, we have had to listen very carefully to each other while writing this chapter, to each other's ideas, words, and, yes, emotions. Even in the cautionary tale told in the first case study above, with Julian and Anne, lessons about listening like a feminist researcher can contribute valuable guidance in our quests to represent our research participants fairly in our reporting. Lisa Bell, in this collection, emphasizes the value of administrators supporting, modeling, and making visible the types of relationship-building, listening, and knowledge co-creation that can occur in the work we do. This type of modeling equally applies to our research—the detailed representations of the work we do.

Lessons in listening—and listening about listening—like a feminist researcher can also inform a theory of practice. When student writers begin to feel that they can trust that tutors will listen to them and that tutors are concerned about them, they may be more likely to open up to them with their developing-writer narratives. As Lape notes, "identifying emotions is a habit of mind and being that tutors can cultivate with practice over time, resulting in deeper intuitions and sharper emotional instincts" (4). Working towards emotional attunement applies to our research in much the same way. For example, like Max, Sara also felt compelled to volunteer her personal story to Corbett, the story of "a rather dysfunctional home life with a pair of alcoholic parents, two older sisters, and a younger brother . . . the story of her life spent balancing taking care of her parents, looking after her little brother and herself, and trying to do well in her studies" ("Learning," 469). Readers might find themselves taken aback at how open Sara was in sharing her backstory with Corbett.

For co-author Kat, it was not until she further reflected on the text that she realized a possible reason Sara shared her deeply personal story. Corbett listened. Despite his identity as a writing center director, a white male, and an authority figure, that connection between identities was somehow made. A balance among emotion, listening, and identity was met, and Sara thrived. She thrived under not just the balance of all three terms, but she modeled it in her sessions and connected students like Max to the narrative of the writing center, who consequently extended it into his own. Writing center scholarship can extend narratives of emotion in listening by taking a closer look at what feministic theory has to offer and what case studies like Corbett's add to the discussion. What further connections can we aspire to co-create via fine-tuned research into our stories of emotion and listening?

WORKS CITED

Babcock, Rebecca, D., and Terese Thonus. *Researching the Writing Center: Towards an Evidence-Based Practice.* Peter Lang, 2012.

Blair, Kristine L., and Lee Nickoson. *Composing Feminist Interventions: Activism, Engagement, Praxis.* The WAC Clearinghouse; UP of Colorado, 2018.Boquet, Elizabeth H. *Noise from the Writing Center.* Utah State UP, 2002.

Briggs, Lynn, C., and Meg Woolbright, editors. *Stories from the Center: Connecting Narrative and Theory in the Writing Center.* National Council of Teachers of English, 2000.

Corbett, Steven, J. *Beyond Dichotomy: Synergizing Writing Center and Classroom Pedagogies.* The WAC Clearinghouse; Parlor Press, 2015.

—. "Learning Disability and Response-Ability: Reciprocal Caring in Developmental Peer Response Writing Groups and Beyond." *Pedagogy: Critical Approaches to Teaching Literature, Language, Composition, and Culture,* vol. 15 no. 3, 2015, pp. 459–75.

Dixon, Elise. "Uncomfortably Queer: Everyday Moments in the Writing Center." *The Peer Review*, vol. 1, no. 2, 2017.

Haen, Mike. "The Affective Dimension of Writing Center Talk: Insights from Conversation Analysis." *WLN: A Journal of Writing Center Scholarship*, vol. 42 no. 9–10, 2018, pp. 2–9.

Harris, Muriel. *Teaching One-to-One: The Writing Conference*. National Council of Teachers of English, 1986.

—. "Talking in the Middle: Why Writers Need Writing Tutors." *College English*, vol. 57, no. 1, 1995, pp. 27–42.

Jurecic, Ann. "Empathy and the Critic." *College English*, vol. 74, no. 1, 2011, pp. 10–27.

Lape, Noreen. "Training Tutors in Emotional Intelligence: Toward a Pedagogy of Empathy." *The Writing Lab Newsletter*, vol. 33, no. 2, 2008, pp. 1–6.

Lawson, Daniel. "Metaphors and Ambivalence: Affective Dimensions in Writing Center Studies." *WLN: A Journal of Writing Center Scholarship*, vol. 40, no. 3–4, 2015, pp. 20–27.

Mackiewicz, Jo, and Isabelle Thompson. *Talk about Writing: The Tutoring Strategies of Experienced Writing Center Tutors*. Routledge, 2015.

Miley, Melissa. "Feminist Mothering: A Theory/Practice for Writing Center Administration." *WLN: A Journal of Writing Center Scholarship*, vol. 41, no. 1–2, 2016, pp. 17–24.

Newkirk, Thomas. "The Narrative Roots of the Case Study." *Methods and Methodology in Composition Research*, edited by Gesa Kirsch and Patricia A. Sullivan, Southern Illinois UP, 1992, pp. 130–52.

Phillips, Sacha-Rose. "Tutor's Column: Shared Identities, Diverse Needs." *WLN: A Journal of Writing Center Scholarship*, vol. 42, no. 9–10, 2018, pp. 26–29.

Ratcliffe, Krista. Afterword. *Composing Feminist Interventions: Activism, Engagement, Praxis*, by Kristine L. Blair and Lee Nickoson, pp. 505–10.

—. "Rhetorical Listening: A Trope for Interpretive Invention and a 'Code of Cross-Cultural Conduct.'" *College Composition and Communication*, vol. 51, no. 2, 1999, pp. 195–224.

Rosenberg, Lauren, and Emma Howes. "Listening to Research as a Feminist Ethos of Representation." *Composing Feminist Interventions: Activism, Engagement, Praxis*, by Kristine L. Blair and Lee Nickoson, pp. 75–91.

Seeley, Gabrielle. "A Delicate Balance: Employing Feministic Process Goals in Writing Center Consulting." *Praxis: A Writing Center Journal*, vol. 3 no. 1, 2005, pp. 1–5.

Woolbright, Meg, "The Politics of Tutoring: Feminism within the Patriarchy." *The Writing Center Journal*, vol. 13, no. 1, 1992, pp. 16–30.

Valentine, Kathryn. "The Undercurrents of Listening: A Qualitative Content Analysis of Listening in Writing Center Tutor Guidebooks." *The Writing Center Journal*, vol. 36, no. 2, 2017, pp. 89–115.

Yoon, Stephanie, R., and Erin B. Stutelberg. "Rose's Writing: The Generative Power of Affect in a High School Writing Center." *WLN: A Journal of Writing Center Scholarship*, vol. 42, no. 9–10, 2018, pp. 18–25.

13 Listening, Reflecting, Responding: Toward a Metic Intelligence for Writing Center Administrators

Erica Cirillo-McCarthy and Elizabeth Leahy

Faculty surveys can help writing center administrators assess institutional perceptions of writing support, but we often get more than we bargain for in our data. As new directors at different institutions, one of our first priorities was to survey our faculty on their perceptions of student writing. Surveys can help new administrators acclimate to campus culture and make decisions, such as framing outreach materials or communicating faculty expectations to tutors (Masiello and Hayward). Therefore, we both recognized this outreach as an essential action in our process of "becoming" (Navickas et al., in this collection). However, as we sifted through our respective data, we were disheartened, though not surprised, to see so many negative comments about student writing. Responses ignored inequities in education and were rife with deficit discourse narratives; furthermore, responses highlighted the disconnect between faculty expectations of the writing center and the reality of our own centers' values, missions, and practices. As we each read through our survey responses, we experienced emotional conflict. We felt sympathy and despair for the students who encountered these outdated and simplified perspectives of writing, and we also felt trepidation about working alongside faculty who see student writing in this reductive way. We reached out to each other for support in processing this emotional conflict. In our shared commiseration upon reading qualitative responses, we asked: How do writing center administrators address and process emotions that result from knowing what faculty think of student writers? Further, would theorizing emotions help us translate conflict into generative action?

Although we first wondered how to move past our emotional reactions to the survey responses, we soon realized the powerful possibilities of confronting our emotional conflict headlong. Our project is partly informed by Alison M. Jaggar's seminal text, "Love and Knowledge: Emotion in Feminist Epistemology," in which she argues that emotions can and should be used in the process of constructing new knowledge. We use Jaggar's definition of emotions as "habitual responses" that "can be attributed only to what are sometimes called 'whole persons,' engaged in the on-going activity of social life" and are challenging to break (159). Emotions are embodied, situated, social experiences. In addition, we were inspired by Susan Miller-Cochran's assertion that "conflict and discomfort are sometimes essential" in moving forward strategically with an ethos of "compassionate administration" (112). We agree that acknowledging and dwelling in these complex emotions positions us to develop a more reflective and empathetic stance in our administrative practice—specifically when confronting conflict during the relationship-building process. Residing in this reflective stance, which is at times uncomfortable and hard work, creates a context to cultivate *metis*—an embodied intelligence often described as cunning, situational, and responsive to conflict (Detienne and Vernant; Hawhee; Dolmage). Because writing center administration requires a certain flexibility and cunningness already, the concept of *metis* seems particularly fitting. By tapping into the generative possibilities of *metis,* we can harness our embodied responses to conflict and rely more increasingly on metic intelligence to guide our decision-making. Similar to other mindful-based approaches to stress and conflict, growing one's metic intelligence is the result of mindful practice of *metis*. The more it is practiced, the more adept practitioners become.

Grounding this chapter in our lived experiences, we argue that writing center directors can use moments of conflict to cultivate their metic intelligence and thus respond more strategically within the restraints of their rhetorical situations. We extend Miller-Cochran's argument and propose a recursive process of listening, reflecting, and responding when faced with conflict. When practiced regularly, this process cultivates administrators' metic intelligence so that emotions evoked in response to conflict are harnessed rather than suppressed. Specifically, engaging in *metis* invites us to tap into emotional responses to work more effectively within our institutional realities to affect material change for our students and tutors; we do this through a process of listening to and reflecting on our emotional reactions. Slowing down to listen and reflect allows us to be more creative and strategic in how we respond to conflict. While our proposed process of listening, reflecting, and responding would not alleviate the conflict writing center administrators face, it allows us to develop our metic intelligence in ways that could serve as part of a more complex, problem-solving process when engaged in challenging faculty relationships.

EMOTIONS AND CONFLICT IN WRITING CENTER ADMINISTRATION

As evidenced in this collection, writing center directors routinely face emotions and conflict in their work. Like Kelin Hull and Marilee Brooks-Gillies, we also see emotions as intertwined with administrative decision-making, and as Genie Giaimo argues, institutional constraints can heavily impact our emotions. In this section, we turn to scholars whose work helps us better theorize emotion and conflict in writing center administration. In her work on compassionate administration, Miller-Cochran acknowledges the ubiquitous nature of conflict in writing administration because ". . .we answer to multiple groups, and those groups often have conflicting goals" (108). She advocates for "sit[ting] with the discomfort" of the emotional conflicts we often experience because it creates a space to "think through how to respond" (111). Roberta D. Kjesrud and Mary A. Wislocki also see the value in acknowledging emotions in administrative work and warn that ignoring the emotions that are inevitable in conflicted collaborations with institutional partners ". . .leaves researchers more, not less, open to bias, because academics who bracket emotion underestimate the extent to which emotions are socially inculcated and manipulated. . ." (103). Finally, Jaggar describes the generative nature of emotions, in particular, "outlaw emotions" that are "conventionally inexplicable" and "challenge dominant conceptions of the *status quo*" that exist to reproduce existing power structures (167). Writing center administrative work can, at times, mean conflict. Ignoring the resulting emotions reproduces limiting perspectives; examining emotions, on the other hand, can serve as a site of inquiry and create a space for meaning-making.

Similar to Kjesrud and Wislocki, Miller-Cochran, and Jaggar, we believe it is important to examine our own responses to conflict. Doing so can shed light on the entrenched binary constructs of "us versus them" that limit action beyond an emotional response. We find it is easy to become frustrated with faculty conflict and fall back on a set of common tropes in our response: *faculty do not care about writing; faculty wrongly believe that first-year composition should teach everything about writing; faculty see us as service workers rather than intellectual equals.* Yet, repeating these responses each time we face conflict with faculty—for example, when reading negative faculty responses—does not serve our practice, does not help us theorize conflict, nor does it help us build writing center programming that better serves students. Ultimately, we seek to recognize how an intentional method of listening and reflecting cultivates metic intelligence and helps develop a better understanding of how to respond productively to moments of conflict. Doing so also makes visible the ways that traditional responses to conflict in the writing center reproduce limiting binary constructs.

Avoidance of emotions in the literature fulfills a long, Western tradition of centering reason and devaluing marginalized, embodied, emotional experiences. But scholars like Laura Micciche compel us to transgress limiting epistemological binary constructs and come to understand and value embodied knowledge. Micciche, like Jaggar, argues for "emotioned epistemologies," a process in which emotions help build understanding rather than hinder it (Micciche, "Staying"). We see building an emotional epistemology of writing centers as a generative path to follow when theorizing the ways emotion and conflict inform writing center administrators' identity and practice. Recently, writing center scholars have begun to center embodied experiences and their corresponding emotions when building new knowledge regarding writing center praxis and racial justice (Condon; Diab et al.; Kern) and embodied and racialized experiences in the writing center (Green; Martinez; García). Our process seeks to join them in disrupting limiting epistemological binaries. Jaggar argues for a new feminist epistemology in which we begin to see emotions as ways of being and of "construct[ting] the world" (159). Seen in this way, emotions demand that a theory be "self-reflexive, to focus not only on the outer world but also on ourselves and our relation to that world, to examine critically our social location, our actions, our values, our perceptions, and our emotions" (Jaggar 170). As we expand our writing center theory to value and validate emotions and embodied experiences, we turn to *metis* as a rhetorical concept useful for writing center directors.

METIS-INFORMED WRITING CENTER ADMINISTRATION

As we began to theorize conflict and emotion in writing center administration, we drew on our own training as rhetoricians. *Metis,* a rhetorical concept that combines fluidity and cunning with embodied knowledge, is useful when describing the savvy stance writing center directors can adopt when facing conflict. *Metis* is more than a rhetorical strategy; it responds to the situational nature of the rhetorical context. Exploring *metis* through ancient texts and practices, Marcel Detienne and Jean-Pierre Vernant argue that *metis* is a constant state of being, a ". . .body of mental attitudes and intellectual behavior[s]" that cultivates a set of skills that can be called upon in a variety of situations (3). Detienne and Vernant emphasize that *metis* is particularly useful for situations that do not have logical and linear characteristics; instead, *metis* serves the interlocutor most when facing ambiguous "disconcerting" situations that "do not lend themselves to precise measurement, exact calculation or rigorous logic" (3–4). *Metis* invites interlocutors to marry embodied responses with intellectual tactics in a way that not only protects the rhetor's emotions but also actively employs them in a fluid and creative decision-making process.

Engaging in *metis* as writing center administrators creates a generative space for identifying effective and timely responses to faculty conflict within the constraints of the rhetorical situation. Debra Hawhee's explanation of cunning intelligence clarifies the situational nature of *metis* as an intelligence that emerges as unpredictable yet responsive action, a way to express the "idea of intelligence as immanent movement" (48). In other words, our bodily responses hold within them strategies to counter conflict. Honing our metic intelligence in order to respond more effectively to conflict means slowing down to listen to our embodied responses.

Reflection is a crucial component to our interpretation of *metis* because it is the mechanism by which we build and improve our metic intelligence. We draw on Micciche's slow agency, Miller-Cochran's intentional administration, and Krista Ratcliffe's rhetorical listening in advocating for this reflective approach. When articulating a slow agency approach to administration, Micciche argues for "residing longer than is comfortable in the complexity, stillness, and fatigue of not knowing how to proceed" ("For" 80). For Miller-Cochran, lingering in such spaces is a key component of compassionate, intentional administration because it allows administrators to listen in order to "grow, change, and innovate," despite the discomfort caused by emotions (111). This discomfort also allows administrators to see the range of possibilities and identify strategies for action. Specifically, Ratcliffe identifies rhetorical listening as a way to "consciously locate our identification in places of commonalities *and* differences" (32). Towards this end, we are proposing a process that seeks to slow down our response to conflict, listen rhetorically, and sit with our discomfort; these actions are key components in engaging in *metis*—which, over time and through repetition, cultivates metic intelligence.

Our three-step process consists of listening, reflecting, and responding when facing conflict. This process allows us to listen to not only our interlocutors but also attend to our emotional and bodily responses to conflict. In describing our process, we hope to meet Jaggar's and Micciche's calls to employ emotions when constructing new knowledge (Micciche, "Staying"). Further, we hope to show how constructing an "emotional epistemology" pushes us past fossilized, binary constructs in our responses; finally, we demonstrate how the feminist practice of slowing down and rhetorically listening allows for a cultivation of metic intelligence. After briefly sketching out this process, we share examples of the process in action as we consider negative comments from our surveys. These examples demonstrate the generative capacity of reading faculty survey responses wherein directors identify connective and collaborative strategies. Rather than relying on internalized commonplaces in our responses, we show how developing our metic intelligence gets us unstuck from these commonplaces and instead trains administrators to rely on empathetic responses that ultimately allow us to identify actionable responses to the conflict.

Our first step in cultivating metic intelligence as writing center directors is listening to the faculty comment and our immediate reaction to it. Taking time to inventory the entire comment is important because we tend to fixate on negative aspects of the comment while ignoring implicit or explicit positive aspects. Listening to our emotional response acknowledges our own emotional stake in the issue, validates our emotions rather than suppresses them, and keeps us from immediately reacting to or dismissing the other party by asking us to slow down.

During the next step, reflecting, we unpack and think critically about the comment and our emotional response. Jaggar warns that uncritical acceptance of emotions does little to further knowledge (169). At times, emotional responses to conflict are rooted in a disciplinary and administrative marginalized identity. Acknowledging these roots, Kjesrud and Wislocki argue for writing center directors to "become more aware of deeply encultured habits of argument and reductive victim-loser/villain-winner schema we carry around in our heads" because "this schema undermine our ability to adopt new ideas or initiate exploratory dialogue around points of conflict" (107). Therefore, we invite writing center directors to contextualize not only comments from stakeholders but also their own emotional responses during moments of conflict. Questions for reflection include:

- What is the cultural or ideological history informing the comment or the response?
- What is the local context informing the comment or the response?
- How might a new response acknowledge the local or institutional context?

Taking time to sit with the faculty comments in this way allows for a more nuanced understanding of the faculty member's expectations and needs; further, mindful reflection helps us excavate our own limiting, internalized tropes while stimulating creative approaches to identifying generative actions.

The previous steps of listening and reflecting lead us to the final step: crafting an action-oriented, metic response that attends to faculty concerns. A response is not always going to engage directly with the other party. In fact, as you will see in our examples, we cannot directly respond to an anonymous survey comment. We can, however, brainstorm responses to the source of conflict. Some questions that help in this final step:

- What are some actionable responses that work both within and against faculty expectations?
- What are productive ways to engage with faculty who share similar concerns?
- In what ways do these concerns connect with larger goals for the center and its role in the institution?

These questions can help identify responses that work within a writing center director's specific institutional context. Thinking critically about emotions and extending our empathy to better understand our interlocutors makes visible a range of *metis*-informed responses.

ACTIVATING *METIS* IN MOMENTS OF CONFLICT: LISTENING, REFLECTING, RESPONDING

In this section, we each narrate our process of listening to, reflecting on, and responding to a particularly vexing comment from our faculty survey. Both of our surveys received IRB approval, but because this section isolates specific survey data, we made a conscious choice to anonymize our narrations. In the first example, the director was able to view the faculty comment within the context of the rest of her faculty survey in order to further understand the professor's experiences and challenges. As a result, she realized new opportunities for targeted outreach on her campus to foster collaborations in supporting discipline-specific writing. In the second example, the director identified several ways she could use this faculty comment to advocate for an increase in resources while also thinking about creative ways to develop outreach for new faculty.

DIRECTOR # 1

My survey was designed to help me understand the campus writing culture. Overall, the 104 responses provided insight into how faculty assigned writing, their awareness of the writing center, and their perceptions of student writing challenges. The survey included a few optional open-ended questions and comment boxes. There were plenty of positive comments, but I fixated on the bad. For example, I received the following explanation from a professor who thought students were "not at all prepared" to do the writing required in their courses.

> . . .in my 3000 level courses, in general, the students cannot write strong papers. I do take [. . .] a (relatively) Spartan approach to assigning papers. This semester, I spent one class period giving them all the basics of what I expect, showing formatting and introducing Turabian footnotes, with unimpressive result. I used to take even less time [. . .] but that gave extremely poor results. I thought that by the time they are in a 3000 level course they could write a cohesive paper with appropriate sen-

tence structure, but I was mistaken. I will work on instituting some of the measures this survey mentions [. . .] but frankly, I am disappointed that I have to. College students, especially ones past the first two years, should be able to write papers without hand-holding and step-by-step guidance. The focus of my classes should be in my field, which is not English.

Below I outline the process of listening, reflecting, and responding to this comment. Engaging in this process challenged my initial interpretation of the comment and helped me discover a potential outreach opportunity on my campus.

Listening. This professor is clearly frustrated by their students' lack of disciplinary writing knowledge, although they do not seem interested in teaching their students to write in their discipline. My initial reaction to this comment was disbelief. I could not believe that this professor viewed spending class time going over assignment guidelines and disciplinary conventions—such as Turabian—as excessive "hand-holding" and beyond the scope of their field. I was amused that they could complain about student writing while doing little to support their students in this writing. This comment was familiar to me because it echoed faculty complaints I had heard before—a desire for students' writing to improve without "wasting" class time on writing, and an assumption that students should have learned the professor's disciplinary and personal writing preferences somewhere else. Recognizing I was reacting emotionally, I sat with the discomfort and listened.

Once I made space to listen to this comment and my reaction, I realized I was overlooking key details. Although aspects of the comment lined up with previous faculty complaints, the comment in its entirety had more nuance and complexity. First, the professor is describing a process wherein they have recalibrated their approach to the paper when they realized their usual method was not enough. Second, they are, although reluctant, receptive to trying new methods: the measures they mention incorporating from my survey. These activities include explaining assignment goals, providing students with rubrics or models, incorporating peer review, and requiring multiple drafts. Even though this professor seems annoyed about devoting more class time to writing, they seem open to implementing these activities. I missed these details previously because my emotional reaction to some of their comments made it difficult for me to do anything other than villainize them, as

Kjesrud and Wisocki caution. However, slowing down and taking stock allowed me to see that my reaction, while genuine, was not going to be productive. Listening also allowed me to notice not just differences but commonalities, as Ratcliffe argues. In this case, I saw common ground in the professor's openness to implementing new classroom activities.

Reflecting. The reflection stage invites practitioners to understand the context of the comment. In order to do so, I examined the rest of this professor's survey responses. They have been a full-time lecturer for 2–5 years, and their experience with the writing center is limited to occasionally referring students to peer tutoring. In an optional, open-ended question about what they believe should be the writing center's purpose, they responded that it should "supplement/remind what students learn in their introductory English/writing class." However, in a series of Likert scale questions asking faculty to agree or disagree with statements about the writing center, this professor disagreed that the writing center should "teach every style of disciplinary writing."

These responses allowed me to think more holistically about this professor's experiences with and expectations for student writing. They are interested in improving their students' writing and are somewhat open to devoting class time to it, but view writing instruction to be the responsibility of introductory English courses. I am struck by this discrepancy. They seem to think there is something taught in introductory writing classes that is fundamental to writing in their discipline. In contemplating this disconnect, I wonder why this professor is reluctant to include more writing support in the class and why they even fail to provide their students with grading criteria. Do they feel it is beneath them? Or do they lack confidence in teaching writing? I look again at the survey and see that when asked to choose the top three characteristics of "good writing" in their field, they broke the rules and chose ten characteristics. This response could mean they have difficulty prioritizing writing concerns and isolating disciplinary writing preferences, which could be why they do not feel comfortable providing grading criteria. I also wonder if this professor's 2–5 years of service impacted their awareness of writing center services and instructional support. During their time on campus, they would have experienced changes in writing center leadership, so they may not be aware of our instructional support. Ultimately, after listening and reflecting, I felt I understood more of this professor's experiences and how to reach out in ways that could engage them in support.

Responding. Before I engaged in this process, I had concluded that my survey demonstrated an outreach gap with seasoned faculty who had been on campus ten or more years, but now I am seeing another outreach gap: faculty who have been with campus 2–5 years who have only known the writing center as being in transition. Their new faculty orientation would not have introduced them to the range of writing center services that are now available. At the beginning of this process, I only focused on the professor's frustration and quickly made assumptions— based on my previous experiences with faculty complaints—about their understanding of the writing center and their commitment to teaching writing. Had I continued with these assumptions rather than sitting with my emotions, I would not have seen the possibilities for strategic engagement with this professor and others like them. This professor is an excellent candidate for instructional support from the writing center. They seem open to devoting class time to writing, although a bit uncertain about it. They recognize that the writing center cannot teach every style of disciplinary writing, but they also seem hopeful that it can help students with transfer.

Although I ca not respond directly to this anonymous faculty member, this process allowed me to develop a *metis*-informed plan for reaching out to faculty. These outreach efforts place the emphasis on improving student writing—in an effort to hook faculty—but ultimately engage faculty in conversations about what they value in writing. In this way I can, as Miller-Cochran has argued, keep my own values in view and craft a response that acknowledges the frustrations these faculty members are experiencing, while strategically planting some seeds about their role in supporting their students with writing. Doing so will allow me to help faculty better scaffold this writing and more effectively communicate their expectations to their students.

DIRECTOR #2

I created an anonymous faculty survey in collaboration with the Office of Institutional Effectiveness, Planning and Research, IEPR, and received 145 complete surveys. Faculty ranked the importance of specific student writing support needs, such as assistance with longer projects, incorporating and synthesizing sources, disciplinary writing, mechanics, and brainstorming. Following that, respondents were asked to identify any writing support their program or department offered and how they personally supported writers in their classroom. A final, open-ended prompt provided respondents a text box to expand upon what they want the writing center to know about better serving their students.

I kept seeing the word "basic" throughout the responses to the final question, and the answers presented a paradox. On one hand, concepts such as clear arguments and logical flow of ideas are so easy—they are basic—and yet on the other hand, faculty do not have the time nor desire to teach them, and students have yet to master them. Faculty identified both concepts and genres as basic: "directly addressing a question and sticking to an argument in their writing;" "basic writing skills;" and "basic grammar, spelling, and punctuation;" and students cannot write "basic things like personal statements and cover letters." In reading these responses, my emotions pinballed from anger to defense to curiosity. I started to see "basic" as code for something and wanted to understand what this adjective meant to faculty who used it to describe both students who did not live up to their expectations and to particular writing strategies or concepts. Therefore, I chose a quote that was illustrative of the rest of the faculty responses in its focus on "basic."

To the final survey prompt, "We want to be able to assist all undergraduate students at every stage of the writing process. Please let us know if there is anything else we should consider as we work toward this goal," one faculty member responded:

> Many [State University] students' writing skills are below college-level. Higher order writing (e.g., independent analysis) is difficult to teach students if they lack basic writing proficiency. I spend an inordinate amount of time correcting basic writing problems that tend to be repeated over and over again by the same students. Student success, including retention, depends on effectively moving students toward higher levels of writing proficiency. I'm new to campus and would greatly appreciate a place to send my students to get help with basic writing that is something akin to a writing boot camp. My time and energy are better spent on my subject content.

Listening. Upon my first attempt at listening, I quickly concluded that this professor thinks carefully about student writing but is frustrated with students' patterns of error. I focused intently on that last sentence and thought, "They think they are too good to teach writing! Don't they know that research shows that writing across the disciplines is a high impact practice that has been proven to support student success" (c.f. Kuh). Then, I put the survey down and silently hoped I never ran into this faculty member. However, listening works best when the practitioner slows down. Listening—slowly and intentionally—affords the opportunity to identify commonalities and thus ways to address conflict (Ratcliffe). Therefore, I had to return to this comment to use my emotions in a generative and solution-oriented way. Only then could I start cultivating my metic intelligence and move towards identifying responses.

When I did slow down the listening, I began to see things differently: first, the respondent understands writing from a writing across the curriculum, WAC, perspective, in that students' growth as writers is a process that continues well beyond first-year composition, and more importantly, that a sustained attention to writing across or in the disciplines supports student success and retention. When I stop and listen to the response, I see a teacher who understands that writing is an integral part of a student's experience at the university. I also see a teacher who might be tired and anxious in their new role at a new institution. Moreover, if they are a newly minted PhD, they also might be exhausted. Slowing down and listening moved me through the initial emotional response rooted in a binary construct of them versus me to a place of empathy and understanding (Micciche, "Slow;" Miller-Cochran; Kjesrud and Wislocki; Ratcliffe).

Reflecting. Moving away from entrenched responses that pit myself against faculty was a surprise result of sitting with my emotions and listening. Reflection, then, prompted me to turn inward and examine my initial reaction. Similar to my co-author, when I skimmed through the qualitative responses, my eyes focused on the negative comments. My defensiveness is rooted in the marginalized identity of writing centers as a discipline and as a practice. This marginalized experience has formulated much of my idea of the relationship between faculty and the writing center. I say idea because that is not the reality. I run a center located in the library, so while not the "center" of the institution, it is far removed from a basement; my role is tenure-track, so I am of equal status to the faculty surveyed. Despite all this, the commonplace of being a misunderstood and marginalized writing center still plays such a large role in framing my responses to negative faculty survey responses. This process of reflection has helped me locate the context informing my defensiveness so that I will change my approach the next time I come across comments such as this. Listening allowed me to revise my typical response to negative talk about student writing—"what do *they* know?"—and reflecting made visible my reliance on the limiting hero versus villain response so that I could begin generating new narratives that did not close off possibilities.

Responding. Upon reading the survey responses, I faced an ambiguous moment that was, as Detienne and Vernant would describe, "disconcerting" and lacked "precise measurement" (3–4); in other words, a moment that called for *metis*. After listening and reflecting, I decide that there is plenty I can do to respond to this faculty member in a *metis*-informed way. I can use the respondent's comment in a WAC proposal I have been writing with my institution's writing program administrator (WPA) to highlight the timeliness of a WAC program on my campus; I can also liaison with our Center for Teaching and Learning to identify and craft faculty-facing workshops on student writing that would speak to faculty members who already value writing in the classroom. Finally, this response has also pushed me to evaluate my writing center's current outreach to new faculty. My responses are situational and actionable while also acknowledging and leveraging the emotional aspect of the rhetorical context. Unfortunately, I do not think I have a better understanding of the word "basic" and the way it was used by faculty in their responses, but I now can identify it as a distraction that delayed my understanding of the larger message and blocked me from identifying responses that generated positive action to best serve students. As I develop my metic intelligence in my administrative role and more deftly identify effective strategies in response to conflict, I will become more adept at spotting these distractions.

CONCLUSION

Whenever we compare notes or talk shop with other writing center directors, our conversations inevitably turn to moments of conflict with disciplinary faculty and other campus stakeholders. We share recurring stories that are familiar to anyone who has worked in a writing center: professors who write infuriating comments on student papers, demonstrate a misunderstanding of the writing center's purpose, or do not wish to explicitly teach writing in their class but are critical of the writing center's approach. Despite their familiarity, these stories still tend to elicit intense emotions grounded in defensiveness. writing center directors' defensive responses are commonplaces for a reason. Writing centers have historically functioned in a state of precarity, borne out of a misunderstanding or devaluation of writing instruction and support. This reality fuels the emotion behind the defensive stance. However, defaulting to these responses—often dismissive of faculty investment in the teaching of writing—prevents directors from engaging with faculty concerns, creates more distance between writing center directors and disciplinary faculty, and limits possibilities for understanding and supporting faculty in the teaching of writing across disciplines. Instead, writing center directors can cultivate their metic intelligence to better engage with faculty concerns and think through how to respond to and adapt to the needs and perceptions of their faculty colleagues.

It is important to acknowledge our emotions, and venting with other directors is often therapeutic. However, it is also important to acknowledge that these emotions, when unexamined, can obscure metic-informed, action-oriented responses to conflict. When we first began developing this process, we were only looking for a way to speak back to negative faculty concerns that reproduced harmful deficit discourses. Along the way, we discovered that we also needed to push back against some of our own entrenched ideas about faculty concerns with writing. In some cases, they were limiting our ability to see a possible way forward. Slowing down to listen and reflect allowed us to see a wider range of responses that worked within the realities of our respective contexts and the variety of constituents with whom we interact and serve.

We do realize that not every situation offers a chance for a slow response. If, for example, during a campus-wide budget meeting, someone proposes slashing your center's budget, you cannot say, "I need a minute to process. Let me do some free-writing." But our hope is that by bringing this process into daily interactions where a slow response is possible, we can begin to hone our metic intelligence in order to better attend to moments of conflict that require swift action—in particular, regarding issues of precarity and sustainability. Writing centers are lauded during flush economic times but are equally scrutinized and often the first to have their lean budgets cut during austere times. Because of this precarity, our practice of serving diverse stakeholders—students, tutors, faculty, institutional administrators—and the role writing centers play in higher educational social justice, writing center directors face conflict and emotion daily. By engaging in our proposed process, writing center directors can become more attentive to emotions and thus cultivate their metic intelligence, subsequently translating conflict into generative action.

WORKS CITED

Condon, Frankie. *I Hope I Join the Band: Narrative, Affiliation, and Antiracist Rhetoric*. Utah State UP, 2012.

Detienne, Marcel, and Jean-Pierre Vernant. *Cunning Intelligence in Greek Culture and Society*. Translated by Janet Lloyd, U of Chicago P, 1978.

Diab, Rasha, et al. "Making Commitments to Racial Justice Actionable." *Performing Antiracist Pedagogy in Rhetoric, Writing, and Communication*, edited by Frankie Condon and Vershawn Ashanti Young, The WAC Clearinghouse; UP of Colorado, 2016, pp. 19–40.

Dolmage, Jay. "Metis, *Mêtis, Mestiza*, Medusa: Rhetorical Bodies Across Rhetorical Traditions." *Rhetoric Review*, vol. 28, no. 1, 2009, pp. 1–28.

García, Romeo. "Unmaking Gringo-Centers." *The Writing Center Journal*, vol. 36, no. 1, 2017, pp. 29–60.

Green, Neisha-Anne S. "The Re-Education of Neisha-Anne S. Green: A Close Look at the Damaging Effects of 'A Standard Approach,' the Benefits of Code-Meshing, and the Role Allies Play in this Work." *Praxis: A Writing Center Journal*, vol. 14, no. 1, 2016.

Hawhee, Debra. *Bodily Arts: Rhetoric and Athletics in Ancient Greece*. U of Texas P, 2005.

Jaggar, Alison M. "Love and Knowledge: Emotion in Feminist Epistemology." *Inquiry*, vol. 32, no. 2, 1989, pp. 151–76.

Kern, Douglas S. "Emotional Performance and Antiracism in the Writing Center." *Praxis: A Writing Center Journal*, vol. 16, no. 2, 2019, pp. 43–49.

Kjesrud, Roberta D., and Mary A. Wislocki. "Learning and Leading through Conflicted Collaborations." *The Writing Center Journal*, vol. 31, no. 2, 2011, pp. 89–116.

Kuh, George D. *High-Impact Educational Practices: What They Are, Who Has Access to Them, and Why They Matter*. AAC and U, 2008.

Martinez, Aja Y. "Alejandra Writes a Book: A Critical Race Counterstory about Writing, Identity, and Being Chicanx in the Academy." *Praxis: A Writing Center Journal*, vol. 14, no. 1, 2016, pp. 56–61.

Masiello, Lea and Malcolm Hayward. "The Faculty Survey: Identifying Bridges Between the Classroom and the Writing Center." *The Writing Center Journal*, vol. 11, no. 2, 1991, pp. 73–79.

Micciche, Laura R. "For Slow Agency." *WPA: Writing Program Administration*, vol. 35, no. 1, 2011, pp. 73–90.

—. "Staying with Emotion." *Composition Forum*, vol. 34, Summer 2016.

Miller-Cochran, Susan. "Innovation through Intentional Administration: Or, How to Lead a Writing Program Without Losing Your Soul." *WPA: Writing Program Administration*, vol. 42, no. 1, 2018, pp. 107–22.

Ratcliffe, Krista. *Rhetorical Listening: Identification, Gender, Whiteness.* Southern Illinois UP, 2005.

14 ALIENATION AND WRITING: WORKING WITH DISPOSITIONS

Lisha Daniels Storey

A s writing center tutors and directors, we are familiar with students identifying themselves as "bad writers," or even dis-identifying themselves: "I'm not a writer." These declarations are often made at the beginning of a session, perhaps as the writer slides a draft across the table with a wince or a nervous chuckle. If we inquire further about writers' prior experiences with writing, this may also sound familiar: "I used to love writing until. . ." followed by either "middle school" or "high school." In writing centers and writing classrooms, I frequently hear students share vivid memories of writing in elementary school and then describe losing interest—as writing became more expository and less imaginative, once the emphasis shifted from creating and sharing writing to passing standardized assessments, or as writing became less personally meaningful.

These familiar declarations invite us to consider how writers' attitudes bear the consequences of prior experiences with writing. Prior experiences can shape the ways writers value and devalue their writing and themselves as writers, often in totalizing ways—a wholesale rejection of writing ability, enjoyment, or identity that tutors encounter in sessions. Even writers who experienced success in school writing, like many peer writing tutors, have vivid memories of negative writing experiences that still resonate strongly; though they may not result in the same self-dismissal, these prior experiences stick. One way to account for the current attitudes we encounter is to approach them as part of students' writing dispositions, shaped via an accumulation of emotions throughout students' writing lives. As Bronwyn Williams explains, the emotions of prior writing experiences play a role in shaping students' "attitudes and dispositions toward literacy practices" (16). A disposition can be understood as a tendency to perceive and respond to a situation, like a writing task, in certain, patterned ways, based on how a writer has emotionally experienced similar situations in the past. A disposition is an embodied tendency, one that registers physiologically—in terms of heart rate and body temperature—as well as emotionally, expressed with verbal language and gesture. Encountering dispositions in writing centers, then, involves embodied ways of thinking and feeling about writing that have been long in the making and that can foreclose other ways of thinking and feeling about writing.

Dispositions that devalue writing are especially important given the historical situation in which they are located—where writing is quite economically valuable. Deborah Brandt, for example, points to writing's role as a "dominant form of manufacturing" in knowledge and informationalized sectors of the economy (3), as the activities of writing, in workplaces as well as beyond them, and as created items of value—commodities such as "knowledge, ideas, data, information, news" (3). In addition to writing in workplaces, writing produces economic value within the informationalized economies of the Internet, which Christian Pulver identifies as "engines of capital circulation and accumulation" (197). Within the economies of Web 2.0, users of "free" Web communication tools offered by companies—such as Facebook—are writers, producing content that generates value as it circulates (Pulver; c.f. Dush). User-created content such as posts, tweets, stories, videos, and even likes and clicks generates revenue and produces valuable digital data—"commodified information" that companies harness for profits (Pulver 195). At the same time, writing's value in schools is largely defined in terms of standardized assessment or in other transactional terms, rather than its meaning or significance for writers. A student may feel like a "bad writer" when writing in school contexts even as they are creating valuable texts in other venues—a practice and status they may or may not claim or even be aware of.

The dynamic of devalued writers within a context of valued writing is not new, as we know from research on literacy myths and crises as well as language difference (Graff; Horner et al.). Literacy researchers have shown how public concern over literacy—often expressed in terms of a "literacy crisis"—reflects literacy's value in terms of rising, not falling, levels of literacy. In other words, literacy crises reflect an increasing value—the need for more literacy and more of certain kinds of literacy—

in terms of a deficit: students and others not meeting this bar. How does this dynamic come to bear on the ways students think and feel about writing? If writing is so valuable, what are students' relationships to this value? How do writers *feel* these values, particularly in school contexts? What other values and relations with writing are available?

In many ways, writing centers already work at the level of writers' dispositions—tutors help them see their writing differently and feel better about it, with the goal of reshaping attitudes about subsequent writing. I suggest we extend this work to learn more about the conditions and consequences of students' attitudes towards school writing. Unenjoyable writing from fourth or sixth grade onward is not simply a feature of writing education in the US. It is not something students endure and put behind them. Rather, our encounters with embodied attitudes from these experiences invite further exploration of the conditions of writing. Understanding writers' dispositions offers insights that can guide writing center practice and research.

Critical affect and emotion studies provide important starting points for exploring writing dispositions beyond individual experiences or attitudes to account for their embodied, social, and political dimensions. The study of emotion and affect spans multiple fields and approaches, with the two terms "emotion" and "affect" naming different configurations of sensation, perception, cognition, expression, and circulation. These configurations have been taken up in writing studies in what Jennifer Trainor identifies as "Critical Emotion Studies," or "CES", the interdisciplinary study of "individually-experienced but historically situated emotions" (646), and what Jenny Edbauer Rice identifies as "Critical Affect Studies," or CAS," which is concerned with "affect and its mediating force in everyday life" (201–02). These studies offer frameworks for writing centers to explore emotion and affect with attention to their complexity as individual, social, and political practices.

In the rest of this chapter, I extend the work of critical affect and emotion studies to think about dispositions as sites of exploration and inquiry for writers and tutors, as ways to think about how emotional relations with writing are shaped by prior experiences with an eye to the material conditions and consequences of these experiences. After discussing what dispositions can mean for writing and writing center studies, particularly in relation to emotion and writing, I will use the Marxist concept of alienation to illustrate dispositions as individually-experienced emotional and material relations to writing. Thinking of alienation as writing disposition can be useful for holding together individual emotional experiences of writing—what writing centers see, hear, and feel from and with writers—in relation to material conditions that shape their writing's value.

Writing Dispositions as Emotional, Social, and Material

Writing centers can use dispositions to think about how writers approach writing situations, and how these attitudes come to take shape. Broadly, dispositions are inclinations toward certain feelings, behaviors, or actions; they are relational, and they involve the blending of affect and thought. The relevant entry in the *Oxford English Dictionary* defines dispositions as a *"state of mind or feeling in respect to a thing or person*; the condition of being (favourably or unfavourably) disposed *towards"* (emphasis added). Dispositions, then, are qualities of mind and feeling that orient or incline us towards things or persons in certain ways, and, as Dana Lynn Driscoll and Jennifer Wells explain, they are features that shape how knowledge or abilities will be used. Their relational aspect means dispositions are not individual phenomena; dispositions include not only the things, persons, or practices towards which we are inclined but also the experiences, contexts, and conditions that shape them.

Writing dispositions involve inclinations to think and feel in certain ways toward writing: to think and feel as if one is a good or a bad writer and to think and feel that writing is difficult, fun, pointless, meaningful. This way of thinking and feeling may not carry through an entire writing situation. Writers may develop a new strategy, encounter a setback, or interpret feedback, including grades, in ways that affirm or challenge their dispositions. As orienting features, dispositions play a role in how writers relate to writing situations and consequently how they act and make sense of their writing. Involving ways of feeling as well as thinking, dispositions are embodied and thus can be durable insofar as they are more like well-worn feeling and thinking pathways.

Writing and writing center studies have engaged with the concept of dispositions in ways related to learning, emotions, and social material dimensions. Recent writing studies research draws from work in education and psychology to examine how dispositions such as self-efficacy and regulation of learning affect writing knowledge transfer and practices across contexts (Driscoll and Wells). A dispositional approach moves away from studying learning as what David Perkins et al. call an "abilities-centric view of intellectual performance" (270) to attend to "not only what people can do, but how they tend to invest their capabilities—what they are disposed to do. . ." (270). Understanding a writer's willingness or ability to transfer what they learn from one context—for example, a first-year writing course—to another involves more than creating conditions for transfer; it also includes the motivations and habits of mind of the writer within those contexts. These habits of mind might include attitudes about the value and relevance of what they have learned in a course, self-efficacy, a sense of control over events and responsibility for outcomes, and an ability to self-regulate learning (Driscoll and Wells).

Writing center studies attending to transfer of learning have also engaged with dispositions, particularly for peer tutor education (Devet; Driscoll). For example, Bonnie Devet considers how dispositions—such as self-efficacy and self-regulation, among others—play a role as tutors apply their learning and gain tutoring experience and how directors can help tutors cultivate such dispositions (130–31). Important for tutors as well as writers is a capacity for taking on the role of learner, which involves an openness to new situations and to understanding how to adjust (130). Similarly, Dana Lynn Driscoll takes up this learner disposition for tutor education using a "preparation for future learning (PFL)" framework (158), which focuses on how tutor education can foster dispositions that support not only the "near connections" of tutoring (164) but also future professional endeavors. In addition to studying transfer, a dispositional view of learning also aligns with writing center scholarship about the roles tutors play in supporting writers' affective concerns. For example, this focus aligns with what Muriel Harris identifies as "evaluation anxiety" and "defeatist convictions that [students] are not good writers" (35). Additionally, Jo Mackiewicz and Isabelle Thompson's research shows how tutors use "motivational scaffolding strategies" to foster "interest, self-efficacy, and self-regulation" (63). Although they do not specifically name dispositions, studies such as these point to ways that writing center interactions involve the emotional elements of motivation and attitude, elements that contribute to dispositions and also serve as expressions of them.

The attention Harris and Mackiewicz and Thompson give to motivation and other affective concerns relates to another strand of disposition scholarship that more directly addresses emotion and affect. Within this scholarship, dispositions involve what seems to be a contradiction:

the accumulation of affect and emotion, which are commonly understood as fleeting phenomena. The key to understanding dispositions as accumulation of affect and emotion is repetition. Even though affect and emotion are transient, registering in relation to immediate stimuli, repetition of these stimuli can cultivate repeated affective and emotional responses. These repeated responses can accumulate as embodied memories, involving the physiological dimensions of affect as well as emotional meaning-making (Watkins; Williams). Through repeated writing situations in school—assignments, feedback, evaluation, and testing—students experience emotions that accumulate as memories and shape dispositions towards writing. For example, students encounter writing situations, like writing a timed essay exam or receiving a score for it, that register as momentary physiological effects—for instance, a churn of the stomach. In addition, students make sense of these experiences and effects with cognitive, social, and rhetorical expression, which—over time—contribute to memory and identity (Williams). A writer might make meaning out of a churning stomach during the timed essay exam, interpreting it as stress, fear, nervousness, or excitement.

We accumulate both emotional and bodily memories through these repeated encounters, as our bodies register writing experiences, like a stomach churn, and we make sense of them as emotion, like fear. Although affective responses are transient, Megan Watkins argues that they also can accumulate through repeated situations as "*bodily* memory" that create a "capacity" for future responses (279). These memories shape dispositions and inclinations to respond to future writing situations in certain ways—for example, the churn in a writer's stomach when they receive a writing assignment in college as well as their interpretation of that churn. Williams considers how writers can accumulate meanings from these repeated affective experiences: "These dispositions accumulate and we begin to define ourselves through them. I become a person who hates traffic jams . . . I become a person who loves—or hates—to read and write" (24). Affect and emotion can interrelate in this accumulation: dispositions are embodied "repertoires" (Wetherell) of meaning-making that are used to interpret new situations; they can incite affective responses of fear, anger, or excitement even before we process and name them as emotions (Williams 20). Dispositions help to explain how a self-identified "bad writer" in our writing center session may be inclined to feel fear, frustration, uncertainty, anger, or a combination of these about their writing—approaching a writing situation *already feel-*

ing like a bad writer. A negative disposition can foreclose other ways for the writer to think and feel about future writing, just as a positive disposition, such as self-efficacy, can orient a writer toward a new situation very differently.

This view of affect and emotion accumulating to form dispositions also involves seeing dispositions as not only individual characteristics but shaped in relation to experiences, contexts, and conditions, such as recurring writing experiences in school. Such an approach follows the vein of critical affect and emotion studies, which explores individual embodied phenomena and experiences as social and political. For example, Lauren Brentnell et al. discuss elsewhere in this collection that the act of crying in the writing center is not only an individual, emotional experience but also one with social, political, and rhetorical effects and meanings. Likewise, Anna Rita Napoleone examines affect in the ways that writers and tutors feel social structures and class boundaries within academic social spaces that produce class differences.

Attending to the social, historical, and material factors of academic social spaces adds to their historically specific logics and practices. These practices include curriculum design, assessment, and teacher-student interactions with informing logics such as competition, individualism, and standardization. Logics and practices produce resources and patterns that people use to make meaning of emotional experiences and, in turn, form dispositions. To use the example of Williams's traffic-hating disposition, a social material approach would look at not only the repeated experiences of frustration in traffic but also the conditions for that experience—the historically specific design of cities and the availability and accessibility of mass transit. The approach would also require considering socially available resources, such as attitudes about the inconvenience of mass transit or marketing schemes that represent vehicular travel in terms of freedom. Similarly, the disposition of hating or loving writing is assembled from the economic, cultural, and social narratives and values that circulate within schools and classrooms, families, and cultural representations of writing.

This accumulation of emotion—in relation with social material conditions—involves what Margaret Wetherell calls "embodied meaning-making" (4), which includes both bodily operations and the socially available materials with which these operations are integrated: "feelings and thoughts, interaction patterns and relationships, [. . .] social relations, personal histories, and ways of life" (14). Dispositions are assembled from socially available resources and patterns writers use to make sense of their feelings about writing experiences. According to Rosemary Hennessy, "sensations . . . never speak for themselves but are always made sense of by the ways of knowing that circulate within a particular social organization or community" (72). A social material approach to dispositions, then, challenges writing educators to think about the conditions and materials for embodied meaning-making, for assembling and mobilizing emotions in the moment, and for producing "embodied memories" (Williams 21–22) of writing that orient writers when making sense of future writing experiences.

These social material processes of embodied meaning-making that orient attitudes and actions are also reflected in Pierre Bourdieu's theory of *habitus*. Bourdieu's theory conceptualizes dispositions in terms of the relations between individuals and institutions, relations that comprise of social *fields* such as education. According to Bourdieu, dispositions are what constitute an individual or institution's *habitus*, "systems of durable, transposable dispositions . . . as principles which generate and organize practices and representations" (53). The dispositions that make up *habitus* are "ways of acting, feeling, thinking, and being" (Maton 51) that are both "durable and transposable" to other situations (53). With these concepts, Bourdieu's theory outlines how humans reproduce the values of social structures in everyday life but in ways that allow for them to act in and on those structures (Eagleton 156).

When applied to academic contexts, examining an individual's *habitus* can reveal important relations between their practices, past, and current situation (Maton 51). For example, Elizabeth Wardle illustrates how school-based dispositions are shaped. She considers how standardized testing regimes can produce "answer-getting dispositions" as part of schools' and students' *habitus*, in contrast to "problem-exploring dispositions" that are more conducive to the demands of writing and other complex tasks. Wardle explains, "Problem-exploring dispositions incline a person toward curiosity, reflection, consideration of multiple possibilities, a willingness to engage in a recursive process of trial and error, and toward a recognition that more than one solution can 'work.' Answer-getting dispositions seek right answers quickly and are averse to open consideration of multiple possibilities." We likely have encountered such dispositions in our writing center sessions. Through participation in the patterned experiences and social relations of schooling, especially as curricula and instruction are bent toward standardized testing, students can come to embody these types of answer-getting dispositions—a desire for "quick and formulaic answers" (Wardle) when approaching an open-ended writing assignment. Dispositions and *habitus* involve not only the relations of individuals and institutions within social fields, but also the relations of perceptions, feelings, and practices. A social material theory of dispositions can be extended to include affect and emotion that can help with exploring writing dispositions. As Trainor explains, "Emotions are structured in ways that relate to the system of values and norms that exist in a social context" (648). She analyzes how "emotional rules" such as "toughing it out" can be taught and performed through "the institutional and social practices of daily life in school" (649–50). These rules "structure" students' orientations in other learning contexts (650). Similarly, writers assemble dispositions not only from explicit instruction but from the *habitus* of education—the habitual ways of seeing and doing that make up the everyday practices of schooling. Repeated practices, rewards, and reinforcements contribute significantly to shaping students' attitudes towards writing. For example, Williams points to the repeated process of submitting writing and receiving grades as an emotionally patterned experience, explaining, "Such ongoing and repeated emotional experiences construct dispositions in which many students expect failure, or at least disappointing nonengagement with their writing, rather than success or learning" (30). He highlights how this exchange is structured around judgment and emotion, whether positive or negative, rather than learning. While a school does not "experience" affect or emotion, the *habitus* of school can structure certain emotional relations with writing.

One important point across these strands is that while dispositions are durable, they are not fixed. Dispositions are ongoing practices shaped and reshaped within the relations of social fields, rather than things or states that we acquire, like discrete skills or items of knowledge. Education is one of many social fields that shape and reshape writing dispositions in different ways, and writing centers participate in this project. A social material approach invites writing centers to consider not only writers' dispositions as sites of engagement and inquiry but also the writing center *habitus* and how this *habitus* relates to the dispositions of higher education. Dispositions, then, offer writing centers a way of viewing writers' emotional relations with writing that is socially and materially situated. With this understanding of dispositions, I propose a social material exploration of one disposition that writing centers encounter: alienation.

ALIENATION AS DISPOSITION

Writers' emotional responses and practices may seem momentary, but they may also be evidence of embodied writing dispositions. Such dispositions are not only individually experienced and expressed but also shaped in relation to social material conditions. Negative dispositions, such as alienation, are worth considering because of their potential to foreclose other experiences and meanings of writing. Alienation is also relevant for thinking about the social material dimensions of dispositions that writers embody as they move through schooling contexts and other sites of social and economic production.

Alienation has been taken up in multiple fields, including philosophy, sociology, and psychology. Broadly, it refers to a state of detachment or estrangement. Scholars and researchers have approached alienation as a subjective experience—having to do with an individual psychological state—or as an objective set of structural social, economic, or political conditions (c.f. TenHouten; Petrović). Alienation has been viewed as an individual experience of detachment from others and from oneself or as a social configuration of relations and conditions that estrange people from each other and from themselves. In considering alienation as a disposition, I suggest combining embodied experience with socially and historically available conditions and resources. More specifically, I will focus on the Marxist concept of alienation to explore a writing disposition that involves a material and emotional relation with writing within economies that shape writing's value.

The Marxist conception of alienation names both a condition and a process in and by which people are estranged or separated from the products of human labor by commodity production and wage labor under the capitalist mode of production. Their work produces things that do not belong to them, and this process secures workers' relation to their own labor and of worker to capitalism. When defining alienation in *Economic and Philosophic Manuscripts of 1844*, Karl Marx includes the language of emotion and in doing so, identifies a material and emotional process:

> What, then, constitutes the alienation of labour? First, the fact that labour is *external* to the worker, i.e., it does not belong to his essential being; that is in his work, therefore, he does not affirm himself but denies himself, does not feel content but unhappy, does not develop freely his physical and mental energy but mortifies his body and ruins his mind. The worker therefore

only feels himself outside his work, and in his work feels outside himself. (74, emphasis original)

Economic and Philosophic Manuscripts is from Marx's earlier work, and while understood as more philosophical compared to the later economic analysis of *Capital*, it is worth exploring to understand alienation in terms of embodied meaning-making. In *Economic and Philosophical Manuscripts*, Marx positions labor as significant human activity involving sensation and emotion, and the condition of alienation involves self-denial, unhappiness, mortification, and ruin of body and mind. Thinking in terms of emotion and affect, alienation can be understood as the felt experience of the contradictions of the capitalist mode of production, where commodity production dominates social relations and forms of value.

Alienation has been articulated in relation to industrialized labor, especially the shift to factory production in the nineteenth and early twentieth centuries, which entailed the transformation of skilled craftsmen's work in assembly line production. This transformation took place via technological development—machinery—and through scientific management of the manufacturing process (McNally). As the mode of production shifted from the skilled work of craftspeople to mechanized assembly-line production creating and relying on deskilled labor, workers were increasingly disconnected from the product and process of their labor and from other workers, and they struggled for control over their working conditions.

This kind of alienation may not seem so applicable for the postindustrial knowledge economy of the United States, including the work of writing. Many jobs in the knowledge and information sectors that students seek seem high-skilled and meaningful, located in team-based workplaces that suggest a move from assembly lines to something more connected and collaborative. The conditions of late capitalism require a different understanding of alienation, one that can make visible their relevance for the work of writing. James Paul Gee et al. consider these dimensions for "the new work order:"

> Work in the old capitalism was alienating. Workers were forced to sell their labor, but often with little mental, emotional, or social investment in the business. Today . . . [t]hey are asked to think and act critically, reflectively, and creatively. While this offers a less alienating view of work and labor, in practice it can

also amount to a form of mind control and high-tech, but indirect coercion. (7)

Although workers today still sell their labor, Gee et al. point out the different qualities of much of that labor. When workers engage in work that is creative rather than rote or standardized, they may find that work more fulfilling. Within this configuration of capitalist production, alienation takes on new forms given the characteristics and uses of writing as economic production and the relationship of writers with the process and product of their work. As Samuel Bowles and Herbert Gintis note, "capitalistic production is at heart a social and not merely a technical process. And alienation is a class and not a technological phenomenon" (74). Research on writing's shift towards content creation and its consequences for writers and content creators shows what alienation can mean for writing in twenty-first century writing economies (see Dush; McNally).

Understanding alienation as a social process is useful for considering the economies students write in as well as those they are preparing to enter. Moving from corporate and workplace settings, alienation is discernible within the social relations of education, where teaching and learning are largely governed by neoliberal education policies, accountability discourses, and standardized curricula and assessment. Neoliberal policies have restructured education according to market logics, evidenced by the dominance of standardized testing and the push for privatization, including the rhetoric of school "choice." Additionally, these policies operate via "accounting practices and their technologies" and other forms of regulation and control that comprise "audit culture" (Soliday and Trainor 126) or what could also be called the "audit *habitus*" of education. This *habitus* has the capacity to shape writing dispositions in students and teachers—for example, the emotional relations with writing that are embodied and transposable to other contexts, such as the "answer-getting dispositions" that Wardle suggests. When writing's purpose is repeatedly tied to assessment, not only to scores and advancement but also to access to resources, this defined value affects the ways writing is taught, the ways it circulates, and the ways students relate to it (Trimbur). Writing centers encounter the enduring, embodied consequences of these relations.

Taken together, the writing and content produced in school, work, and Web contexts is commodified, producing value in ways that writers and creators do not define or have control over. These writing economies call for writers with certain skills and require dispositions that shape not only how those skills will be used but also how writers relate to the process and product of their writing. The problem posed by alienation is not that writing has no value, it is the extent that writers have a say in defining or determining it. The means of production may have changed in certain economic sectors; however, the kernel of social relations remains, ready to take new forms and extract value from meaningful human activity. Declaring oneself a "bad writer" or "not a writer" suggests a capacity to surrender writing's value to the economic logics and processes of profit-making, to be claimed by corporations. Other meaningful uses and values of writing—for example, for critical reflection, for social justice—are largely, though not entirely, foreclosed. The alienated writer, in Marx's words, "only feels himself outside his work, and in his work feels himself outside himself" (74).

WORKING WITH DISPOSITIONS: IMPLICATIONS FOR WRITING CENTERS

Writing centers can understand writing dispositions, such as alienation, in terms of the conditions and available resources for experiencing and making sense of writing and its value in school. A disposition like alienation is possible when much of the sanctioned writing that students experience does not connect them with the work of writing and the ways they can identify value in that work. The texts encountered in school are published works that have been revised, copy edited, and typeset. Their value takes the form of the finished product and its consumption within the classroom, for the purposes of quiz, exam, or timed essay. The work put into creating value is not visible: sentences, paragraphs, and sections that have been rearranged, removed, and rewritten; feedback from readers, editors, and publishers; the reader's role in making meaning. Also unaddressed are other forms of value for the writer, whether monetary compensation, CV lines, new insight gained through writing, or even the emotional dimensions of that writing—experiences of doubt, excitement, or any number of forms of embodied meaning-making involved.

One role that writing centers play in writers' lives is making the work of writing visible in these many dimensions, and helping writers make meaning of those dimensions. In doing so, writing centers provide "a distinctly different emotional experience of learning" that can "help reshape their dispositions toward literacy practices" (Williams 34). Tutors may already be familiar with this role and its impact, evidenced in the visible relief a writer conveys when a tutor agrees that writing conclusions is just hard or expresses excitement and interest in a new idea. Writing centers can be characterized by what Soliday and Trainor call an "artisanal approach" (143) to writing education that is less alienating for students, allowing them to develop a sense of authorship and the ability to approach ill-structured problems. In line with this artisanal framework, writing centers articulate their work in terms of serving the role of "authentic reader" and providing feedback at "the point of need" (Soliday and Trainor 137). Without the immediate result of a grade at the end of the session, the conversation between writer and tutor can focus on the writer's goals and concerns, as well as their learning (Williams 34). However, while writing centers may not directly engage with the transaction of evaluation and grades, they are not neutral spaces located outside the reach of writing economies. Part of reshaping dispositions involves acknowledging the ways that values are at work—not only those of the assignment at hand but also those of prior experiences.

Understanding writing dispositions as embodied and as social and material invites members of the writing center community to think beyond the boundaries of a particular session or semester. If we include in our work helping writers reflect on and reshape dispositions, we acknowledge the ways that emotions and values are at play—not only those of the assignment at hand but also those of prior writing experiences. A writer may make progress with one assignment, only to return intent on finding "the thesis" for their next essay. Thinking about a disposition like alienation can be particularly useful for approaching sessions with reluctant writers who come without drafts, notes, ideas, or even motivation to brainstorm with the tutor—sessions my tutors tend to struggle with. A dispositional approach can help tutors, especially inexperienced ones, make a shift from thinking there's nothing to work with, or that the writer first needs to "return with something," to seeing what's present and engaging with the writer's attitudes and experiences. By understanding dispositions like alienation as embodied, memory-rich relations with writing and value, tutors and directors can approach their work with appreciation, curiosity, and empathy for writers' attitudes and the ways they have been shaped. We can be attentive to the layers, patterns, and memories at play in a writer's concern with a grade, difficult writing prompt, or their identification as "bad writer." We can partner with writers to find alternate uses and values for writing, including using writing for discovery and shaping thinking.

Reshaping writing dispositions takes place for tutors as well as writers. Tutor education is an important venue for investigating our own writerly dispositions: how they have been assembled and how they inform our tutoring. In my experience, reshaping dispositions is no small thing, as those familiar with "imposter syndrome" may understand. As Chavannes et al. discuss in this collection, graduate students, including those taking on leadership roles in writing centers, can experience feelings of imposter syndrome as they develop academic and professional identities. As the first in my family to obtain a four-year degree, I struggled as a graduate student with the position and identity of "expert" and "colleague" that I was being trained to take on. I could critique the social material conditions of my experiences, but I *felt* something else—something difficult to put into words—that seemed stitched into me. My work in writing centers helps me recognize and work against this inclination to claim a professional identity, and the concept of dispositions has helped me make sense of this experience. Our work with peer tutors invites them to do the difficult work of investigating and reshaping dispositions to take on what may be new values: collaborative learning, writer agency and authority, difference as norm rather than deficit. This dispositional approach underscores the difficulty and the importance of these efforts, especially when bringing in the social material forces that work with and upon capitalism in ways that shape writers' emotional relations with writing and with other writers—white supremacy, class hierarchy, homophobia, ableism. Del Russo's project of cultivating critical empathy in their writing center, in this collection, provides a promising direction for tutor education.

Writing centers are in a position to provide different emotional experiences of learning for writers but also to contribute research into writing dispositions that can support tutor education, tutoring practices, and instruction and advocacy beyond the center. Partially removed from other sites of writing, centers can create spaces for writers and tutors to explore emotional dimensions of writing with curiosity about prior experience. Research that explores writing memories, attitudinally marked features of talk about writing, and emotional responses to feedback are some possible ways that writing centers can investigate dispositions and contribute to understanding the emotional accumulation around students' relations with writing, how writers make sense of dispositions, and how dispositions are reshaped. Research can also investigate relations shaped by the conditions of writing and how these contribute to writers' dispositions—admittedly retrospective when it comes to prior school writing, but possible for current writing conditions, following Soliday and Trainor's study. Applying the Marxist concept of alienation to dispositions provides a way to explore student writers' experiences and attitudes in terms of the social and material contexts of writing education and writing economies. Students' dispositions are a starting point for learning more about writers and the conditions for writing. Dispositions also invite us to support writers with finding alternate values of writing and forging writerly identities. This is not to suggest that writing centers endeavor to help writers love writing, or even enjoy it; rather, addressing alienation calls us to envision different relations with writing, to name what those can be. Working within a capitalist system of commodification and alienation, writers can claim writing and its value as a powerful tool for making meaning, thinking deeper, communicating with others, and meeting human needs in other ways.

Works Cited

Bourdieu, Pierre. *Logic of Practice*. Translated by Richard Nice, Stanford UP, 1990.

Bowles, Samuel, and Herbert Gintis. *Schooling in Capitalist America: Educational Reform and the Contradictions of Economic Life*. Haymarket Books, 2011.

Brandt, Deborah. *The Rise of Writing: Redefining Mass Literacy*. Cambridge UP, 2015.

Devet, Bonnie. "The Writing Center and Transfer of Learning: A Primer for Directors." *The Writing Center Journal*, vol. 35, no. 1, 2015, pp. 119–51.

"Disposition, N." *Oxford English Dictionary*, Oxford UP, 2020.

Driscoll, Dana Lynn, and Jennifer Wells. "Beyond Knowledge and Skills: Writing Transfer and the Role of Student Dispositions." *Composition Forum*, vol. 26, 2012.

—. "Building Connections and Transferring Knowledge: The Benefits of a Peer Tutoring Course Beyond the Writing Center." *The Writing Center Journal*, vol. 35, no. 1, 2015, pp. 153–81.

Dush, Lisa. "When Writing Becomes Content." *College Composition and Communication*, vol. 67, no. 2, 2015, pp. 173–96.

Eagleton, Terry. *Ideology: An Introduction*. London: Verso, 1991.

Edbauer Rice, Jenny. "The New 'New': Making a Case for Critical Affect Studies." *Quarterly Journal of Speech*, vol. 94, no. 2, 2008, pp. 200–12.

Gee, James Paul, et al. *The New Work Order: Behind the Language of New Capitalism*. Westview P, 1996.

Graff, Harvey. *The Labyrinths of Literacy: Reflections on Literacy Past and Present*. U of Pittsburgh P, 1995.

Harris, Muriel. "Talking in the Middle: Why Writers Need Writing Tutors." *College English*, vol. 57, no. 1, 1995, pp. 27–42.

Hennessy, Rosemary. *Profit and Pleasure: Sexual Identities in Late Capitalism*. Routledge, 2000.

Horner, Bruce, et al. "Language Difference in Writing: Toward a Translingual Approach." *College English*, vol. 73, no. 3, 2011, pp. 303–21.

Mackiewicz, Jo, and Isabelle Thompson. "Instruction, Cognitive Scaffolding, and Motivational Scaffolding in Writing Center Tutoring." *Composition Studies*, vol. 42, no. 1, 2014, pp. 54–78.

Marx, Karl. "Economic and Philosophic Manuscripts of 1844." *The Marx-Engels Reader*, 2nd ed., edited by Robert C. Tucker, W.W. Norton and Company, 1978, pp. 66–125.

Maton, Karl. "Habitus." *Pierre Bourdieu: Key Concepts*, edited by Michael Grenfell, Acumen, 2008, pp. 49–65.

McNally, Michael. "Enterprise Content Management Systems and the Application of Taylorism and Fordism to Intellectual Labor." *Ephemera*, vol. 10, no. 3/4, 2010, pp. 357–73.

Perkins, David, et al. "Intelligence in the Wild: A Dispositional View of Intellectual Traits." *Educational Psychology Review*, vol. 12, no. 3, 2000, pp. 269–93.

Petrović, Gajo and Norman Geras. "Alienation." *A Dictionary of Marxist Thought*, 2nd ed., edited by Tom Bottomore, et al., Harvard UP, 1991, pp. 11–15.

Pulver, Christian. "Web 2.0 Writing as Engine of Information Capital." *Economies of Writing: Revaluations in Rhetoric and Composition*, edited by Bruce Horner, et al., Utah State UP, 2017, pp. 191–202.

Soliday, Mary, and Jennifer Seibel Trainor. "Rethinking Regulation in the Age of the Literacy Machine." *College Composition and Communication*, vol. 68, no. 1, 2016, pp. 125–51.

TenHouten, Warren. *Alienation and Affect*. Taylor and Francis, 2016.

Trainor, Jennifer Seibel. "From Identity to Emotion: Frameworks for Understanding, and Teaching Against, Anticritical Sentiments in the Classroom." *JAC*, vol. 26, no. 3/4, 2006, pp. 643–55.

Trimbur, John "Composition and the Circulation of Writing." *College Composition and Communication*, vol. 52, no. 2, 2000, pp. 188–219.

Wardle, Elizabeth. "Creative Repurposing for Expansive Learning: Considering 'Problem-Exploring' and 'Answer-Getting' Dispositions in Individuals and Fields." *Composition Forum*, vol. 26, 2012.

Watkins, Megan. "Desiring Recognition, Accumulating Affect." *The Affect Theory Reader*, edited by Melissa Gregg and Gregory Seigworth, Duke UP, 2010, pp. 269–85.

Wetherell, Margaret. *Affect and Emotion: A New Social Science Understanding.* SAGE Publications, Ltd., 2012.

Williams, Bronwyn. *Literacy Practices and Perceptions of Agency: Composing Identities.* Routledge, 2017.

15 Is It Enough? An Interrogation of the Wellness Turn in Writing Centers

Genie Giaimo

There is a recent and growing interest in wellness and self-care practices in writing centers and writing studies more broadly (Degner et al.; Mack and Hupp; Mathieu); however, much of the current research functions as a litmus test that identifies the growing need for these kinds of support, rather than necessarily offering larger heuristics for the field. This makes sense because of the relative novelty of wellness and self-care work in writing centers. Other research focuses on writing center administrators and that population's experience of burnout and work-related stress (Caswell et al.). It is clear from our field's turn to wellness studies that there are significant issues with how we labor in our field; we are constantly switching jobs, dropping out of the profession entirely, and struggling with burnout, overwork, budgetary cuts, etc. Many of these issues circle around but do not name or interrogate the cause of this wellness crisis in our field. In this chapter, I will make explicit what I believe to be a largely unexamined, yet ever-present, issue that our field faces: writing centers are in crisis because of the austerity measures taken by neoliberal higher education institutions. Conversations that center on wellness sometimes fail to identify how austerity has contributed to problematic labor practices in our field. Because wellness is also predicated on the material conditions in which workers labor, we need to do more work to ask these questions of our writing centers' wellness interventions: *is it enough*? Are our current interventions in writing center training and staff support enough? Are the studies on mental health, burnout, and attrition in our field enough? In short, is what we are doing as a field enough?

Of course, in asking these questions, I am also asking writing center administrators to kick these questions up the administrative chain to ask what universities and colleges are doing to support the work and mission of writing centers—and other—workers. While our field has demonstrated interest and concern in the affective and material conditions under which we labor, it is unclear what we consider to be the responsibilities of those above us in the administrative hierarchy. As middle managers and—largely—student laborers, we have limited power, time, and money to make many of the changes that are necessary for the sustainability of our centers. Therefore, I point upwards to the administrators that ultimately control the fates of our programs and ask them, as well, if what they are doing to support us is enough?

We cannot rest at asking these questions, however. We must also change how we think about writing center work as labor in a contextual relationship with upper administrators and the institution. Turning our focus inward will not solve the systemic issues our field faces. In other words, analyzing the affective dimensions of writing center work at the micro level is simply not enough. We need to challenge our current administration practices and our relationship to upper administration and our institutions. While the discourse around writing center work is saturated in the language of affect at the micro level, scholars must also attend to the structural elements underpinning writing center work, which affect their material realities. Precarity, for example, profoundly affects our affective responses to and experiences of writing center work.

In this chapter, I offer a game-theoretical framework for engaging with upper administration that understands our choices to cooperate or coerce as interdependent agents with varying power levels. I interrogate how writing center labor functions within a constellation of responsibility centered management (RCM) to heighten mental health concerns among students and employees, as well as foster improvement-minded growth impulses in student-support units, all of which impact our labor. To avoid further exploitation while working in a neoliberal institution, we need to understand our positionality relative to agents with more power and who have incentives to coerce us. Our field's turn to wellness is one such impulse to confront these tensions; however, it should not be our only response to austerity in higher education.

Why Game Theory?

There are, of course, many different theories that one can apply from outside the field of writing centers to problematize our relationship to labor and to develop new models of writing center administration. In the previous chapter, Lisha Daniels Storey utilizes the Marxist concept of alienation to explore how student writers experience writing education by examining the dispositions writers acquire over time. Storey critiques our educational system and students' experience of it through lodging a critique against its economically-motivated underpinnings.

Here, I utilize game theory, which is a strategy-based approach to engagement with other agents that attempts to produce specific and preferential outcomes. Game theory can help writing center administrators situate *how* we administer writing centers in relation to outsiders who often have more power than we do and who often operate with different goals and knowledge than we have. It also provides a proactive way to plan our responses to austerity. As the COVID-19 pandemic has demonstrated, there is profound uncertainty and precarity in higher education; this is no less true in the writing center-management dynamic. Through game theory, writing center administrators can build long-term strategies that respond to austerity at the macro—rather than micro—level. Currently, it seems, much of our research attempts to stop the gap of austerity through more interventions and more labor from writing center administrators and their staff members. This is an intensive, uncompensated, and ultimately local approach to systemic issues our field faces. We need to consider structural changes alongside these more local interventions if we hope to stem the tide of cutbacks, furloughs, freezes, and other measures.

Our Field's Involvement in the Neoliberal University

Recently, there has been an upswing in wellness research in our field. Scholars have explored the tutors' mental health concerns (Degner et al.), experience of stressors (Simmons et al.), administrative burnout (Jackson et al.), and a host of mindfulness training interventions (Mack and Hupp; Johnson; Featherstone et al.; Concannon et al.; Emmelhainz). This is perhaps because wellness is hopeful; it is aspirational; it is the belief that, with enough research, support, and training, our staff will be able to handle any situation that is thrown their way. Some of us, myself included, may also believe it is our duty to prepare student workers for occupational hazards beyond writing center work, such as those that may arise in their academic and professional lives. Wellness is the alluring practice that we hope will fill in the gaps in our tutors' support structures. For me, wellness is personal because I have watched my working-class family run their bodies and their minds into the ground at jobs that do not nourish them and in conditions that are far less than equitable.

Wellness training, however, only gets a workplace so far when the working conditions are untenable or the university refuses to support its contingent labor with fair wages and access to basic benefits. These are issues that we agonize over—even though they are often far above our paygrade and over which we have little to no control. We cannot do wellness work alone, and we should not expect our workers to either.

We have responded to RCM even if we do not realize we are doing it. We justify our purpose through scheduled appointments, no-show and usage rates, demographic breakdowns, assignment and support requests, and a host of other factors that are dutifully placed into semester and year-end reports. We administrators are taught to believe that if we use enough empirical evidence in our arguments to the "powers that be," then our needs will be met. We will secure more funding. We will secure that additional staff or tenure-track line. We will be vindicated, through reason and data, and our labor will be justly rewarded. Yet, often, we write these reports with "bean counting" in mind rather than context (Lerner 1). The practice of bean counting encourages growth and development but can be a muddled—if not empty practice—if it lacks specific goals or plans. Furthermore, the situation on the ground is far from ideal. Administrators take on too much work with too little support. We manage staff that come with their own unique needs, in addition to the varied needs of the writers we support. And we often face budgetary cuts, made without our input, or other kinds of adverse conditions that arise with no forewarning. Couple these cuts with "the inconsistency of expectations and rewards across different institutions" for writing center administrator labor (Perdue et al. 284), and we see a landscape in which RCM has created a free market full of units competing against each other for money through enrollment numbers, credit hours, majors, and ambiguous or outright unethical hiring practices.

In a way, we were primed for RCM approaches to our work. Historically speaking, writing centers have expanded their roles as institutions change and new demands arise. In their earliest iterations, writing centers were created in response to institutional pressures and were often embedded into the curriculum of the university (Boquet). They changed again in the mid-twentieth century to respond to the open access movement in higher education and to include peer tutors and an informal educational model (Boquet). Perhaps writing centers are changing again to respond to the explosion of wellness needs clients—and tutors, alike—bring to the writing center. If writing centers, as Boquet argues, produce and sustain "hegemonic institutional discourses" (466), we need to interrogate where the sudden explosion in interest about wellness and self-care comes from. It is not just from a well-meaning but unmoored conviction; it comes from a response to our previous and largely uncritical production of labor for the university and our disgust with late-stage capitalism and its influences on higher education. However, rather than interrogating what we should be provided with, we respond to austerity with wellness. Once again, we have turned inward and created a plan to provide for others. Service to the institution is rooted deeply into the psyche of our profession; we need to start digging out the roots.

As other authors (Hull and Brooks-Gillies; McKinney et.al; Navickas et.al.) in this collection, I recognize the need for our field to reframe how we describe and enact writing center work through understanding and defining the emotional elements of that work. These elements are frequently linked with figurations of wellness that are guided by the neoliberal university's enactment of austerity measures. Like the authors in this collection (Hull and Brooks-Gillies; Grutsch McKinney et al.; Navickas et al.), I recognize the need for our field to reframe how we describe and enact writing center work through understanding and defining the emotional elements of our work, which I see as inexorably linked with wellness guided by the neoliberal university's enactment of austerity measures. Like Storey, I draw attention to the economic elements of writing center work and the structural limitations of individual writing centers to enact change at the institutional level. This work is often overshadowed by the more immediate, emotional exigencies placed upon writing centers and their workers at the micro level.

A GAME-THEORETICAL APPROACH TO WRITING CENTER ADMINISTRATION

I invite readers to join in a thought experiment, using game theory, where writing center administrators compete with other players in the institution for resources and support. As Francesco Guala suggests, "Game theory is aimed at modeling and understanding people's behavior, in particular when the outcome of their actions depends not only on what they do, but also on other people's decisions" (240). A game theoretical model acknowledges the interconnectedness between players, environments, and outcomes: one decision maker's environment and incentive structures affect the choices of the other player or players and vice versa. The primary purpose of game theory, as Viliam Ďuriš and Timotej Šumný note, "is to analyse conflicting situations and to find the best strategy to maximize the profit" (758). "Profit," in this instance, can refer not only to money but also to any objectively good outcomes for the player. While getting additional money is one potentially positive outcome for a writing center, so, too, are things like subjective satisfaction, "mission accomplished" moments, or feelings that one's work is meaningful and effective. Some "rules" for negotiating within a game include:

1. There have to be at least two agents or participants in the game.
2. Each agent or participant has to make some type of choice.
3. The choices they make affect the rewards or penalties that occur for all the players.

There is a "convention in game theory of assuming common knowledge of the game that is being played" (Guala 244). In other words, there is an assumption that the players are rational actors who are aware of each other's knowledge and preferences (241). Game theory does not necessarily account for individual actors whose behavior may not be rational, whose knowledge is partial or relatively limited, or whose incentives are obscure. Yet, these are often the conditions that we labor under within higher education, so this game theory model provides contingencies for these real-world conditions.

To apply game theory to writing center work—or any work, for that matter—we must recognize players are not always rational and do not always have common knowledge of the game. Furthermore, the players' difference of interests, knowledge, and power contribute to potential material inequities such as labor exploitation. Writing center administrators are often in a one-down position in terms of power and knowledge levels when compared to upper administrators; therefore, they have a disadvantage in terms of options in the game. While power imbalances may be quite difficult to change, writing center administrators can access more knowledge as they become aware of the game they play against upper-administration and, so armed, play the game with better odds in their favor. Power hierarchies cannot be separated from game theory insofar as they significantly affect how two players can and will engage with each other.

As a caveat, the writing center field is idiosyncratic. Some folks are tenure-track or tenured. Some are in upper administration. Some are staff members. Some are part-time lecturers. Some are graduate students. Some are co-located and not staffed by a writing center administrator. We, writing center administrators, are in different social environments that have different incentive structures. In other words, we are all playing different games with our administrators and other funding agents. Therefore, the choices that some writing center administrators make in a given situation of a game might be effective for them while being ineffective for other administrators in other writing centers, who are playing different games. Regardless of the situation, any individual will benefit from thinking intentionally about their particular environment and decoding the game that they are playing to, potentially, win it. Writing center administrative work already includes games where the director is assessing—or being asked to assess—what the value or worth of a writing center is and conveying that to an administrator in order to secure more support or maintain current funding levels. Of course, funding matters, as does assessment, but their frequent tethering in scholarly research (Lerner; Essid; Reardon; Lape; Ryan and Kane; Giaimo) ought to be interrogated. Funding should not be predicated on a growth model that optimizes labor over workers. In other words, our field often frames itself within the language of the neoliberal university (Monty)—the Fordist model of production—in usage rates, foot traffic, clients, and hours. Yet, when austerity measures come down the chain of command, these data do not protect us from cuts. Often, we are working in a system that seems logical when, in fact, it is driven by the illogic of capitalism. A game-theoretical model challenges writing center administrators to ask whether our desired outcomes are, in fact, rational ones. For example, as a writing center administrator, you may seek out additional funding for programming and expanding the writing center, but what if the growth model you seek comes at a steep cost to yourself—and your ever-expanding duties—and to your staff? In other words, what motivates us to play a game is only part of this equation; we also must consider if our desired outcome is, in fact, one that will be a "win" in the long term. Who, in other words, are we playing this game for and to what end?

What follows is my characterization of different types of game outcomes (see Table 1). In a win-win game, there are ways for both parties to make choices that allow them both to come out ahead. In a lose-lose game, it is almost certain that both parties will come out for the worse in the end. In a win-lose game, one party will "win" while the other will "lose." In this game, the players are natural antagonists.

Table 1. Different game outcomes

Game Outcome	Player 1	Player 2
Win-Win	+ Outcome	+ Outcome
Lose-Lose	– Outcome	– Outcome
Win-Lose (Zero Sum)	– Outcome	+ Outcome
Win-Lose (Zero Sum)	+ Outcome	– Outcome

While win-win is arguably the best outcome, and one we, as writing center administrators, ought to aspire, and lose-lose is one that we ought to avoid, it seems like writing center administrators are usually stuck somewhere in the middle: in the win-lose game. Win-lose, or zero-sum, is a game with an uneven outcome, with one winner and one loser. Though it might be possible and desirable to move from a win-lose game to a win-win game through cooperation between players—where goals are compatible or shared—what is more likely is a prisoner's dilemma situation. With a prisoner's dilemma, two people are under duress, and due to structural incentives, are less likely to cooperate than they are to defect for individual gain. Like other institutions under intense financial and other pressures, those in a university setting are less likely to work towards a common goal. The zero-sum game provides the best opportunity for enacting knowledge against the other player to secure a desired goal. It is also, often, the situation under which writing center scholars write about assessment and funding—if we have enough of x data we will secure y money. Of course, the amount of knowledge that both players bring to the game, as well as their desired respective outcomes, profoundly affects how the game is played.

Knowledge Levels and Incentives
in Game Negotiation

The spectrum of knowledge between two players—in this case, the writing center administrator and the upper administrator—can profoundly affect both the outcome of the game and players' preparation for it. Both parties can have no, partial, or full knowledge of the other. Securing an outcome is contingent on each player's level of knowledge of the other and their intentions. For example, if the objective for the writing center administrator is to secure additional writing center support while the upper administrator is looking for either a static budget or even a reduced one, it makes sense to understand what knowledge and goals these two players have going into the game. If the upper administrator has no knowledge of the writing center, the writing center administrator, or the writing center administrator's desire for more support, it is less likely that they will be willing to provide additional funding because they are either unaware of the writing center's value or because they do not place a value on it. If, however, they have partial knowledge about the writing center, then the writing center administrator needs to assess their knowledge of the administrator—their values, as well as their desired outcomes in the negotiation process. In either instance—no knowledge or partial knowledge—the writing center administrator will likely need to educate the upper administrator.

In the instance where the upper administrator lacks knowledge about the writing center, which almost certainly sets-up a lose-lose or a win-lose scenario, the writing center administrator can make the writing center familiar to them, within reason. Some possible actions may include holding an open house, promoting the center through branding and marketing, or giving the upper administrator opportunities to meet with stakeholders and staff members. Only after the first step of providing knowledge to the upper administrator does it make sense to reveal one's desired outcome—of securing additional funding or whatever other objective—from them.

In the instance where the writing center administrator lacks knowledge about the upper administrator's desired outcome for the game, which will likely result in a lose-lose or win-lose scenario, the writing center administrator needs to get more information. They may ask the upper administrator what types of initiatives they have supported in the past or learn more about their strategic plan or mission for the school.

The writing center administrator may also identify alternative support models for the writing center, prior to entering a conversation with the upper administrator. The writing center administrator may also need to determine what kind of power the administrator has to make important decisions about funding.

Of course, there are all kinds of outcomes based on different situations where both players play with varying levels of knowledge about the other player's motivations and intentions. Sometimes, giving the upper administrator more information can lead to decision-making that results in a lose situation for the writing center administrator—think here about a school looking to cut expenditures and landing on the writing center because it appears to be "losing" money in RCM's credit-generating funding structure. Sometimes, educating is not the best option for the writing center administrator. The upper administrator's incentives can, after all, be adversarial to the writing center administrator. However, because this is not a closed system, it is also possible for the writing center administrator to suggest possible incentives that are compatible with the upper administrator's and that they might not yet be aware of. That shift would allow for the elusive win-win outcome.

While game theory is a useful model to understand and engage in writing center administration, I also share action items below that I have gleaned from such an engagement with this model. Of course, this is a partial list. However, despite all the advice, models, and planning that I offer in this chapter, it is also critical to recognize that many writing center administrators might face lose-lose situations—perhaps due to austerity measures being imposed because of the purported economic fallout from COVID-19—that are not their fault. There comes a time when no amount of strategy, data, forecasting, or other proactive behavior may make much of a difference. In these instances when the situation is dire, I encourage writing center administrators to take care of themselves and their workers. Do your best to advocate. Start an American Association of University Professors, AAUP, chapter (www.aaup.org/). Speak with local unions. But, in the end, as the title of this piece suggests, it might simply not be enough. And that is not on you. Rather, it is an effect of late-stage capitalism acting upon an already precarious industry: education.

ACTION 1: WRITING CENTER ADMINISTRATORS NEED TO STOP COVERING THE GAPS IN NEED AND SUPPORT WHEN AUSTERITY MAKES WRITING CENTER LABOR UNSUSTAINABLE.

Writing center administrators are not educated in leveraging the power of "no" or speaking back to the administration about the consequences of their actions. Just recently, conversations about COVID-19 and austerity measures have populated professional social media platforms—early into a worldwide crisis, colleges and universities cut administrator and tutor compensation and pulled center funding. Yet, for the most part, in conversations where austerity measures are implemented, writing center administrators try to brainstorm ways to justify or otherwise combat these decision-making processes with research and data. Some writing center administrators seem poised to work the same amount, or more, for even less compensation. Some are wondering how to balance the safety of their staff with institutional directives to resume in-person classes. In better times, leveraging the power of "no," is incredibly important; however, in times of crisis, it is necessary. To prepare for this crisis and the next one, we need to interrogate writing center administrative models that are predicated on improvement and growth. When our institutions make our work less tenable by the day, we need to stop looking inward to fill those gaps and, instead, reconfigure our work expectations.

While improvement models give purpose and order to what otherwise might be an overwhelming tide of emotional needs that come washing through the center's doors daily, this model also facilitates an eradication of boundaries—*I'll just answer this one email* or *I'll just take one more client*—which hastens burnout among center workers. It also denies the material conditions of our work and reinforces inequality related to compensation, job security, and invisible labor, all of which disproportionately affect people of color, LGBTQ+ folks, and women. Therefore, we need to develop other administrative and management models that leverage the power of "no" as Katelyn Parsons suggests in her piece on creating boundaries in writing center work.

ACTION 2: WRITING CENTER ADMINISTRATORS NEED TO DEVELOP PROACTIVE MODELS OF WRITING CENTER ADMINISTRATION.

In shifting the focus off ourselves and what we can do individually in favor of a more collaborative model that assesses and responds to the behavior of interrelated actors that are operating under competing incentives, we can break out of the writing center administrator-as-savior role. Game theory helps guide actors to their own optimal outcomes within the context created by the other actors. Institutional context is frequently incentivized to escape responsibility and push unsustainable models onto writing center administrators and our labor; therefore, we need to devise strategies for how best to pursue our goals even within this very un-ideal context. In place of growth models and a belief that assessment work and data will finally give us institutional and scholarly legitimacy, I argue that game theory can help us prioritize, strategize, and advocate for our writing centers while reframing our thinking about how we position our labor within the larger context of the university. Our current labor model forces us to see the trees and not the forest—in other words, we are reacting rather than behaving proactively for the betterment of the writing center, its staff, and clients. Game theory offers a proactive model through which to conceive writing center labor and negotiation between writing center administrators and upper administration.

ACTION 3: WE NEED TO ACT COLLECTIVELY TO REIMAGINE WRITING CENTER WORK AS SUSTAINABLE AND ORIENTED TOWARDS SOCIAL JUSTICE.

Perhaps because many writing centers only have one full- or part-time writing center administrator, writing centers tend to operate in isolation. This is an issue for many reasons, including: the overburden of expectations for the lone administrator; the lack of a sounding board or natural ally; and the individualistic rather than collective organizational structure. For time- and resource-strapped writing center administrators, there are communal approaches that we can take to our work. We might connect laterally with departments, such as student wellness, counseling services, and even human resources for training, support, and other initiatives. We might call upon upper administration to support our workers and our clients.

However, we also need to take necessary actions when support fails to materialize. Action may take the form of conducting a salary parity study across student and staff employment rates and offering tutors a raise. It may mean putting into place flexible work policies so that workers can attend to personal and familial needs without fear of losing their jobs. It may mean reorienting our work towards anti-racist practices and policies that directly support our tutors of color, particularly our Black tutors. More generally, this means asking pointed questions of administrators during campus interviews, yearly budgetary meetings, and other opportunities that may arise about the value they place upon our labor—be it student labor, adjunct labor, staff or faculty labor—and, ideally, setting-up intermittent discussions about writing center work. These discussions should include both qualitative and quantitative data, but they should also showcase the affective dimensions of writing center work, which we perform daily in our centers, and which often go unacknowledged and overlooked. In the end, however, after all this work, there may be a time when we, as writing center administrators, say *this is enough*, and we stop growing, stop offering, and stop running to catch up with needs that are not being acknowledged or understood by upper administration. The outcomes of doing otherwise, in addition to burnout and psychological damage to workers, especially underrepresented workers, is a reduced standard of services for clients.

ACTION 4: OUR FIELD NEEDS TO DEVELOP AN ADVOCACY WING THAT LOBBIES STATE LEGISLATURES AND ENGAGES IN RE-ACCREDITATION OF COLLEGES AND UNIVERSITIES.

Among practitioners in other fields, such as mental health workers, boundaries are part of their everyday work; they have set schedules, set caseloads, and set protocols for disruptive or distressed individuals. On the other hand, writing center workers—administrators and staff—do not have best practices for disengaging from emotionally volatile or dangerous sessions. There are no field-specific standards for the number of clients a tutor ought to work with per day or even what the appropriate or recommended length of an individual session ought to be. We lack these standards for our tutors and our administrators though, collectively, some centers work with tens of thousands of writers each year and hire staffs of sixty to one hundred—or more—tutors. Because of this, it is necessary for our field to develop an advocacy wing that lobbies state legislatures and engages in re-accreditation of colleges and universities. In many areas, we are failing to play similar games with players outside of our immediate lines of reportage, such as state legislatures, accrediting boards, and professional organizations. We need to do more as a field to extend discussions and work regulation to larger systems of power.

To do so, however, we need guidelines that go beyond the current scope of standards for writing centers and their support in higher education provided by the International Writing Centers Association (IWCA,

"Position Statements"), which asks only for the bare minimum: physical space for a center, some type of compensation and professional development for writing center administrators, training for staff, and more. With guidelines like this, it is no wonder that we are unequipped to play a game with specific and long-term positive outcomes—a "win"—against upper administrators; we, as a field, are unsure of what long-term outcomes we are playing for. Therefore, we must first clearly define our desired outcomes before commencing negotiations for our centers. I argue that we need specific standards for writing center labor that advocate for fair compensation, training, and support for our workers, and that include specific best practices that address and support the emotional labor we undertake. These standards may include recommended session "caseloads" for individual tutors, standards for session length, or advocacy for more full time and tenure-track administrators with more robust administrative support. We also need regulation of writing center administrator positions, advocacy for mentorship, and support for junior administrators working under faculty. Finally, we need more evidence to support our practices, which can help to inform and shape labor standards. Obviously, this conversation is just beginning.

I will say that despite the pressure that many writing center administrators feel to constantly develop new programs and services, growth should not be something that we continuously aspire to in our work. At times, we must remain stable, or perhaps even reduce our centers to align with the support that we are given. We, writing center administrators, ought not to drain ourselves in pursuit of support to justify and grow our centers, only to continuously play catch-up with our growth model. Nor should we optimize our resources and produce efficiency in the hope that this will somehow result in more resources. RCM should not drive the strategic planning for our centers. We need to recognize that we, and our staff, are finite labor with limits and that we are deserving of investment and external support.

CONCLUSION

In *Undoing the Demos*, Wendy Brown argues that neoliberal reasoning is shifting all sectors of current life towards economization; she notes, "all conduct is economic conduct; all spheres of existence are framed and measured by economic terms and metrics, even when those spheres are not directly monetized" (10). The university has not escaped this paradigm shift, and while writing center administrators have tried, in some ways, to change with the times by providing more and better assessment to justify the work of writing centers, somewhere during the past two decades, we have done more with an ever-shrinking piece of the pro-verbial pie. Perhaps this economization of our work is why we are turn-ing towards wellness and self-care; we are burnt out, stressed out, and unable to continue using the models we have labored with for so long; clearly, they are not working. In this way, we need to reclaim wellness before it is appropriated by neoliberal institutions and becomes a tool for further optimization of our work force's productivity at the expense of actual, substantive health. We cannot ignore or normalize toxic work environments, structural exploitation, or occupational hazards; wellness training cannot fix high-level structural issues in the system, nor can it ameliorate the experiences of burnout among practitioners in our field—at least, not in any long-term way. We need to find a model that rejects neoliberal reasoning and recognizes self-care and wellness as radical acts that may work against the business as usual—improvement—models of the writing center. Game theory can be used to test the waters of inter-personal engagement at individual centers and help frame how our field contributes to institutions of higher education. It is my hope that this model helps writing center administrators to understand how they, as players, can affect the outcomes of the "game" through their decisions and actions. While opposing an player or players might have motiva-tions and incentives that are at cross-purposes or obscure, this model offers a shorthand for negotiations, as well as helping to know when to walk away from the playing table if the scenario happens to be unwin-nable. If we can know more about the other player's context, perhaps we can adjust our actions for a better outcome or attempt to shift the rules of engagement.

Approaching writing center work through a game-theoretical model can help writing center administrators to think about the macro level, rather than the micro level, of programmatic planning and advocacy. For example, the material conditions of our labor inform not only how we play the game against administrators but also inform the decisions we make and the goals we set. In framing the outcomes of my person-al administrative work and decision-making through various win-win, win-lose, and lose-lose scenarios, I have developed strategic plans that are far more flexible and that are highly vigilant of potential exploitation. It is a more proactive, rather than reactive, strategy. While cooperation with the other player may be a viable strategy, so might obstruction or collective action that allows players to pool resources in order to get more power. In short, few strategies are off the table as we decide what goals to set for our staff, our centers, and ourselves. Game theory helps us to put our work into context and consider the underlying motivations of those playing with and against us, even as we consider potential outcomes and plan our next moves.

WORKS CITED

Boquet, Elizabeth H. "'Our Little Secret': A History of Writing Centers, Pre- to Post-Open Admissions." *College Composition and Communication*, vol. 50, no. 3, 1999, pp. 463–82.

Bouillon, Marvin L., et al. "The Revenue Side of the Responsibility-Centered Management (RCM) Model at Regional State University." *Journal of Case Studies*, vol. 34, no. 2, 2016, pp. 111–20.

Brown, Wendy. *Undoing the Demos: Neoliberalism's Stealth Revolution*. Zone Books, 2015.

Caswell, Nicole, et al. *The Working Lives of New Writing Center Directors*. UP of Colorado, 2016.

Concannon, Kelly, et al. "Cultivating Emotional Wellness and Self-Care through Mindful Mentorship in the Writing Center." *WLN: A Journal of Writing Center Scholarship*, vol. 44, no. 5–6, 2020, pp. 10–17.

Degner, Hillary, et al. "Opening Closed Doors: A Rationale for Creating a Safe Space for Tutors Struggling with Mental Health Concerns or Illnesses." *Praxis: A Writing Center Journal*, vol. 13, no. 1, 2015, pp. 28–38.

Ďuriš, Viliam, and Timotej Šumný. "Modelling Behaviour on a Game Theory Principle." *TEM Journal—Technology Education Management Informatics*, vol. 7, no. 4, 2018, pp. 758–61.

Essid, Joe. "Working for the Clampdown? Being Crafty at Managed Universities." *The Writing Lab Newsletter*, vol. 30, no. 2, 2005, pp. 1–5.

Emmelhainz, Nicole. "Tutoring Begins with Breath: Guided Meditation and Its Effects on Writing Consultant Training." *WLN: A Journal of Writing Center Scholarship*, vol. 44, no. 5–6, 2020, pp. 2–9.

Featherstone, Jared, et al. "The Mindful Tutor." *How We Teach Writing Tutors*, edited by Karen Gabrielle Johnson and Ted Roggenbuck, *WLN Digital Edited Collection*, 2019.

Giaimo, Genie. "Focusing on the Blind Spots: RAD-Based Assessment of Students' Perceptions of a Community College Writing Center." *Praxis: A Writing Center Journal*, vol. 15, no. 1, 2017, pp. 55–64.

Guala, Francesco. "Has Game Theory Been Refuted?" *The Journal of Philosophy*, vol. 103, no. 5, 2006, pp. 239–63.

IWCA. "Position Statements." *International Writing Centers Association*, writingcenters.org/position-statements/.

Jackson, Rebecca, et al. "Writing Center Administration and/as Emotional Labor." *Composition Forum*, vol. 34, 2016.

Johnson, Sarah. "Mindful Tutors, Embodied Writers: Positioning Mindfulness Meditation as a Writing Strategy to Optimize Cognitive Load and Potentialize Writing Center Tutors' Supportive Roles." *Praxis: A Writing Center Journal*, vol. 15, no. 2, 2018, pp. 24–33.

Lape, Noreen. "The Worth of the Writing Center: Numbers, Value, and the Rhetoric of Budget Proposals." *Praxis: A Writing Center Journal*, vol. 10, no. 1, 2012.

Lerner, Neal. "Counting Beans and Making Beans Count." *Writing Lab Newsletter*, vol. 22, no. 1, 1997, pp. 1–3.

Mack, Elizabeth, and Katie Hupp. "Mindfulness in the Writing Center: A Total Encounter." *Praxis: A Writing Center Journal*, vol. 14, no. 2, 2017, pp. 9–14.

Mathieu, Paula. "Being There: Mindfulness as Ethical Classroom Practice." *The Journal of the Assembly for Expanded Perspectives on Learning*, vol. 21, 2016, pp. 14–20.

Monty, Randall. "Undergirding Writing Centers' Responses to the Neoliberal Academy." *Praxis: A Writing Center Journal*, vol. 16, no. 3, 2019, pp. 37–47.

Parsons, Katelyn. "Just Say 'No': Setting Emotional Boundaries in the Writing Center is a Practice in Self-Care." *WLN: A Journal of Writing Center Scholarship*, vol. 44, no. 5–6, 2020, pp. 26–29.

Perdue, Sherry Wynn, et al. "Centering Institutional Status and Scholarly Identity: An Analysis of Writing Center Administration Position Advertisements, 2004–2014." *The Writing Center Journal*, vol. 36, no. 2, 2017, pp. 265–293.

Reardon, Daniel. "Writing Center Administration: Learning the Numbers Game." *Praxis: A Writing Center Journal*, vol. 7, no. 2, 2010.

Ryan, Holly, and Danielle Kane. "Evaluating the Effectiveness of Writing Center Classroom Visits: An Evidence-Based Approach." *The Writing Center Journal*, vol. 34, no. 2, 2015, pp. 145–172.

Simmons, Erik, et al. "Is Tutoring Stressful?: Measuring Tutors' Cortisol Levels." *WLN: A Journal of Writing Center Scholarship*, vol. 44, no. 5–6, 2020, pp. 18–25.

Epilogue

Kelly Concannon and Janine Morris

Kelly Concannon and Janine Morris. When we began circulating the CFP for *Emotions and Affect in Writing Centers* at the 2018 IWCA conference, there's no way we could have anticipated how the world would change between then and now, as we bring this collection to a close in 2021. The COVID-19 pandemic resulted in many financial, familial, and personal challenges for individuals and writing centers alike. Further, calls for racial justice echo through higher education and our field as we work to account for and address the systemic and institutional racism and inequities that permeate our spaces and work. While calls for change existed prior to summer 2020 (see chapters by Brentnell et al., Chavannes et al., Storey, Giaimo, and Napoleone on power structures and intersectional imbalances within writing centers), authors in this collection completed their chapters prior to our current moment.

In this epilogue, we invited contributors to reflect on how their views of emotions and affect may have changed over the course of the last year and where they see conversations about affect and emotions in writing centers moving from here. We also asked them to consider how their chapters respond to the social, political, and educational changes that have happened because of the pandemic and in response to social injustice across the US. Finally, we asked authors to consider the practical applications or lessons suggested by emotion and affective work. We organized contributors' statements according to those that focus specifically on the changes to and emotions involved in tutoring and working in writing centers and those that consider how writing centers might collectively move forward given the significant events of this past year.

In this conclusion, we note how embracing virtual modalities and the move away from physical writing center spaces has changed the emotional and affective dimensions of tutoring practices. Many of the chapters in this collection focus on the implications of emotions and affect in face-to-face tutoring sessions in physical spaces. As the authors suggest below, the move online has called for increased attention to listening, rapport-building, and efforts to see and understand one another. The move online has also caused us to rethink our own health and personal boundaries and what community means in writing centers. Acknowledging shared fears and stressors, recognizing the limitations of our work, and seeing one another as fully human are necessary for coping and getting through the hardships many are facing.

Another theme echoed in this conclusion is the role individuals and administrators in writing centers now play. Adaptability is highlighted and authors here reflect on how they have grown and changed, along with their tutors and centers, in response to the pandemic. As administrators ourselves, we recognize the calls authors are making to be more empathetic, flexible, adaptable, and less focused on professional identity. Authors reflect on ways the larger writing center community has responded to the exigencies of this past year and emphasized the importance of supporting one another as we address the shared challenges our writing centers face.

MOVING WRITING CENTERS ONLINE AND EMOTIONS IN VIRTUAL TUTORING SESSIONS

Neal Lerner and Kyle Oddis. Our chapter focuses on the question of what "listening" might look like in online synchronous writing center sessions. The shift to completely online, one-to-one writing instruction as a result of the pandemic creates additional exigency for this question, one we found was not necessarily answered by closely examining a familiar practice in writing center work no matter the modality: asking questions. Our aim to enact Krista Ratcliffe's ideas of "rhetorical listening" in writing center work seems well within reach but frustratingly elusive. Attention to the emotional lives of student writers and writing consultants seems more important now than ever, given Zoom fatigue, social isolation, and understandable anxiety about the future—whether in regards to our health or our finances. We do hope that this attention to affect and emotion in online writing center sessions will help us realize the often-lofty goals we have for our centers, particularly our goals for diversity, equity, and inclusion. We also need to describe what it might look like in order to help our staffs achieve those goals. We will keep looking.

Luke Iantorno. My chapter examines how writing center tutors and administrators at Texas Tech University experienced emotional labor in response to job-related stressors in face-to-face interactions. Given that the Writing Centers of Texas Tech—much like other writing centers across the country—have been fully online since March 2020, future studies in affect and emotion could examine if and to what extent working for extended periods in online learning spaces—like WCOnline and Zoom—have compounded issues related to emotional labor and occupational stressors.

In my own experiences as a writing consultant in 2020, the shift to a fully-online writing center in response to the COVID-19 health crisis created new opportunities to discuss with my colleagues' issues of workspace-homespace interference, how to best welcome visitors to our virtual writing center, and how to develop rapport with clients on the opposite end of a computer screen. Our weekly, online, professional development meetings also provide us the opportunity to evaluate how the pandemic has redefined the space and place of writing centers. In the course of these conversations last year, I often reflected on how affect and emotion now shape the work we do with others in online spaces. Specifically, has it been easier or more difficult for us to display genuine positive emotions during our online interactions with clients and co-workers? Does the virtual divide between computer screens increase emotional performance and emotional regulation? Has screen fatigue and a lack of in-person communication resulted in higher instances of emotional exhaustion and burnout? Investigating questions like these, whether for future research projects or for continuing tutor training and professional development, could certainly allow us as an academic community to refine, rethink, and rework our understanding of emotional labor in writing centers.

Mike Haen. Going forward, I believe writing centers will need to think about the affordances and limitations of face-to-face instruction and different modes of online instruction—for example, Zoom and email instruction—for students as well as tutors. For example, September 2020 exchanges on the WCenter Listserv speak to the difficulties that writers and tutors have had with screen fatigue and general burnout from online writing and interactions about writing. While convenient in certain ways, online writing center teaching—whether via Zoom or other video platforms, email instruction, or Google Doc feedback—seems to present certain drawbacks. Exploring these drawbacks from the perspectives of tutors, writers, and administrators is a promising avenue for future research. Conversations about affection and emotion in writing center work can proceed in many different directions. I believe future conversations can benefit from consistent reflection on our practice as instructors and the place of positive and negative affect within it; open dialogue about the affordances and limitations of different modes of instruction; and inquiries informed by a range of methods and epistemologies that build upon prior lines of research in writing center studies.

TAKING CARE: BLENDING PERSONAL AND PROFESSIONAL IDENTITIES

Katherine Villarreal. I see the work of emotion and affect flow in and out of our writing center like Chanel No.5; it is remarkable and memorable, but you cannot quite shake the lingering scent of what is missing in our spaces—experiences, voices, and perspective from tutors, administrators, and students. If we begin to focus our work not only on the "right" thing to do but also on individuals' writing center experiences, we can develop more practices and opportunities for everyone to excel. We need to continue listening to one another and looking past the text in front of us to see the person on the other side. One way to encourage mutual understanding is to reflect on embracing the vulnerability lingering in the air and encourage reconnecting with clients during sessions. For example, the emotion and energy of movements like BLM should not be excluded from sessions; in fact, tutors should have discussions about equality, racism and oppression with students, energizing our sense of purpose. I focus now more than ever on just sitting back and listening, relating to the odd-ness of these times with my clients and colleagues, and making myself more sympathetic than ever—well past being just a tutor and, instead, seeing myself as a fellow spectator. I try to remind those I work with that we are all in this together and only we can write these pages in our history books as we deem fit.

Lisa Bell. In writing center work, we claim to assist with writing and learning, but we often lack a clear understanding of the learners we work with and fail to see ourselves—tutors and administrators—as learners.

In our shift towards more research-based practices, we must understand and address learners as fully human. This includes looking at large-scale numerical data as well as narratives from local learners.

This need to better understand learners and their contexts was amplified in 2020 as systemic inequality was visible and visceral at our individual institutions and on the nightly news. In addition to highlighting inequality and issues of access, the cultural upheaval of 2020 revealed significant divisions in our societies and our failure, both in and out of academia, to listen and learn from and with each other. As humans committed to building more equitable and accessible educational systems and societies, participation, common ground, and validation are needed, as is an awareness of how we support and sustain each other's efforts and confidence in this ongoing, collaborative work.

Within writing centers, our programming should not be one-size-fits-all—or most. What we offer as opportunities for learning interactions must reflect the range of learners within our communities. Beyond thinking of learners in terms of cognitive ability, we should build services that reflect the relational capital and life contexts of learners. At my writing center, that means providing one-on-one sessions, in-person and online. It means offering live workshops for those tutors and writers ready to engage in learning in real time and shared space and asynchronous, interactive writing resources for those who need additional time and space to fully engage mentally, emotionally, or linguistically in learning exchanges. What we know and what our research continues to show us is that writers are more than just individuals attached to assignments, they are fully human learners who work with and within writing centers.

Lisha Daniels Storey. As I think about my chapter on alienation in relation to the social, political, and educational climate of the last year, I stop short at the scale and magnitude of the conditions under which writers, tutors, and writing center directors have had to make writing education—let alone our daily lives—work. The conversations around writing that take place in our centers become sites of connection and struggle over the purpose, value, and emotions of writing—not as a retreat from these larger social conditions but with an increased awareness of these conditions and their sometimes muted, sometimes amplified pressures on our bodies and our words.

In this moment and with an eye to the future, my writing center is one space that my tutors and I can organize with intention—our purpose has been brought into sharper relief this year. More practically, even as my tutors and I work through the pedagogical and technical adaptations to online synchronous tutoring, I have become more attentive to the practice of rapport-building. I find myself shifting their attention away from thinking about building rapport only in the first few minutes of the session, an item to check off the list. Building rapport is different in an online context without the same bodily and spatial cues. With online sessions, I find myself inviting tutors to think about how we build rapport throughout the session, not before we get to the writing or separate from the writing, but through the work of engaging meaningfully with writing and the writer. It may be overly ambitious for me to hope that this kind of work, this engagement with dispositions, can give writers and tutors a sense of what they can make—and remake—that, in turn, fortifies their ownership of our world. But, with others, I see, in uncertain futures, radical possibilities.

Rachel Robinson, Lauren Brentnell, and Elise Dixon. Our chapter focuses on the act of crying in the physical space of writing centers, but now the physical space of the center is often our own homes. Certainly, like most people experiencing the pandemic, crying in our homes has occasionally been a part of life. We suggested three potential benefits to crying: crying as community and relationship-building; crying as writing process; and crying as social justice literacy. When we socially distance and quarantine, crying as community and relationship-building seems difficult and perhaps even impossible—finding ways to do this online is even more challenging than in a physical writing center. Many of us are already having difficult conversations about how to build and continue relationships during the pandemic, so we suggest incorporating conversations about crying into those.

At the conclusion of our chapter, we suggest that being a crybaby in the writing center has positive social justice implications if considered carefully. If that is so, how does crying in the privacy of our homes—during a pandemic and aftermath of a political coup—become something fruitful? We are not sure about the answer to that question. What we do know is that crying has been and continues to be an effective coping mechanism for the difficulties in our own and our writing lives and that the tears of the people who have lost loved ones during the pandemic are powerful parts of our collective story. We want to take this time to honor the tears shed for the lives of those lost to racial and discriminatory violence and to COVID-19.

COMMUNITY BUILDING AND DISCIPLINARY IDENTITIES

Kelin Hull and Marilee Brooks-Gillies. We were keenly aware of the embodied and emotional implications for both ourselves as administrators and for consultants as we moved to all-online programming with only a few days' notice before our spring break. While we were attentive to the logistical and practical elements of moving our programming online, we were focused on ways to foster and support our community of consultants and writers. We understood the need to be transparent and authentic with our embodied experiences while attending to the emotional needs of the writing center: instill confidence and encourage togetherness. As administrators, this felt overwhelming and exhausting. Consultants pulled together rapidly to create guidance for online consulting and training for the few consultants who had never consulted online. We offered weekly office hours in Zoom, attempting to make them sound more friendly by calling them "chillin' with Kelin" and "tea with Marilee." Meanwhile, our university asked instructors to move to asynchronous course models in the wake of the pandemic, and consultants and writers shared with us how important our synchronous programming was to help them feel supported.

Based on these experiences, we share a few takeaways:

- Through conversation with stakeholders and university administrators, we can continue to make visible the fiercely relational nature of writing center work, but our voices do not enact immediate change.
- Community is an activity and one that we as leaders in the community must model, which has a heavy emotional cost at all times but especially in times of upheaval.
- Attention to the emotional, embodied relationality of our work goes beyond our own campuses, and we need to find ways to support each other in a profession that is often misunderstood on our campuses. Our centers are made and remade in relationship with and among the larger network of writing centers as well as our own local contexts.

Kate Navickas, Kristi Murray Costello, and Tabatha Simpson-Farrow. Through our chapter, we determined that emotional labor is related to a writing center administrator's sense of their ideal identity as an administrator or who they want to be in this role. We discussed how this pressure or inspiration, depending on the moment, permeates every decision we make for our centers. During times of transition, the writing center administrators were more likely to over-scrutinize their actions in terms of whether or not they aligned with their administrative values and felt anxiety when context, work, or other challenges resulted in actions that did not align with their sense of an ideal writing center administrator. We argue, too, that the interviews demonstrate the value of sharing, especially with an administrative predecessor, about one's emotional labors, feelings, and experiences.

Connecting with one another is always meaningful but has become increasingly important for our professional and mental health as we navigate the unprecedented hurdles and isolation brought upon by the COVID-19 pandemic, institutional austerity measures, and the persistence of racism and white supremacy. Our research showed that writing center administrators naturally begin to let go of some of the anxiety of the "ideal writing center administrator identity" as they become more comfortable and confident in their own decision-making; however, 2020 and the pandemic thrust all administrators into a set of ongoing transitions involving tough choices constrained by more complicated contexts than normal. Thus, now we would add that during times of upheaval, emotional labor may be more consistently fraught for all administrators, regardless of whether they are transitioning into or out of new positions. Inversely and more optimistically, though, we have the hope that by merely having weathered the pandemic and other crises with our centers intact that we have also, out of necessity, shed some of the pressures of the ideal writing center administrator identities that can haunt us.

Nicole Chavannes, Monique Cole, Jordan Guido, and Sabrina Louissaint. Since March 2020, our lives have changed, and we understand, even more, the importance of our roles as leaders and how our emotions influence our lives and interpersonal relationships. No matter the modalities of our future work, we believe that writing center leadership teams will have to balance the emotional well-being of their centers by making staff and students feel like they are safe, while also trying to meet the expectations of their university. Going forward, we think that research regarding emotions and affect will likely take a more nuanced approach, focusing on the various identifiers associated with writing center leadership, staff, consultants, and clients. In addition, we think a focus on the environments where writing center work takes place needs continuous examination in relation to emotion and affect. We recognize the importance of mental and emotional awareness in performance as both students and leaders. Emotional challenges are almost constant, so acknowledge feelings, take a break if necessary, and do not put so much pressure on yourself. We are in important roles, but we do not have to be perfect all the time. We are not imposters in our writing center environments. We belong and deserve to be here.

Anna Rita Napoleone. One practical outcome of my chapter is that we should read emotional experiences not as individualistic but, rather, in relation to systems. Doing so might allow us to engage, reflect, and respond in new ways. We often seem to deal with emotion through a deficit model: we behave as if we, the tutors and the administrators, are there to empower and give confidence to others as if it is ours to give, which suggests a white-male-savior model, even when it is done with the best of intentions. Perhaps reflecting on emotions as systemic can reveal the connections between individuals and systems, thereby shifting how we understand and confront those feelings.

Emotion as a consequence of systems may be a way to better understand how difference is marked in individual moments and sessions. Also, how difference gets marked in tutorials via emotions may be a way to think about how to research and assess writing center practices. For example, how are we engaging with writers whose feelings of inadequacy speak to a system that values white, monolingual, middle-class norms? In tutor education, it is important to talk with tutors about the feelings that emerge for them in tutoring sessions, and then reflect on how those feelings translate into their engagement with tutees. Administrators can do the same. What the writing center can do is expand its space so as to give writers, tutors, and administrators pause and then work collectively to confront the systems behind those feelings. More research on how difference gets marked via emotions may help us better assess our writing center practices.

Genie Giaimo. Since I first drafted my chapter on game theory and writing center administration, in some ways, I am only *more* affirmed in my sense that our field needs to address how late-stage capitalism has hollowed many elements of higher education, including services and programs related to the work we do in writing centers. Since spring 2020, our profession seemed to be first on the chopping block at several institutions. With the attack on tenured faculty and the shuttering of entire academic departments, I am affirmed that even the most secure among us—which are few—are not safe. In effect, none of us are safe so long as most of us labor precariously in our field.

While this precarity begs many of the questions that I ask about affect and writing center work, I am also reminded that writing center folks are compassionate and often energetic people who can mobilize fairly quickly and effectively. Even as schools closed all over the world, I also observed several, radical changes in how we labor. Suddenly, we were sharing documents and training guides. We were regularly convening in large-scale support meetings. We were sharing information on how to protect and support tutors and other writing center workers. We were drafting statements and action lists about racial justice, worker rights, and pandemic protocols. Without the prompting, really, we connected across affiliate organizations, social media, and email to create a community of support and a community of care. I hope we can take a page from activist politics and work to provide mutual aid and care to our local communities—and, in turn, accept this kind of care from others. We need to be willing to disrupt, to slow down, and to pull back. In short, we need to stop accepting that the new normal is dictated by disaster capitalism and austerity politics. We need to find a way that recruits our emotionality—our affect—for intentionally anti-racist and, dare I say, anti-capitalist collective endeavors.

Kelly Concannon and Janine Morris. It is our hope that these reflections serve to keep conversations of emotions and affect in motion—as we stay true to much of the research on emotions and affect and its impact on writing center work. As contributors reflect on how to move forward and conceptualize this work within a new political, social, and cultural climate, we imagine that this work will continue to inspire others to actively create spaces to interrogate and engage in discourses of and around emotions and affect. Thus, these shifts function to alter individual and structural practices that create space and allow us to engage in productive change.

Contributors

Lisa Bell is Coordinator of the Utah Valley University Fugal Writing Center and President of the Rocky Mountain Writing Centers Association. Her recent research and publications in writing center studies focus on online tutoring and support for multilingual writers.

Lauren Brentnell is an instructor in the Department of English at the University of Northern Colorado. Their research focuses on incorporating trauma-informed, care-based practices into institutional contexts, including writing classrooms, programs, and centers. They received their PhD in Rhetoric and Writing from Michigan State University. Currently, they serve as a managing editor for *constellations: a cultural rhetorics journal* and the secretary of the CCCC Queer Caucus. Recent publications include "Living Oklahoma: A Memoir About Trauma and Rebuilding in Academia," a chapter in the digital collection *Pixelating the Self*, published through *Intermezzo*, and "The Hidden and Invisible: Vulnerability in Writing Center Work" forthcoming with Dixon and Robinson.

Marilee Brooks-Gillies is Assistant Professor of English and the Director of the University Writing Center at Indiana University-Purdue University Indianapolis. She currently serves as President of the East Central Writing Centers Association and on the IWCA Social Justice and Inclusion Task Force. Her scholarship is situated within cultural rhetorics and writing center studies with an emphasis on place-making in communities of practice. Her work has been published in the *Journal of Multimodal Rhetorics*, *The Peer Review*, and *enculturation*. She is an editor of *Graduate Writing Across the Disciplines* as well as special issues of *Across the Disciplines* and *Harlot*. When she is not writing, mentoring, teaching, or trying to sleep, she enjoys hiking with her family and crocheting.

Nicole I. Caswell (she, her, hers) is Associate Professor of English and Writing Center Director at East Carolina University. She researches writing assessment, emotion and affect, and writing centers. Sheis the co-author of *The Working Lives of New Writing Center Directors*.

Nicole Chavannes is a graduate of the Master's program in Composition, Rhetoric, and Digital Media at Nova Southeastern University where she was previously a graduate assistant coordinator of NSU's Writing and Communication Center. She is an Assistant Director of Graduate Admissions of NSU's Halmos College of Arts and Sciences. Her research focuses on mindfulness and creative approaches to writing center work as well as ontological security among transmediated-storyworld fandoms. She has presented at regional and national conferences, including SWCA, PCAS and ACAS, and PCA and ACA. Her work has also appeared in *WLN: A Journal of Writing Center Scholarship*.

Erica Cirillo-McCarthy is Assistant Professor of English and directs the Margaret H. Ordoubadian University Writing Center at Middle Tennessee State University. Her research has been published in *Praxis: A Writing Center Journal*, the *Journal of Global Literacies, Technologies, and Emerging Pedagogies* and in multiple edited collections, including in the inaugural *WLN: A Journal of Writing Center Scholarship* digital edited collection, "How We Teach Writing Tutors." She can be reached at erica.cirillo-mccarthy@mtsu.edu.

Monique Cole graduated with a Master's Degree in Composition, Rhetoric, and Digital Media from Nova Southeastern University, where she worked as a Graduate Assistant Coordinator in the NSU Writing and Communication Center. Her research focuses on social media and writing centers. She has presented her research twice at the Southeastern Writing Center Association, SWCA, conference. Her work has also appeared in the *Communication Center Journal*.

Kelly Concannon is Associate Professor of Writing in the Department of Communication, Media, and the Arts at Nova Southeastern University, where she is also a Faculty Coordinator in the Writing and Communication Center. Currently, she teaches a variety of undergraduate and graduate courses, including basic writing, college writing, advanced composition, gendered images in popular culture, the teaching of writing, writing center praxis, and history and theory of rhetoric. Dr. Concannon's research interests include community engagement, service learning, feminist theory, social justice education, writing center theory and practice, and literacy studies. Her book, *Peace and Social Justice Education*, was published in the winter of 2015. She has published book chapters in *Teaching Peace through Popular Culture*, *The School Violence Reference Handbook*, and *A History of Evil in Popular Culture*. Further, she has published in major journals, including *Reflections: A Journal of Public Rhetoric, Civic Writing, and Service Learning*, *The Journal of Feminist Scholarship*, *Academic Exchange Quarterly*, *enculturation*, *Community Literacy Journal*, *Journal for Expanded Perspectives on Learning*, *College Literature*, and *The Journal of Advanced Composition*. She has presented at national and regional conferences and serves as an undergraduate mentor for the *Undergraduate Journal of Service Learning and Community-Based Research*.

Steven J. Corbett is Director of the University Writing Center and Associate Professor of English at Texas A and M University, Kingsville. He is the author of *Beyond Dichotomy: Synergizing Writing Center and Classroom Pedagogies*, 2015, and co-editor with Michelle LaFrance and Teagan E. Decker of *Peer Pressure, Peer Power: Theory and Practice in Peer Review and Response for the Writing Classroom*, 2014, with Michelle LaFrance of *Student Peer Review and Response: A Critical Sourcebook*, 2018, and with Jennifer Lin LeMesurier, Teagan E. Decker, and Betsy Cooper of *Writing in and about the Performing and Visual Arts: Creating, Performing, and Teaching*, 2019. His articles on writing and rhetoric pedagogy have appeared in a variety of journals, periodicals, and collections.

Celeste Del Russo is Associate Professor in Writing Arts and the Writing Center Director at Rowan University. Her research interests include tutor education and writing center issues around social justice, access, and inclusion. Her work has been published in *Praxis: A Writing Center Journal*, *WLN: A Journal of Writing Center Scholarship* and in edited collections including, *Linguistic Justice on Campus: Pedagogy and Advocacy for Multilingual Students* and *Writing Centers and Learning Commons*. Her favorite part of writing center work is collaborating with tutors and writing center friends.

Elise Dixon is Director of the Writing Center at the University of North Carolina at Pembroke, where she is Assistant Professor in the English, Theatre, and Foreign Languages Department. Her teaching and research focus on queer, cultural, and multimodal rhetorics as well as writing center studies. Much of her work is focused on how marginalized communities and organizations empower themselves through collaborative writing and making. Her scholarship has appeared in *The Writing Lab Newsletter, The Peer Review Journal, The Journal of Veterans Studies,* and in multiple book chapters.

Genie Giaimo is Assistant Professor and Director of the Writing Center at Middlebury College in Vermont. She is editor of the digital edited collection *Wellness and Care in Writing Center Work,* 2021, and several peer reviewed articles and book chapters. For more information, visit her website: geniegiaimophd.weebly.com/.

Jackie Grutsch McKinney is Professor of English and Writing Center Director at Ball State University. She is the author of *Peripheral Visions for Writing Centers,* and *Strategies for Writing Center Research,* and co-author of *The Working Lives of New Writing Center Directors.*

Jordan Guido (He/Him) is a Master's student in the Composition, Rhetoric, and Digital Media Master's Program at Nova Southeastern University. He is also a graduate assistant coordinator in the NSU Writing and Communication Center. His research focuses on Queer rhetorics, and he has presented at regional and national conferences, including the Southeastern Writing Center Association conference.

Mike Haen is a PhD candidate in the Department of English at the University of Wisconsin-Madison. He currently teaches undergraduate writing courses and works with UW writing center colleagues on various projects and initiatives across the university and within the Greater Madison community. In addition to a forthcoming article in *The Writing Center Journal,* his recent work has appeared in *Composition Studies, Studies in Applied Linguistics and TESOL,* and *WLN: A Journal of Writing Center Scholarship.* Using audiovisual recordings of one-to-one conference talk and detailed transcripts, his current project examines a new writing fellow's interactional practices when working with students to identify areas for revision, revise their central arguments, and acknowledge and resolve writing troubles and complaints. Through this research, he challenges conventional practices promoted in tutor education literature, and he underscores how subtle interactional choices can shape conferencing relationships in big ways.

Kelin Hull is Visiting Lecturer of English and Assistant Director of the University Writing Center at Indiana University-Purdue University Indianapolis. Her scholarship is positioned within cultural rhetorics and writing center studies with an emphasis on the rhetoric of community. She has presented at international and regional writing center conferences and is the founder of Kindness Week at the University Writing Center. Outside of her professional life, Kelin is an avid cook, gardener, hiker, and traveler who loves adventuring with her family.

Luke A. Iantorno is Assistant Professor of English and the Writing Center Director at Webber International University. He previously worked for Texas Tech University as an English instructor and writing consultant. His research interests include writing center theory and pedagogy and the culture of Romantic era apocalypticism and sensibility. In his off-time, he plays tabletop roleplaying games, loses himself in suspense-horror films, and is a volunteer referee for women's flat-track roller derby.

Rebecca L. Jackson (she, her, hers) is Professor of English and Director of the MA Rhetoric and Composition program at Texas State University. She is co-author of the *The Working Lives of New Writing Center Directors* and co-editor with Jackie Grutsch McKinney of *Self+Culture+Writing: Autoethnography for/as Writing Studies* forthcoming from Utah State UP.

Elizabeth Leahy is Assistant Professor in the Library and director of the Writing and Communication Center at the University of Tennessee-Chattanooga. Her work is featured in *Praxis: A Writing Center Journal, Rhetoric Review,* and in the collection *WAC and Second Language Writers: Research Towards Linguistically and Culturally Inclusive Programs and Practices.* She can be contacted at elizabeth-leahy@utc.edu.

Neal Lerner is Professor and Chair of the English Department at Northeastern University, where he teaches undergraduate and graduate courses on writing studies, creative nonfiction, and the teaching of writing. His most recent book is *Reformers, Teachers, Writers: Curricular and Pedagogical Inquiries* from Utah State UP, 2019, and his current project is building a public digital archive of the Northeastern Writing Program history.

Sabrina Louissaint completed her Master's degree in Composition, Rhetoric, and Digital Media at Nova Southeastern University, NSU. In her position as a Graduate Assistant Coordinator in the NSU Writing and Communication Center, she explored different avenues to grow in professional development and leadership. Her research focuses on writing centers, community engagement, and social justice. She has presented her research at the Southeastern Writing Center Association conference.

Janine Morris is Assistant Professor of writing in the Department of Communication, Media and the Arts at Nova Southeastern University, NSU. She is also a faculty coordinator at NSU's Writing and Communication Center and is the 2020–2022 Southeastern Writing Center Association President. Her recent work has appeared in a number of edited collections and in *WLN: A Journal of Writing Center Scholarship* and *Southern Discourse in the Center.*

Kristi Murray Costello is Associate Chair of Writing Studies and General Education at Old Dominion University. She is an editor of the collection, *The Things We Carry: Strategies for Recognizing and Negotiating Emotional Labor in Writing Program Administration*, co-edited alongside Courtney Adams Wooten, Jacob Babb, and Kate Navickas. Her recent publications include "In Their Own Words: Student Responses Illuminate Dissatisfaction and Differences Regarding FYW Research," published in Tricia Serviss and Sandra Jamieson's *Points of Departure: Rethinking Student Source Use and Writing Studies Research Methods* and her article, "From Combat Zones to Contact Zones: The Value of Listening in Writing Center Administration," published in *The Peer Review*. Kristi lives in Norfolk, VA, with her partner, Liam, and their adorable dog, Rafa—pictures available upon request.

Anna Rita Napoleone is the Director of the University of Massachusetts Amherst Writing Center and the Site Director for the Western Massachusetts Writing Project. She has a PhD in Rhetoric and Composition from the University of Massachusetts Amherst. Her research focuses on classed literacy practices in higher education, how social class and affect impact teachers' pedagogy and how class intersects with global, racial, and gendered literacies. She has published in *Pedagogy* and has contributed to and edited collections such as *Examining Education, Media, Dialogue Under Occupation*, and *Out in the Center.*

Kate Navickas is the Director of the Cornell Writing Centers and teaches in the Knight Institute for Writing in the Disciplines at Cornell University. She is an editor, along with Courtney Adams Wooten, Jacob Babb, and Kristi Murray Costello, of the collection *The Things We Car-*

ry: Strategies for Recognizing and Negotiating Emotional Labor in Writing Program Administration. As a contributor to the collection, Navickas explores the relationship between emotional labor and disciplinary narratives informing the transition from graduate school into administration. Other recent publications include an interview with Minnie Bruce Pratt for *Pedagogy* and the *Composition Forum* article, "The Perpetual 'But' in Linguistic Justice Work: When Idealism Meets Practice," co-written with Nicole Gonzales Howell, Rachael Shapiro, Shawna Shapiro, and Missy Watson. Kate lives in central New York and survives the winters alongside her partner, Adam, three gray cats, and their Boston terrier, Olive.

Kyle Oddis researches values and tools in writing assessment, writing curriculum and pedagogy, and digital archives at intersections of writing analytics and data ethics. Kyle is the Project Manager for the Northeastern University Writing Program Digital Public Archive and is an instructor of composition and rhetoric, literature, and writing in the business administration professions. Kyle is the former Assistant Director and Director of Programming of the Writing Center at Northeastern University in Boston, where she is pursuing a PhD in English writing studies. Her research also appears in the *Writing Center Journal* and *The Journal of Writing Analytics.* She is a poet, amateur yogi, and former kickboxer.

Rachel Robinson is a PhD candidate in the Writing, Rhetoric, and American Cultures Deptartment at Michigan State University, studying the rhetoric and embodiment of imposter syndrome in academic spaces through feminist and cultural rhetorics perspectives. From 2018–2019, she served with Elise Dixon as Interim Assistant Co-Director of the Writing Center @ MSU. Before returning to school in 2016, she served as the Assistant Director of the writing center at Appalachian State University in Boone, NC, and, prior to that, as the Assistant Director of the writing center at Middle Tennessee State University in Murfreesboro, TN, her hometown. She has also worked with the Red Cedar Writing Project, a Michigan branch of the National Writing Project, since the summer of 2017. Recent publications include "Big Happy Family" with Baldwin, Brentnell, Donelson, Dixon, and Firestone, *TPR*, vol. 2, 2018, and several chapters in *COMPbiblio: Leaders and Influences in Composition Theory and Practice* with Allison Smith and Karen Wright, Fountainhead Press, 2007. In 2019, she and Elise Dixon co-edited a special issue on *TPR: The Peer Review* focusing on (re)defining welcome in the writing center.

Tabatha Simpson-Farrow is the Writing Center Director at Arkansas State University. She is an editor of the third edition of *Pack Prints*, a custom instructional text used in Arkansas State's first-year writing program. In addition to emotional labor, her research interests include an exploration of burnout theory as it applies to contingent faculty as well as the effects of co-curricular tutor training on writing center campus impact. Between academic semesters, Tabatha enjoys long naps and the company of three cats, a Great Dane, and her partner, Jeremy.

Lisha Daniels Storey is Director of the Scarbrough Center for Writing and Assistant Professor of Writing at Austin College in Sherman, Texas. She traces her writing center roots back to the University of Massachusetts Amherst Writing Center, where she tutored and served as Assistant Director while earning her PhD, and to the Center for Writing and Speaking at Agnes Scott College, where as a peer tutor she learned how much she enjoys working with and through writing with others. Her research interests include writing centers, tutor education, and writing economies.

Katherine Villarreal is an Interdisciplinary EC-6 Education major and lead peer writing tutor for the University Writing Center at Texas A&M University, Kingsville, where she does nonprofit animal rescue work and foster care. She has presented at several writing center conferences on topics like feminist perspectives and diversity in writing center practice. She was named South Central Writing Center Association 2020 Outstanding Tutor of the Year. Katherine is newly married as of 2020 to her husband, Marshall, and they share a home with five pets: Maple, Avocado, Pizza, Potato, and PopTart.

INDEX